THE NEW CAMBRIDGE SHAKESPEARE

GENERAL EDITOR
Brian Gibbons, *University of Münster*

ASSOCIATE GENERAL EDITOR
A. R. Braunmuller, *University of California, Los Angeles*

From the publication of the first volumes in 1984 the General Editor of the New
Cambridge Shakespeare was Philip Brockbank and the Associate General Editors
were Brian Gibbons and Robin Hood. From 1990 to 1994 the General Editor
was Brian Gibbons and the Associate General Editors were A. R. Braunmuller
and Robin Hood.

A MIDSUMMER NIGHT'S DREAM

Professor Foakes offers a new perspective on Shakespeare's most popular comedy,
and also a profound archetypal play.

The introduction describes the two main traditions in the stage history of
A Midsummer Night's Dream, one emphasising charm and innocence, the other
stressing darker suggestions of violence and sexuality, and relates them to similar
traditions in critical interpretation, showing that both are necessary to a full
understanding of the play.

Illustrations show the variety of ways in which the play has been staged, including
Peter Brook's 1970 production. The editorial commentary is especially concerned to
help the reader visualise the play in performance.

THE NEW CAMBRIDGE SHAKESPEARE

All's Well That Ends Well, edited by Russell Fraser
Antony and Cleopatra, edited by David Bevington
The Comedy of Errors, edited by T. S. Dorsch
Hamlet, edited by Philip Edwards
Julius Caesar, edited by Marvin Spevack
The First Part of King Henry IV, edited by Herbert and Judith Weil
The Second Part of King Henry IV, edited by Giorgio Melchiori
King Henry V, edited by Andrew Gurr
The First Part of King Henry VI, edited by Michael Hattaway
The Second Part of King Henry VI, edited by Michael Hattaway
The Third Part of King Henry VI, edited by Michael Hattaway
King Henry VIII, edited by John Margeson
King John, edited by L. A. Beaurline
King Lear, edited by Jay L. Halio
King Richard II, edited by Andrew Gurr
Macbeth, edited by A. R. Braunmuller
Measure for Measure, edited by Brian Gibbons
The Merchant of Venice, edited by M. M. Mahood
The Merry Wives of Windsor, edited by David Crane
A Midsummer Night's Dream, edited by R. A. Foakes
Much Ado About Nothing, edited by F. H. Mares
Othello, edited by Norman Sanders
Pericles, edited by Doreen DelVecchio and Antony Hammond
The Poems, edited by John Roe
Romeo and Juliet, edited by G. Blakemore Evans
The Sonnets, edited by G. Blakemore Evans
The Taming of the Shrew, edited by Ann Thompson
Titus Andronicus, edited by Alan Hughes
Twelfth Night, edited by Elizabeth Story Donno
The Two Gentlemen of Verona, edited by Kurt Schlueter

THE EARLY QUARTOS
The First Quarto of King Lear, edited by Jay L. Halio
The First Quarto of King Richard III, edited by Peter Davison

A MIDSUMMER NIGHT'S DREAM

Edited by
R. A. FOAKES

Professor of English, University of California, Los Angeles

CAMBRIDGE
UNIVERSITY PRESS

Published by the Press Syndicate of the University of Cambridge
The Pitt Building, Trumpington Street, Cambridge CB2 1RP
40 West 20th Street, New York, NY 10011–4211, USA
10 Stamford Road, Oakleigh, Melbourne 3166, Australia

© Cambridge University Press 1984

First published 1984
Reprinted 1987, 1988, 1990, 1994, 1995, 1997

Printed in Great Britain at the
University Press, Cambridge

Library of Congress catalogue card number: 84–203

British Library Cataloguing in Publication Data

Shakespeare, William
A midsummer night's dream. – (The New Cambridge Shakespeare)
I. Title   II. Foakes, R. A.   III. Series 822.3'3   PR2827

ISBN 0 521 22194 3 hardcovers
ISBN 0 521 29389 8 paperback

THE NEW CAMBRIDGE SHAKESPEARE

The *New Cambridge Shakespeare* succeeds *The New Shakespeare* which began publication in 1921 under the general editorship of Sir Arthur Quiller-Couch and John Dover Wilson, and was completed in the 1960s, with the assistance of G. I. Duthie, Alice Walker, Peter Ure and J. C. Maxwell. *The New Shakespeare* itself followed upon *The Cambridge Shakespeare*, 1863–6, edited by W. G. Clark, J. Glover and W. A. Wright.

The New Shakespeare won high esteem both for its scholarship and for its design, but shifts of critical taste and insight, recent Shakespearean research, and a changing sense of what is important in our understanding of the plays, have made it necessary to re-edit and redesign, not merely to revise, the series.

The *New Cambridge Shakespeare* aims to be of value to a new generation of playgoers and readers who wish to enjoy fuller access to Shakespeare's poetic and dramatic art. While offering ample academic guidance, it reflects current critical interests and is more attentive than some earlier editions have been to the realisation of the plays on the stage, and to their social and cultural settings. The text of each play has been freshly edited, with textual data made available to those users who wish to know why and how one published text differs from another. Although modernised, the edition conserves forms that appear to be expressive and characteristically Shakespearean, and it does not attempt to disguise the fact that the plays were written in a language other than that of our own time.

Illustrations are usually integrated into the critical and historical discussion of the play and include some reconstructions of early performances by C. Walter Hodges. Some editors have also made use of the advice and experience of Maurice Daniels, for many years a member of the Royal Shakespeare Company.

Each volume is addressed to the needs and problems of a particular text, and each therefore differs in style and emphasis from others in the series.

PHILIP BROCKBANK
Founding General Editor

v

CONTENTS

ILLUSTRATIONS

Illustrations 1, 2, 3 and 5 are reproduced by permission of the Shakespeare Centre Library, Stratford-upon-Avon; illustrations 6, 7 and 8 by permission of the Governors of the Royal Shakespeare Theatre and Angus McBean; illustrations 9 and 10 by permission of the Shakespeare Centre and the Governors of the Royal Shakespeare Theatre; and illustration 4 by permission of the Victoria and Albert Museum

PREFACE

Innocent fantasy or sinister nightmare – *A Midsummer Night's Dream* seems, in the twentieth century at any rate, to yield anything we might wish to find in it. The stage history and the history of its treatment in criticism alike show how this apparently simple and delightful play can yield strange and complex resonances, profundities as fathomless as Bottom's dream. In the Introduction I have therefore dealt at some length with the stage history of the play, and its bearing upon critical interpretation. In the Commentary, too, there is much emphasis upon staging, groupings of characters and the significance of stage directions. I hope this will help the reader in what is perhaps the most difficult aspect of studying a play-text – I mean in visualising in the imagination what action is taking place, and how the characters relate to one another on stage. The sources of the play have been analysed in detail by Kenneth Muir in *The Sources of Shakespeare's Plays*, and by H. F. Brooks in his edition of the play, and most of them are readily available in Geoffrey Bullough's *Narrative and Dramatic Sources of Shakespeare*, vol. I. I have not attempted to duplicate their work, but have rather tried to show, on the one hand, how Shakespeare transformed his source-materials, and to distinguish, on the other, between genuine sources, consciously used as such, and images, ideas, hints drawn, probably unconsciously, from the capacious storehouse of a well-read dramatist's memory. Over all, I have tried to keep the Commentary and other editorial matter brief, so as not to intervene more than is necessary between the reader and the play, but only to display and elucidate its richness of meaning.

I am grateful to many colleagues and friends who have willingly talked over problems or helped in various ways, and to the staff of a number of libraries, especially the Huntington Library in San Marino, and the Shakespeare Centre Library in Stratford-upon-Avon. The work of two recent editors of the play, Stanley Wells and H. F. Brooks, has made my task much lighter than it might have been, but also, I am glad to say, left me plenty to do in presenting the play with a very different emphasis from theirs. To the General Editors, especially Brian Gibbons, and to Paul Chipchase of Cambridge University Press, I am indebted for their guidance, and their sharp eyes in noticing errors or inconsistencies; they are, of course, in no way responsible for any that remain.

R. A. F.

ABBREVIATIONS AND CONVENTIONS

1. Shakespeare's plays

The abbreviated titles of Shakespeare's plays have been modified from those used in the *Harvard Concordance to Shakespeare*. All quotations and line references to plays other than *A Midsummer Night's Dream* are to G. Blakemore Evans (ed.), *The Riverside Shakespeare*, 1974, on which the *Concordance* is based.

Ado	*Much Ado about Nothing*
Ant.	*Antony and Cleopatra*
AWW	*All's Well That Ends Well*
AYLI	*As You Like It*
Cor.	*Coriolanus*
Cym.	*Cymbeline*
Err.	*The Comedy of Errors*
Ham.	*Hamlet*
1H4	*The First Part of King Henry the Fourth*
2H4	*The Second Part of King Henry the Fourth*
H5	*King Henry the Fifth*
1H6	*The First Part of King Henry the Sixth*
2H6	*The Second Part of King Henry the Sixth*
3H6	*The Third Part of King Henry the Sixth*
H8	*King Henry the Eighth*
JC	*Julius Caesar*
John	*King John*
LLL	*Love's Labour's Lost*
Lear	*King Lear*
Mac.	*Macbeth*
MM	*Measure for Measure*
MND	*A Midsummer Night's Dream*
MV	*The Merchant of Venice*
Oth.	*Othello*
Per.	*Pericles*
R2	*King Richard the Second*
R3	*King Richard the Third*
Rom.	*Romeo and Juliet*
Shr.	*The Taming of the Shrew*
STM	*Sir Thomas More*
Temp.	*The Tempest*
TGV	*The Two Gentlemen of Verona*
Tim.	*Timon of Athens*
Tit.	*Titus Andronicus*
TN	*Twelfth Night*
TNK	*The Two Noble Kinsmen*
Tro.	*Troilus and Cressida*

| Wiv. | *The Merry Wives of Windsor* |
| WT | *The Winter's Tale* |

2. Editions

Alexander	*William Shakespeare: The Complete Works*, ed. Peter Alexander, 1951
Brooks	*A Midsummer Night's Dream*, ed. Harold F. Brooks, 1979 (Arden Shakespeare)
Cam.	*The Works of William Shakespeare*, ed. W. G. Clark, John Glover and W. Aldis Wright, 9 vols., 1863–6 (Cambridge Shakespeare)
Capell	*Mr. William Shakespeare his Comedies, Histories, and Tragedies*, ed. Edward Capell, 10 vols., 1767
Chambers	*A Midsummer Night's Dream*, ed. E. K. Chambers, 1897 (Warwick Shakespeare)
Cuningham	*A Midsummer Night's Dream*, ed. Henry Cuningham, 1905, rev. edn 1930 (Arden Shakespeare)
Dyce	*The Works of William Shakespeare*, ed. Alexander Dyce, 6 vols., 1857
F	*Mr. William Shakespeares Comedies, Histories, & Tragedies*, 1623 (First Folio)
F2	*Mr. William Shakespeares Comedies, Histories & Tragedies*, 1632 (Second Folio)
F4	*Mr. William Shakespeares Comedies, Histories, & Tragedies*, 1685 (Fourth Folio)
Halliwell	*The Complete Works of Shakespeare*, ed. J. O. Halliwell, 3 vols., 1852
Hanmer	*The Works of Shakespeare...Carefully Revised and Corrected by the former Editions*, ed. Thomas Hanmer, 6 vols., 1744
Johnson	*The Plays of William Shakespeare*, ed. Samuel Johnson, 8 vols., 1765
Knight	*The Pictorial Edition of the Works of Shakespeare*, ed. Charles Knight, 8 vols., 1839–43
Malone	*The Plays and Poems of William Shakespeare*, ed. Edward Malone, 10 vols., 1790
NS	*A Midsummer Night's Dream*, ed. Sir Arthur Quiller-Couch and John Dover Wilson, 1924, rev. edn 1968 (New Shakespeare)
Pope	*The Works of Shakespeare*, ed. Alexander Pope, 6 vols., 1723–5
Q1	*A Midsommer nights dreame*, Imprinted at London for Thomas Fisher, 1600 (first quarto)
Q2	*A Midsommer nights dreame*, Printed by James Roberts, 1600 (in fact by William Jaggard, 1619: second quarto)
Rann	*The Dramatic Works of Shakespeare*, ed. Joseph Rann, 6 vols., 1786–91
Rolfe	*A Midsummer Night's Dream*, ed. W. J. Rolfe, 1877
Rowe	*The Works of Mr. William Shakespear*, ed. Nicholas Rowe, 6 vols., 1709 (second edition also 1709)

Rowe[3]	*The Works of Mr. William Shakespear*, ed. Nicholas Rowe, third edition, 8 vols., 1714
Singer	*The Dramatic Works of William Shakespeare*, ed. S. W. Singer, 10 vols., 1826
Staunton	*The Plays of Shakespeare*, ed. Howard Staunton 3 vols, 1858–60
Steevens	*The Plays of William Shakespeare*, ed. George Steevens, 10 vols., 1773
Theobald	*The Works of Shakespeare*, ed. Lewis Theobald, 7 vols., 1733
Var. 1778	*The Plays of William Shakespeare*, with the corrections and illustrations of various commentators, to which are added notes by Samuel Johnson and George Steevens, 10 vols., 1778
Warburton	*The Works of Shakespeare*, ed. William Warburton, 8 vols., 1747
Wells	*A Midsummer Night's Dream*, ed. S. W. Wells, 1967 (New Penguin Shakespeare)
White	*Mr. William Shakespeare's Comedies Histories Tragedies and Poems*, ed. Richard Grant White, 6 vols., 1883
Wright, Aldis	*A Midsummer Night's Dream*, ed. W. Aldis Wright, 1877 (Clarendon Shakespeare)
Wright, Martin	*A Midsummer Night's Dream Edited from the Quarto of 1600*, Martin Wright, 1968

3. Other works, periodicals, general references

Bullough	*Narrative and Dramatic Sources of Shakespeare*, ed. Geoffrey Bullough, I, 1957
Chambers, *Shakespeare*	E. K. Chambers, *William Shakespeare: A Study of Facts and Problems*, 2 vols., 1930
conj.	conjecture
EETS	Early English Text Society
ELH	*ELH: A Journal of Literary History*
Folks	Martin Folks, conjectural emendations in Theobald
Geneva	Geneva translation of the Bible (1560)
Golding	*Shakespeare's Ovid: being Arthur Golding's Translation of the Metamorphoses*, ed. W. H. D. Rouse, 1961
Greg	W. W. Greg, *The Shakespeare First Folio*, 1955
Henslowe's Diary	*Henslowe's Diary*, ed. R. A. Foakes and R. T. Rickert, 1961
Kökeritz	Helge Kökeritz, *Shakespeare's Pronunciation*, 1953
Linthicum	M. Channing Linthicum, *Costume in the Drama of Shakespeare and his Contemporaries*, 1936
McKerrow	R. B. McKerrow, *Printers' & Publishers' Devices in England and Scotland 1485–1640*, 1913
MLQ	*Modern Language Quarterly*
Muir	Kenneth Muir, *The Sources of Shakespeare's Plays*, 1977
North	*The Lives of the Noble Grecians and Romans, compared together by...Plutarke...translated...into French by Sir James Amyot, and...into English by Sir Thomas North* (1579, reissued 1595)

OED	*The Oxford English Dictionary*, ed. Sir J. A. H. Murray, W. A. Craigie and C. T. Onions, 13 vols., 1933
Onions	C. T. Onions, *A Shakespeare Glossary*, 2nd edn, 1946
Qq	Both quartos
SD	stage direction
Shakespeare's England	*Shakespeare's England: An Account of the Life and Manners of his Age*, ed. Sidney Lee and C. T. Onions, 2 vols., 1916
Sisson	C. J. Sisson, *New Readings in Shakespeare*, 2 vols., 1956
SJ	*Shakespeare Jahrbuch*
SQ	*Shakespeare Quarterly*
S.Sur.	*Shakespeare Survey*
subst.	substantively
Thirlby	Styan Thirlby, conjectural emendations in Theobald
Tilley	M. P. Tilley, *A Dictionary of the Proverbs in England in the Sixteenth and Seventeenth Centuries*, 1950 (references are to numbered proverbs)
Tyrwhitt	Thomas Tyrwhitt, *Observations and Conjectures upon Some Passages of Shakespeare*, 1766
Williams, 'Discord'	Gary Jay Williams, '"The concord of this discord": music in the stage history of *A Midsummer Night's Dream*', *Yale/Theatre* 4 (1973), 40–68
Williams, 'Vestris'	Gary Jay Williams, 'Madame Vestris, *A Midsummer Night's Dream* and the web of Victorian tradition', *Theatre Survey* 18 (1977), 1–22

INTRODUCTION

Date and occasion

The dating of Shakespeare's earlier plays remains largely speculative, and in the absence of hard information, it is tempting to look for topical allusions or particular events – in the case of *A Midsummer Night's Dream*, a wedding – which might provide a point of reference for the play. The best evidence for dating this play remains, in fact, its nature and style, for it shares with a group of plays written about 1594–7 the mastery of lyrical drama achieved by Shakespeare in the mid 1590s; there is good reason, therefore, to accept the usual dating of the play within a chronology that probably goes as follows:

1594–5	*Love's Labour's Lost*
1595	*Richard II*
1595–6	*Romeo and Juliet*
1595–6	*A Midsummer Night's Dream*
1596–7	*The Merchant of Venice*

In all of these plays there is a conscious display of poetic and rhetorical skills and devices. In *Love's Labour's Lost* Shakespeare took delight in shaping for his characters 'a set of wit well played', as they engage in virtuoso games of repartee, exchanging balanced speeches, and capping one another's riddles or rhymes. Even in this intellectual play Shakespeare's deeper concerns emerge in his dramatisation of the limitations of wit, and the contrast between words and deeds, as, for instance, between the impressively latinate word 'remuneration' and the three farthings it represents. The primary emphasis nevertheless is on words, as it is in *Richard II*, in which the great set speeches of Gaunt and Richard himself carry the emotional weight of the play, and make Bullingbrook's deeds appear, by contrast, of less concern. Here again is a good deal of rhyme, formal antithesis, and stichomythia. *Romeo and Juliet* too contains rhyming passages, stichomythia, and great verse cadenzas, such as Mercutio's Queen Mab speech in 1.4; it makes memorable the passion of the lovers in speeches that have caused this to become perhaps the best-known of all love stories, yet the dialogue of the lovers is highly artificial, and its lyrical power is generated as much by its relation to the conceits and rhetoric of love poetry (exemplified, for instance, in the great vogue for sonnets at this time) as by its reference to character: so the thirteen-year-old Juliet summons night with a witty image of Phaëton whipping the horses of the sun:

> Gallop apace, you fiery-footed steeds,
> Towards Phoebus' lodging; such a waggoner
> As Phaëton would whip you to the west,
> And bring in cloudy night immediately.

(*Rom.* 3.2.1–4)

1

In *Richard II* even the gardeners speak in verse, but in the other plays Shakespeare was developing his skills in creating prose characters, such as Costard in *Love's Labour's Lost* and the Nurse in *Romeo and Juliet*. These skills come to fruition in the speeches of Shakespeare's first great clown figure, bully Bottom; through him romantic ardour is genially mocked in *A Midsummer Night's Dream*, even as the dramatist's poetic skills are ravishingly displayed. There is no need to suppose that Shakespeare was deliberately repudiating *Romeo and Juliet* in using a similar story, that of 'Pyramus and Thisbe', for the 'tragical mirth' (5.1.57) of Peter Quince's play in Act 5, but it seems that he had the earlier play in mind.[1] The common ground between the stories, 'lovers disregarding parental opposition, meeting in secret and, through mistiming at a rendezvous, coming to a tragic end, the heroine killing herself over the hero's dead body',[2] suggests an element of conscious burlesque. Although the parents are not present in 'Pyramus and Thisbe', Shakespeare began by thinking of them, for Quince includes them in his casting for the play (1.2.49–52), and at the end Bottom leaps up to cry 'the wall is down that parted their fathers'. The natural assumption is that Shakespeare first treated the story seriously in his tragedy, and afterwards exploited its possibilities for burlesque and farce in a comedy.

The Merchant of Venice, which is generally thought to follow *A Midsummer Night's Dream* in the sequence of Shakespeare's plays, brings harsher and more discordant notes to clash against the poetic charm of Belmont, notably in Shylock and the lonely figure of Antonio, and in enmeshing the music and amorous fancy of the lovers within a dramatic world dominated by the cash-nexus. This takes comedy, rather uncomfortably, and at the cost of an anticlimactic fifth act, into new territory for Shakespeare, and to this extent may be seen as an advance on his previous plays. All these plays are often grouped among his early works, and it is as well to notice, therefore, that, on the usual chronological reckoning, *A Midsummer Night's Dream* was the twelfth play Shakespeare provided for his company to act.[3] The apprentice years were well past, and this is a harmonious, finely structured play of great stylistic variety, and complexity of meaning. It stands to his later comedies as *Hamlet* does to the later tragedies. Other plays may, through their range, intensity or complexity, establish new boundaries for these genres, and the general vote is more likely to be awarded to, say, *Twelfth Night* as the 'greatest' of the comedies, and *King Lear* as the highest achievement among the tragedies. None, however, has the archetypal quality and general appeal of the two earlier works, which are known to all who know anything of Shakespeare as a dramatist.

This needs to be kept in mind in considering speculations about an occasion for which *A Midsummer Night's Dream* may have been written. Because the play is designed to culminate in the wedding celebration of Theseus and Hippolyta, many

---

[1] See Glynne Wickham, '*A Midsummer Night's Dream*: the setting and the text', in *Shakespeare's Dramatic Heritage*, 1969, pp. 184–6, and C. L. Barber, *Shakespeare's Festive Comedy*, 1959, p. 152 and n.

[2] Brooks, p. xliv.

[3] A terminal date is provided by the listing by Francis Meres in his *Palladis Tamia Wits Treasury* (1598), p. 282, of the plays by Shakespeare he was aware of, among them *Love's Labour's Lost*, *A Midsummer Night's Dream*, *The Merchant of Venice* and *Romeo and Juliet*.

have conjectured that it must have been written to grace a specific event, a wedding in a noble household. Two possible occasions would have been the marriage between Elizabeth Vere and the Earl of Derby on 26 January 1595, and that between Elizabeth Carey and Thomas Berkeley on 19 February 1596. There is no evidence to connect the play with either ceremony, and, as Wells points out, while aristocratic weddings were sometimes enhanced by formal entertainments, these usually took the form of a masque, and the first play known to have been provided specifically for such an occasion was Samuel Daniel's pastoral *Hymen's Triumph* (1614), written about twenty years later, when courtly entertainments had become much more elaborate.[1] If an occasion must be sought, then the second is more plausible in terms of date, and both the bride's grandfather, Lord Hunsdon, and her father, Sir George Carey, were successively patrons of Shakespeare's company, which might suggest another kind of link. The play contains what is probably a graceful compliment to Queen Elizabeth as a virgin queen, throned 'by the west' (2.1.158 ff.), and while it is not necessary to link this with a specific occasion, she was involved in celebrations relating to the wedding of Elizabeth Vere, and, although there is no evidence to connect her with the nuptials of Elizabeth Carey, she may have had something to do with them, as the bride was her god-daughter.

The best reasons for seeking an occasion for the play do not concern its nature as a wedding play, for in this respect it is simply a variant of Shakespeare's characteristic mode of romantic comedy; *As You Like It*, for example, ends with the god of marriage, Hymen, celebrating the coupling of four pairs of lovers. Two other aspects of the play provide better grounds, though in my view still not very convincing ones, for linking it with a specific event or date. One is the influence of Lyly on this play,[2] which led G. K. Hunter to link it with *Love's Labour's Lost* as marked off from Shakespeare's other comedies 'because the occasion of these plays is aristocratic rather than popular'.[3] Those, indeed, who take it for granted that *A Midsummer Night's Dream* was written for a courtly wedding tend to see it as a play for intellectuals, imbued with a 'sophisticated Renaissance philosophy of the nature of love in both its rational and irrational forms'.[4] As against this, it has to be acknowledged, as Hunter shows, that Shakespeare 'remains true to himself' in a play which is in the line of most of his other work in appealing just as readily to unsophisticated audiences. A second feature of the play which has prompted scholars to look for topical explanations is the demand it makes on casting, and in terms of music. The play has four named fairies, and several other parts that boys would have played (Hermia, Helena, Titania, Hippolyta). It is possible that for a production in a private household, extra resources would have been available, perhaps, as Paul Siegel prettily speculates, more boys to play fairies and to dance with lighted tapers at the end in benediction of an actual wedding pair. The fairies carrying tapers in *The Merry Wives of Windsor* 5.5 are often adduced as analogous; there Evans says 'twenty glow-worms shall our lanthorns be',

[1] A point made by Wells, p. 14.   [2] See p. 5 below.
[3] G. K. Hunter, *John Lyly: The Humanist as Courtier*, 1962, p. 318.
[4] Paul H. Olson, '*A Midsummer Night's Dream* and the meaning of court marriage', *ELH* 24 (1957), 95–6; see also Paul N. Siegel, '*A Midsummer Night's Dream* and the wedding guests', *SQ* 4 (1953), 139–44.

and if the number need not be taken literally, it suggests that more than a few fairies were present. Like *A Midsummer Night's Dream*, *The Merry Wives of Windsor* has been associated with a possible private performance, specifically for a feast on 23 April 1597 when Sir George Carey was among those newly admitted to the Order of the Garter. The connection looks neat, but the arguments about this play are again speculative; it is difficult to see how Shakespeare could have fitted it in during a busy writing period in 1597, it is not mentioned by Francis Meres, and it could belong to a date nearer 1602, when it was published.[1]

The title page of the first quarto of *A Midsummer Night's Dream* presents it as it has been 'sundry times publickely acted' by the Lord Chamberlain's Men, and Shakespeare, who acted with the company, must have known that they had the resources to stage it. In his ingenious study of the number of actors required to perform the early plays, William A. Ringler, Jr, has claimed that Shakespeare 'to the very end of his writing career adhered to his original basic pattern of a cast of 16 actors';[2] he shows how the twenty-two speaking parts in the quarto could have been played by eleven or twelve adults and four boys, on the assumption that there were four fairies only in the 'train' of Titania and Oberon, and that these were played by the same adult actors who took the parts of Flute, Starveling, Snout and Snug. This might seem to be flying in the face of the late-nineteenth-century stage-tradition in doubling adults as fairies, but it is more plausible than to suppose that Shakespeare wrote for a special occasion on the assumption that a private patron would provide several boys to swell the company. At any rate, it is pointless to speculate further about a possible occasion for the play, and it does not affect the dating of its composition in 1595–6.

Sources

The word 'source' is clumsy in relation to a play like *A Midsummer Night's Dream*. Shakespeare used or adapted names, ideas, images or hints for incidents from various works he certainly knew, and echoed a number more, so that a long list of works can be compiled that probably contributed in some way to the play. The detection of these has its own fascination and is useful in so far as they illustrate the workings of Shakespeare's imagination, but the most notable feature of the play is the dramatist's inventiveness, brilliantly fusing scattered elements from legend, folklore and earlier books and plays into a whole that remains as fresh and original now as when it was composed. The range of reference underlying it deserves attention also, however, because it helps to explain something of the archetypal force of the comedy, showing the dramatist's instinct for seizing on whatever might articulate and enrich the web of meanings and relationships developed in it.

[1] For Meres, see above, p. 2 and n. The case for a 1597 date is presented in full by William Green in *Shakespeare's Merry Wives of Windsor*, 1962.
[2] 'The number of actors in Shakespeare's early plays', in G. E. Bentley (ed.), *The Seventeenth-Century Stage*, 1968, pp. 110–34; the quotation is from p. 126. See also Stephen Booth, 'Speculations on doubling', in *King Lear, Macbeth, Indefinition, and Tragedy*, 1983, pp. 131–4.

A play so much concerned with transformation transforms its sources, none more so than the work which has recently been proposed as 'the primary influence' on it, and indeed a major source for it, namely John Lyly's *Gallathea* (?1585; printed 1592).[1] Shakespeare certainly knew the plays of Lyly, and in *A Midsummer Night's Dream* he built up the action 'in the manner of Lyly, by balancing a number of self-contained groups, one against the other',[2] and presenting each group in turn. In drawing attention to Lyly's influence in this general way, G. K. Hunter pointed especially to *Sapho and Phao* (not published until 1632) and *Midas* (1589; printed 1592), in which Midas's head is 'metamorphosed' (4.1.168) into an ass's head, anticipating Bottom's transformation. In her more recent essay, Leah Scragg claims that *Gallathea* was much more directly influential on Shakespeare's play in its concern with love in relation to 'a pervasive process of metamorphosis'.[3] Lyly's plot begins from the disguise of two girls, Gallathea and Phyleida, as boys, so that neither will be made the victim in the sacrifice of a virgin. Lyly plays variations on the effect of this change as they fall in love, until at the end one or other of the girls is to be transformed into a boy so that they can marry. However, *Gallathea* is not much more than an elegant debate on love and chastity, passion and virtue, and the action has to be resolved in the end by a compromise arranged between Venus and Diana. The subplot, involving the three sons of a miller and their dealings with a mariner, an alchemist and an astronomer, has no connection with Shakespeare's play, apart from the dance of fairies Lyly inserted in 2.3, and Lyly's balanced prose, written for his schoolboy actors, appears stylised, monotonous and thin when set against the variety of textures in Shakespeare's language, and the rich play of metaphor and image in *A Midsummer Night's Dream*. Whatever hints Shakespeare picked up from Lyly he developed beyond recognition, so that the differences are far more remarkable than the similarities, and G. K. Hunter's account of Lyly's impact on Shakespeare remains persuasive; he assessed Lyly's dramatic achievement sympathetically, and showed too how Shakespeare went beyond him in *A Midsummer Night's Dream* to create 'a whole realm of action whose poetic atmosphere is alone sufficient to characterize the ideas it contains'.[4]

The framing device of the play – the wedding celebrations of Theseus – Shakespeare developed from the narrative in Chaucer's *The Knight's Tale*, which refers to the conquest by Theseus of the Amazons and their queen, Hippolyta (1, 866–83), and the great 'solempnytee' and feast of the wedding (compare 'the night / Of our solemnities', 1.1.10–11).[5] In Chaucer's poem Theseus is represented as a keen hunter, riding out 'With hunte and horn and houndes him bisyde' (1, 1678;[6] compare 4.1.100 ff.). Chaucer stresses the wisdom, dignity and great state of Theseus, and

[1] Leah Scragg, 'Shakespeare, Lyly and Ovid: the influence of "Gallathea" on "A Midsummer Night's Dream"', *S.Sur.* 30 (1977), 125–34, p. 133. This essay has been supplemented and reworked in *The Metamorphosis of Gallathea: A Study in Creative Adaptation*, 1982, pp. 57–77.
[2] Hunter, *John Lyly*, p. 318; the section in this book on 'Lyly and Shakespeare', pp. 298–340, remains the best study of their relationship.
[3] Scragg, 'Shakespeare, Lyly and Ovid', p. 128.   [4] Hunter, *John Lyly*, p. 327.
[5] See Ann Thompson's useful account of *Shakespeare and Chaucer*, 1978, esp. pp. 88–94.
[6] Line references are to the text as arranged in *The Works of Geoffrey Chaucer*, ed. F. N. Robinson, 2nd edn, 1957.

Shakespeare clouded his picture by taking from Sir Thomas North's translation of Plutarch's 'Life of Theseus' the names of various women he was there said to have loved and abandoned (2.1.77–80). Shakespeare's Theseus, if Oberon (and Plutarch) can be believed, had doted like the lovers in the play, whose story also owes something to Chaucer. In *The Knight's Tale* Theseus returns home to Athens after his wedding to be stopped by a 'compaignye of ladyes' (1, 898) kneeling in the highway and seeking his help against the 'tiraunt Creon' (1, 961) of Thebes, who has refused to allow them to bury their husbands, killed in battle. Theseus in turn slays Creon, and in the fight takes prisoner two young knights, friends and cousins, Palamon and Arcite, who both fall in love with Emily when, from their prison tower, they see her setting out to 'do May observance' (1, 1047, 1500; compare 1.1.167). Their story, involving their meeting in a wood after Arcite's release and Palamon's escape, and their quarrel arising from a clash between love and friendship, suggested the escape of the lovers to a wood in *A Midsummer Night's Dream*, as well as their quarrels and eventual reconciliation. Shakespeare, of course, creates two pairs of lovers and transfers the emphasis on friendship and 'sisters' vows' (3.2.199) to the girls, Hermia and Helena. In Chaucer's tale, Theseus, out hunting on a May morning, comes upon Palamon and Arcite fighting one another for the love of Emily; in the play, Theseus, again out hunting, encounters the two pairs of lovers asleep in 4.1, supposing they have risen 'early to observe / The rite of May' (4.1.129–30). Shakespeare also borrowed the names Philostrate and Egeus from Chaucer; Philostrate is the alias adopted by Arcite at 1, 1428, and Egeus is the name of the old father of Theseus (1, 2838, 2905). Shakespeare transformed the company of ladies who complain to Theseus at the beginning of *The Knight's Tale* into Egeus complaining against Hermia in 1.1.

Shakespeare probably derived the general idea for a King and Queen of Fairies who quarrel between themselves, and intervene in the affairs of human beings, from Chaucer's *Merchant's Tale*. Chaucer's king and queen are called Pluto and Proserpine, and the outcome of their debate about love, sex and the relations of wife and husband, in which Pluto attacks and Proserpine defends the treacheries of women, is that Pluto restores the sight of the old man January in time for him to see his wife, May, making love to the young squire Damian in a pear tree, while Proserpine ensures that May has the wit to persuade January to believe he imagined what he saw. Like Pluto and Proserpine, Oberon and Titania take sides in their support respectively for Hippolyta and Theseus, but Shakespeare richly develops the basic idea by making his fairy king a lover of Hippolyta, and Titania a lover of Theseus, by inventing their quarrel over the Indian boy, and by providing them with a train of fairies and adding Puck; although in Chaucer's tale Pluto is King of the Fairies, no fairies appear, and he is somewhat oddly accompanied by 'many a lady' (IV, 2228).

The name Oberon derives from the romance *Huon of Bordeaux*, translated by Lord Berners (first published 1533–42), and well enough known to have provided matter for a play, no longer extant, in the repertory of the Earl of Sussex's Men in 1593–4,[1] and for incidents in Robert Greene's play *The Scottish History of James IV* (?1590),

---

[1] It was performed three times in December 1593 and January 1594; see *Henslowe's Diary*, p. 20.

which turns history into romance, and gives Oberon a marginal role at the opening and later on when he brings on fairies dancing in rounds. In *Huon of Bordeaux* Oberon and his fairies are associated with the east; they inhabit a wood, they can create illusory storms and dangers, all 'fantasie and enchauntments', and they can make mortals think they are in paradise. When Huon encounters them he is on his way to Babylon to see a maid, 'the most fairest creature in all *Inde*',[1] and this may have suggested to Shakespeare the association of Oberon and Titania with India (2.1.69, 124). The name Titania is a patronymic used several times by Ovid in the *Metamorphoses* in reference to descendants of the Titans, such as Pyrrha (I, 395), Latona (VI, 346), Diana (III, 173) and Circe (XIV, 382, 438). Shakespeare apparently borrowed the name from the Latin, since Arthur Golding never uses it in his translation of the *Metamorphoses* (1567, reprinted for the fourth time in 1593), which the dramatist knew well, and which provided him with a version of the Pyramus and Thisbe story.

If Oberon comes from romance, and Titania from classical legend, Puck seems to have originated as a generic name in Old English for mischievous, or sometimes malicious, spirits, and came to be used in the sixteenth century as a specific name for a 'shrewd and knavish sprite' (2.1.33) also known as Hobgoblin and Robin Goodfellow.[2] Many of Puck's attributes in *A Midsummer Night's Dream* were traditional – his mocking laughter 'Ho, ho, ho', (3.2.421), his broom to sweep 'behind the door', so helping housemaids who left milk for him (5.1.367–8), and his ability to take on any shape (2.1.46–55). Shakespeare makes him merry and impish, a practical joker acting more in fun than malice, and so perhaps established a popular image of Puck, who is elsewhere sometimes depicted as devilish, as in *Wily Beguiled* (1602).[3] Puck or Robin Goodfellow was a familiar figure in Shakespeare's day, in legend, ballad and drama, and he appears with his broom in Jonson's masque *Love Restored* (1616). Bullough and most editors take it for granted that Shakespeare picked up hints for his Puck from Reginald Scot's *Discoverie of Witchcraft* (1584); certainly Scot summarises the traditional characteristics of Robin, though I doubt whether Shakespeare needed to consult him to learn what was common knowledge. Scot interestingly records that belief in such spirits was passing away: 'heretofore Robin Goodfellow, and Hobgoblin were as terrible, and also as credible to the people, as hags and witches be now: and in time to come, a witch will be as much derided and contemned and as plainlie perceived, as the illusion and knaverie of Robin Goodfellow'.[4] Shakespeare gave him immortality by transforming him into his 'merry wanderer of the night' (2.1.43).

Puck was probably played by an adult actor, as in *Grim the Collier of Croydon* (1600),[5] where he appears as the clownish servant of the devil, for he is called a 'lob' or bumpkin by a fairy at 2.1.16. The fairies in the play are, by contrast, imagined

---

[1] *The Boke of Duke Huon of Burdeux*, ed. S. L. Lee, EETS, 2 vols., 1882–3, ch. 21, I, 64; Bullough, I, 391, reprints the 1601 edition, ch. xx.
[2] See M. W. Latham, *The Elizabethan Fairies*, 1930, pp. 223 ff., and K. M. Briggs, *The Anatomy of Puck*, 1959.
[3] See Briggs, *Anatomy of Puck*, pp. 71 ff.   [4] *The Discoverie of Witchcraft*, p. 131.
[5] This play, probably by William Haughton, was written for the Admiral's Men, the major rivals to Shakespeare's company.

as tiny, and Shakespeare teases the imagination of his audience by requiring them to accept that his actors were as diminutive as their names Cobweb and Mustardseed suggest. In her study of *The Elizabethan Fairies*, M. W. Latham found no early references to fairies as diminutive, and supposed Shakespeare to have originated a literary fashion for presenting fairies as tiny, innocuous and associated with flowers (as at 2.1.10–15). The influence of *A Midsummer Night's Dream* may well have been potent in the presentation of fairies as tiny and charming in drama (as in *The Maid's Metamorphosis* (1600)) and poetry (as in Michael Drayton's *Nymphidia* (1627)), but K. M. Briggs and others have shown that fairies much smaller than the three-foot-high dwarf Oberon in *Huon of Bordeaux* were common enough in lore and legend; references abound to fairies ranging from the really minute, the size of bees or wasps, to the very small at twelve or eighteen inches tall.[1]

Fairies might be malevolent, as is made clear in *Cymbeline*, where Imogen prays for protection from 'fairies and the tempters of the night' (2.2.9), and in *Hamlet*, where Marcellus says that at Christmas 'No fairy takes, nor witch hath power to harm' (1.1.163). Oberon explicitly distinguishes the fairies in *A Midsummer Night's Dream* from witches and tempters of the night: 'we are spirits of another sort' (3.2.388). Shakespeare's fairies belong, like those in *The Merry Wives of Windsor* 5.5, to an equally strong tradition of more kindly fairies,[2] who may pinch sluttish housemaids, but reward those who do well and say their prayers, and bring them good fortune, as in Greene's *James IV*, where Oberon's interventions are all benevolent, or in Lyly's *Endymion*, in which fairies, as the servants of Cynthia (or Diana, the moon), pinch Corsitas for his 'trespass' against her and afflict him with spots, but kiss the hero Endymion. In *Huon of Bordeaux*, Oberon says he 'was never devyll nor yll creature',[3] and the image of fairies as well-disposed to the good was encouraged by Spenser's *Faerie Queene*, in which Oberon becomes a quasi-sacred figure as father of Gloriana, who allegorically represented Queen Elizabeth.[4] The traditional sense of fairies as 'friendly' to human beings, or at least as rewarding the good and punishing the idle or bad, is, however, modified by Shakespeare in *A Midsummer Night's Dream*, in which he transforms his fairies on the one hand into Oberon and Titania, who have human passions and jealousies, and on the other hand into their train of delightfully innocuous figures, whose main office is tending their queen, protecting her from beetles, spiders and other night-creatures (2.2.9–23), and serving Bottom on her behalf as airy spirits (3.1.142 ff.). In envisaging them so, Shakespeare perhaps took a hint from the fairies with 'fair faces' who dance and sing in Lyly's *Endymion* 4.3 and dance and play in *Gallathea* 2.3, for in his company of boy-actors, it seems probable that the smallest and most nimble performed these parts. All the fairies join at the end in song and dance

---

[1] See Latham, *Elizabethan Fairies*, pp. 66–79, Briggs, *Anatomy of Puck*, pp. 56–70, and the extensive list of early references to diminutive fairies in Brooks, p. lxxii and n. In *Rom.* 1.4.55–6, Mercutio speaks of Queen Mab, the 'fairies' midwife', as no bigger than 'an agate-stone / On the forefinger of an alderman'.

[2] Falstaff in this play is especially put out by Hugh Evans masquerading as a 'Welsh fairy' (5.5.81), and Brooks, pp. lxxiii–lxxvi, thinks Shakespeare may have been influenced by an acquaintance with Welsh folklore.   [3] *Huon of Burdeux*, ch. 24; 1, 69 in Lee's edn.

[4] *Faerie Queene*, II, x, 75 ff.; see also Brooks, p. lxxvi.

1   Titania's awakening (Act 4, Scene 1); an engraving of 1803, after the painting of 1785–90 by Henry
Fuseli. Bottom is shown surrounded by evil spirits, with a group of good fairies behind Oberon to the
left

to bless the house of Theseus, so that the final image is of creatures who have power to
ward off evil.

Shakespeare needed no other source than imagination working on life to create
Bottom, Quince and the mechanicals – together with the presence in his company of
the well-known clown Will Kemp and the slighter comedian Richard Cowley, a nicely
matched pair who later created the parts of Dogberry and Verges.[1] Bottom's
transformation is a brilliant invention, linking him and his crew to the fairies and the
lovers, and also to a range of well-known tales and legends of men changed into
monsters. These go back to Circe in the *Odyssey*, and her power 'most monstrous
shapes to frame' is also described in the *Metamorphoses*, translated by Arthur Golding
(XIV, 63); there were, however, two famous stories of men changed to asses. One was
the legend of the foolish King Midas, who refused to accept the general verdict that
Apollo had beaten Pan in a musical contest, and was therefore punished by the god,
who changed his ears into ass's ears, leaving the rest of his body human (Golding's
Metamorphoses XI, 165–216). This story was dramatised by John Lyly in his *Midas*
(1589; published 1592), in which Apollo inflicts 'The ears of an ass upon the head

---

[1]   These actors are named in speech headings for the parts in Act 4, Scene 2, in the 1600 quarto of *Much
Ado About Nothing*; see Greg, p. 279.

of a king' (4.1.149–50), until eventually when Midas repents his folly, as the stage direction at 5.3.121 puts it, 'The ears fall off.'

The other well-known tale of the transformation of a man into an ass occurs in Apuleius, *The Golden Ass*, translated by William Adlington (1566; other editions in 1571, 1582 and 1596).[1] In Book 3, ch. 17 Apuleius persuades his mistress Fotis, the servant of a witch, to steal a box of ointment and anoint him with it, in the expectation that he will be changed into a bird, only to find that he is completely transformed into an ass and, what is worse, treated as one by other asses and horses, and by the thieves who take him and use him as a beast of burden. Apuleius as an ass is made to serve the thieves, and later helps a young maid they have captured to escape; she promises to reward him: 'I will bravely dress the haires of thy forehead, and then will I finely combe thy maine, I will tye up thy rugged tayle trimly...I will bring thee daily in my apron the kirnels of nuts, and will pamper thee up with delicates' (Book 6, ch. 23). This may have given Shakespeare a hint for Titania's courtesies to Bottom. If these antecedents were not enough, Shakespeare could also have found in Reginald Scot's *Discoverie of Witchcraft* the story of a young English visitor being transformed into an ass by a witch in Cyprus (Book V, ch. iii), and a description of a charm to 'set an horsse or an asses head upon a mans shoulders' (Book XII, ch. xx).

This is the most notable of many changes of shape and transformations in the play, and probably the most pervasive influence on it is that of Ovid's *Metamorphoses*, mainly as mediated through the translation of Arthur Golding (1567). Shakespeare may have known the Latin text,[2] but he would in any case have found in Golding's Ovid the story of Cupid's gold and leaden arrows (1.1.170; I, 565 ff.), the personification of Hiems as an old man (2.1.109; II, 39); the story of Apollo and Daphne (2.1.231; I, 581 ff.); the legend of Philomel (2.2.13; VI, 542 ff.); the story of the battle between Hercules and the Centaurs (5.1.45; XII, 236 ff.); the description of the death of Orpheus at the hands of the Bacchanals (5.1.48; XI, 1 ff.); and the tale of Cephalus and Procris (5.1.194; VIII, 874 ff.), as well as other suggestions for images.[3] Golding's Ovid was also the main source for the story of Pyramus and Thisbe (IV, 68 ff.), and it was this version on which Shakespeare based the narrative action of the play staged by the mechanicals. Not only the general alignment of the 'tedious brief scene' of Pyramus and Thisbe with the story as told in Golding confirms this as the source, but the correspondence of a number of details which are different in other versions, such as the mantle dropped by Thisbe (5.1.141; IV, 125); the 'crannied hole' (5.1.156; IV, 83); 'Ninus' tomb' (5.1.137; IV, 108); and the mulberry tree (5.1.147; IV, 110).

Shakespeare probably knew several versions of the story, beginning with Chaucer's *Legend of Good Women*, where it is treated seriously and with some delicacy as a moral tale about true love. Other treatments, including Golding's, fall into unintended absurdities, and offered matter for Shakespeare to use or parody. Golding pads out his unwieldy lines with a liberal use of the pleonastic 'did', which Quince's prologue picks up to comic effect.

[1] In Bk. 1, ch. 4, another Circe figure is described in Meroe, a witch who has the power to turn 'divers persons into miserable beasts'.   [2] See p. 7 above.
[3] See, for example, Commentary at 3.2.101 and 4.1.110–11.

> Did scare away, or rather did affright;
> And as she fled, her mantle she did fall,
> Which Lion vile with bloody mouth did stain...   (5.1.140–2)

Shakespeare also exaggerated the courtesy the lovers found in Golding's wall by having Snout play the part.[1]

> O thou envious wall (they sayd,) why letst thou lovers thus?
> What matter were it if that thou permitted both of us
> In armes eche other to embrace? Or if thou thinke that this
> Were overmuch, yet mightest thou at least make roome to kisse.
> And yet thou shalt not finde us churles: we thinke ourselves in det
> For the same piece of courtesie, in vouching safe to let
> Our sayings to our friendly eares thus freely come and goe.   (IV, 91–7)

Golding's fourteen-syllable line breaks down into the measure of part of the 'new Sonet of Pyramus and Thisbe' written by I. Tomson and included in *A Handful of Pleasant Delights* (1584) by Clement Robinson and others:[2]

> Oh Gods above, my faithfull love
>   shal never faile this need:
> For this my breath by fatall death
>   shal weave *Atropos* thread.

This is, in effect, the same rhythm as Pyramus's

> Thy mantle good –
> What, stained with blood?
> Approach, ye Furies fell!
> O Fates, come, come,
> Cut thread and thrum,
> Quail, crush, conclude, and quell.[3]   (5.1.266–71)

Shakespeare may have known also the version, written in rattling fourteeners, much cruder than Golding's, in *A Gorgious Gallery of Gallant Inventions* (1578), and possibly Thomas Mouffet's *The Silkewormes, and their Flies: described in verse* (1599), which incorporates the story of Pyramus and Thisbe because silkworms feed on the leaves of mulberry trees, which were stained, according to Ovid (Golding, IV, 150–1), by the blood Pyramus shed.[4] Mouffet's quite astonishing incompetence as a poet, and blindness to the possible implications of the language he used, together make his version read like a parody. It is almost conceivable that he found hints in *A Midsummer Night's Dream*; I find it more difficult to believe that Shakespeare took the trouble to read his verse treatise in manuscript, and used it for his play.[5] Many of the verbal

---

[1] A point made by Muir, pp. 66–77.
[2] See the edition by Hyder E. Rollins, 1924, p. 37, and Bullough, I, 409–11.
[3] Muir, pp. 70–2, draws attention also to some verbal echoes.
[4] The evidence is set out by Muir, pp. 72–7, who first noticed a possible connection with Mouffet's curious verse tract, and who says Shakespeare 'appears to have taken most' from this version, a view accepted by Brooks, p. lxxxvii.
[5] Like Bullough (I, 375), I remain sceptical about a connection between Mouffet's poem and Shakespeare's play; it is hardly surprising that there should be verbal 'links' between the various versions, since the

links between the play and versions of the story may be fortuitous, and perhaps we can be certain only of Shakespeare's use of Golding, and general burlesque of the absurdities, sillier redundancies and mannerisms of the outmoded versifiers of the age.

One further very specific debt to Golding's Ovid is to be found in Titania's speech on the disorder in nature caused by her quarrel with Oberon in 2.1.81–114, where Shakespeare combined images from the description of the seasons (II, 33–9) with suggestions from various accounts of Deucalion's flood, plagues and curses (I, 295–344; V, 593–603; VII, 678–706). Other minor but significant echoes contribute to the play; the title of Quince's play appears to be a parody of the printed title of Thomas Preston's *Cambyses* (1570) (see Commentary 1.2.9–10) and Bottom's alliterative 'part to tear a cat in' burlesques a passage in John Studley's translation of Seneca's *Hercules Oetaeus* (1581) (see Commentary 1.2.24–31). Bottom's account of his vision takes off from a passage in St Paul's Epistle to the Corinthians (4.1.205–7). Some material for the development of Theseus, his amorous adventures, and devotion to Hercules, was taken from Plutarch's 'Life of Theseus', as translated by Sir Thomas North (1579) (see, for instance, Commentary 2.1.78–80 and 5.1.47). Various other links have been detected, none of them so secure as to command belief, and these are dealt with briefly in the Appendix, pp. 144–5 below. It is exciting to discover connections, to track Shakespeare as a snapper-up of unconsidered trifles, hoarding like a magpie what others did not value, and transmuting it, at opportune moments, into dramatic gold. At the same time it is important to ask continually whether Shakespeare needed to go to a source for what was common property, or could have been on tap as flowing from an unconscious or subconscious assimilation of what was, so to speak, in the air, the common materials of the culture and discourse of his age. Judged on these terms, the other sources that have been claimed for incidents or passages in *A Midsummer Night's Dream* are dubious; all the same, the texture of the play derives a large part of its richness and complexity from the many imaginative strands Shakespeare drew from legend, folklore, literature and drama, and wove inextricably together to our lasting delight.

The play on the stage

A Midsummer Night's Dream was probably performed at court on 1 January 1604,[1] but otherwise nothing certain is known about productions before the closing of the theatres in the Commonwealth period. That it retained its popularity is suggested by the fact that a 'droll' extracted from it, called *The Merry Conceited Humours of Bottom the Weaver*, was published separately in 1661, and then included in Francis Kirkman's collection of farces, *The Wits* (1673), as 'Sundry times Acted In Publique and Private'. The play did not appeal to Restoration taste; only one performance is known, in

basic vocabulary of the story remains much the same. What is surprising is that all authors after Chaucer who narrated it tended to turn it unwittingly into farce, and Shakespeare seized on this potential for absurdity.

[1] Dudley Carleton reported in a letter (15 January 1604) to John Chamberlain the acting of a 'play of Robin goode-fellow', followed by a masque; see Chambers, *Shakespeare*, II, 329.

September 1662, when Pepys saw it and noted the good dancing, but altogether found it 'the most insipid ridiculous play that ever I saw in my life'.[1] Then in 1692 the play was reshaped into a spectacular opera with music by Henry Purcell, and produced by Thomas Betterton as *The Fairy Queen*. The text was cut and altered, Hippolyta omitted, and the play of 'Pyramus and Thisbe' transferred to Act 3. Each act ended with a transformation scene, one of which featured swans swimming on a river with a bridge over it in the form of two dragons, and, at the end of Act 5, a 'transparent Prospect of a Chinese Garden'; the cast included savages and haymakers, there were songs by Coridon and Mopsa, a nymph, Phoebus Apollo and a Chinese, and numerous dances. The play, in other words, became 'an elaborate vehicle for the Baroque music and spectacle',[2] which 'wonderfully satisfy'd' the court and the town, according to John Downes.[3] The importance of this is that it established a way of adapting the play for performance that persisted, with variations, into the twentieth century.

Various other operatic adaptations of the play, or parts of it, were staged in the eighteenth century. The most notable, David Garrick's version *The Fairies* (1755), retained fewer than 600 lines of the original text, omitted all characters but the lovers and fairies, and incorporated 28 songs, including some from other plays such as *The Tempest*, and lyrics culled from other poets such as Dryden.[4] The first major adaptation in the nineteenth century was that by Frederic Reynolds in 1816 at Covent Garden. This new operatic treatment retained a good many of the lyrics Garrick had introduced, but set them to new music, and was innovatory in its scenic splendours, setting a fashion for antiquarian spectacle, and ending with a pageant of the 'Triumphs of Theseus', taken from various legends, amongst them the 'Cretans, the Amazons, the Centaurs, the Minotaur, Ariadne in the Labyrinth, the Mysterious Peplum or Veil of Minerva, the Ship Argo, and the Golden Fleece'.[5] This operatic version by Reynolds formed the basis of other adaptations before 1840, which are notable only for the first use, in Alfred Bunn's Drury Lane production in 1853, of the overture written by Mendelssohn in 1826.[6]

The acclaimed production by Mme Lucia Vestris which opened in November 1840 at Covent Garden was momentous in restoring most of Shakespeare's text to the stage; she cut only about 400 lines, and seems to have established the style of cutting for the rest of the nineteenth century. She also reduced the number of songs to fourteen, and set the fashion for a woman to play Oberon, the part taken by Madame Vestris herself, who sang nine songs (see illustration 2). Although this seems to have been the first production since the Restoration which attempted to present the play 'as an organic and integrated whole',[7] it still treated it largely as an operatic spectacular, with antiquarian settings, crowds of female fairies dressed in white gauze in the romantic tradition of ballet, and effects such as Puck ascending on a mushroom for

---

[1] *The Diary of Samuel Pepys*, ed. Robert Latham and William Matthews, 11 vols., 1970–82, III, 208 (29 September 1662).
[2] Williams, 'Vestris', p. 2.   [3] *Roscius Anglicanus*, 1708, p. 43.
[4] Williams, 'Discord', esp. p. 47. See also Trevor Griffiths, 'A neglected pioneer production: Madame Vestris' *A Midsummer Night's Dream* at Covent Garden, 1840', *SQ* 30 (1979), 386–96.
[5] G. C. D. Odell, *Shakespeare – From Betterton to Irving*, 2 vols., 1920, repr. 1963, II, 113.
[6] Williams, 'Discord', p. 52.   [7] Williams, 'Vestris', p. 9.

2   Madame Lucia Vestris as Oberon in her production at Covent Garden, 1840: she restored Shakespeare's text, but set a fashion for female Oberons (brunette contraltos contrasting with soprano Titanias), and for crowding the stage with fairies, influencing Charles Kean (illustration 3)

3   Charles Kean's production at the Princess's Theatre, 1856: the palace of Theseus in Act 5, with a crowd of ninety fairies dancing; Oberon and Puck were played by actresses

his (her) first entry. Although in this way it maintained the tradition of treating the play as more like an opera with ballet, this production differed significantly from previous ones to the extent that the scenic effects were generally based on Shakespeare's text. This production greatly influenced later Victorian staging of the play, the most intelligent and sensitive production being that by Samuel Phelps at Sadlers Wells in 1853.[1] By this time the incidental music composed by Mendelssohn in 1843, and first used by Ludwig Tieck at Potsdam in that year, had become available, adding thirteen pieces to the overture, and from Charles Kean's production in 1856 until the production at the Old Vic in 1954, was 'the music customarily used' for performances on the English-speaking stage.[2]

The association of Mendelssohn's music with the play became so close that its 'enchanting strains' were felt as 'true Shakespeare',[3] and the habit of treating *A Midsummer Night's Dream* as a musical extravaganza, with the text often heavily cut, persisted into the twentieth century. In addition to scenic spectacles and troops of balletic fairies – sometimes played by women, sometimes by infants – producers often allowed their fancy to run riot in 'upholstering' the play, as in the use of electric fireflies in Augustine Daly's 1888 staging, or the innovation of a fight between a spider

[1] See the review by Henry Morley, reprinted in *Victorian Dramatic Criticism*, ed. George Rowell, 1971, pp. 102–5.
[2] According to Williams, 'Discord', p. 57; he also notes the use of this music as recently as 1965 in a production at the Yvonne Arnaud Theatre, Guildford.
[3] Percy Fitzgerald, *Shakespearean Representation*, 1908, cited in Williams, 'Discord', p. 65.

and a wasp in Frank Benson's treatment of it in 1889.[1] In his productions in 1900 and 1911, Beerbohm Tree used not only Mendelssohn's music for the play, but a number of other pieces by him as well, and once again had a female, singing Oberon.[2] The Mendelssohn spectacular version of the play reached its climactic form in the many productions by Max Reinhardt between 1905 and 1939, his most famous treatment of it being the film he made in Hollywood in 1935.[3] Other composers were drawn to write music to accompany *A Midsummer Night's Dream*, the most notable being Carl Orff,[4] but for a century or so after 1840 the music of Mendelssohn, and the tradition of lavish spectacle almost always marked the staging of this play (see illustrations 2–3 and 5–6).

Against this background the important production by Harley Granville-Barker at the Savoy Theatre in 1914 was revolutionary.[5] It made use of an apron stage, had only two set scenes, and aimed at clarity and simplicity, presenting the action, except for two intervals, in a fast-moving continuous performance with a full and uncut text. The parts of Oberon and Puck were restored to male actors. Floating gauzes were used to suggest a woodland, and three locations (Athens, the palace of Theseus, and the forest) were symbolised by the use of curtains of different colours.[6] Fairies were differentiated from mortals by their stylised movements and a covering of gold paint. In other words, Granville-Barker abandoned realism and sought to achieve a 'unity of atmosphere appropriate to the whole play'.[7] The golden fairies seemed to some reviewers at the time like Cambodian or Indian deities; Puck stood out from them in a scarlet cloak, wearing a wig covered with berries; 'with Theseus looking like a god, Hermia like a Tartar maiden, Helena like a Grecian Gretchen with flaxen hair, and Lysander and Demetrius with a touch of Japanese in their costume',[8] the total image was 'other-worldly', suggesting a remote dream-world (see illustration 4). At the same time, it recognised the conscious artifice of the play, presenting Bottom and his crew as figures from the Warwickshire countryside. Towards the end of 3.2, when Oberon directed Puck to intervene in the lovers' quarrel and set things right, Puck took over as stage-manager, 'motioned for the lights to be dimmed, and then bent down as if raising the drop cloth as it ascended to bring in Demetrius and Lysander'.[9] Thus Granville-Barker daringly (for his time) not only abandoned the tradition of scenic illusion, but emphasised the artifice of his production by making Puck for the

---

[1] Sally Beauman, *The Royal Shakespeare Company*, 1982, p. 35; Williams, 'Discord', pp. 62–3.

[2] Williams, 'Discord', pp. 63–4.

[3] For an account of Reinhardt's work, see J. L. Styan, *Max Reinhardt*, 1982, esp. pp. 54–61. In some respects this director's treatment of *A Midsummer Night's Dream* was revolutionary, for he was the first in Germany to bring out on stage the magic and delight of the play, and to move away from naturalism in his treatment of it in a long series of productions.

[4] See Williams, 'Discord', pp. 67–8; Winton Dean, 'Shakespeare in the opera house', *S.Sur.* 18 (1965), 75–93, pp. 87, 90, and Carl Orff's own account of his various musical settings for the play, 'Musik zum Sommernachtstraum. Ein Bericht', *SJ* 100 (1964), 117–34.

[5] The best brief account of it is J. L. Styan's in *The Shakespeare Revolution*, 1977, pp. 95–104; see also C. B. Purdom, *Harley Granville-Barker, Man of the Theatre, Dramatist and Scholar*, 1955.

[6] Critics disagree on what the colours were; white, pink and blue according to Odell, who saw the production (*Shakespeare – From Betterton to Irving*, II, 463); grey, pink and green according to Styan, *Shakespeare Revolution*, p. 97.   [7] Styan, *Shakespeare Revolution*, p. 97.

[8] *Ibid.*, p. 101.   [9] *Ibid.*, p. 103.

4   Harley Granville-Barker's production at the Savoy Theatre, 1914: Oberon (Denis Neilson-Terry) confronting Titania (Christine Silver) in Act 2, Scene 1, before a symbolic forest painted on a curtain. The gilded fairies wore exotic costumes, oriental in inspiration, part Cambodian, part Byzantine

moment apparently the controller of mechanical devices at the Savoy Theatre. He made the spectators aware that they were in a theatre, but sought to involve them in a world of poetic and dramatic rather than scenic illusion, yielding to a 'self-surrender as immediate and complete as possible'.[1]

This production also abandoned Mendelssohn's music in favour of English folk music arranged by Cecil Sharp. Its abrupt break with the traditional staging of the play shocked many critics and reviewers, horrified some, and delighted those who saw in Norman Wilkinson's 'futuristic' designs and Granville-Barker's radically innovative treatment of the actors and the text an exciting liberation from the overburdened approach habitual in the nineteenth century. Granville-Barker's writings[2] in the next two decades perhaps influenced academics rather more than his practice affected directors working in the theatre. In 1920 at Stratford W. Bridges-Adams returned to Mendelssohn, a female Puck, and traditional bands of skipping children representing fairies, and was acclaimed in *The Observer* for being 'not freakish, or futurist, or rebellious'.[3] His 1932 production, with designs by a now much less adventurous Norman Wilkinson, was staged with even greater scenic splendour, focusing in the forest scenes on a great hollow oak tree, which shifted to give the

[1] Granville-Barker, *Associating with Shakespeare* (an address delivered at King's College, London, on 25 November 1931), 1932, p. 12, cited by Styan, *Shakespeare Revolution*, p. 111. Styan saw this as 'an extra-dramatic device by which Barker's audience could be compelled to accept the mode of the play as one of conscious non-illusion' (p. 103), meaning scenic illusion, not stage-illusion. It is important not to confuse these; see pp. 39–40 below.
[2] Notably his *Prefaces to Shakespeare*, 5 vols., 1927–47, and his 'From *Henry V* to *Hamlet*' (the Annual Shakespeare Lecture, British Academy, 1925).
[3] On 25 April 1920; cited by Styan, *Shakespeare Revolution*, p. 134.

5 The persistence of the balletic tradition: Tyrone Guthrie's production at the Old Vic, 1937–8, with Dorothy Hyson as Titania, replacing Vivien Leigh, attended by twenty-two fairies

audience 'the impression that we were exploring the wood'.[1] The challenge made by Granville-Barker was perhaps not taken up in any substantial way until George Devine, who had worked in experimental theatre with Michel Saint-Denis, arrived in Stratford to direct the play in 1954 in a production which aimed to avoid 'conventional prettinesses'.[2] A formal set, with 'groups of stylized metallic trees', was used to emphasise the comedy of the strongly-played mechanicals and the hide-and-seek antics of the lovers; against these, the fairies were marked off by their strangeness, being feathered and bird-like in appearance and in the sounds they made (see illustration 7), while Puck's movements often resembled those of a chimpanzee.

The reviewers were not very satisfied with these fairies, but the production recovered something of the sinister undertones suggested in Henry Fuseli's remarkable illustrations dating from between 1780 and 1794, which were exhibited in Boydell's Shakespeare Gallery and reproduced in the volumes of prints brought out by John and Josiah Boydell in 1803. In Fuseli's drawing of Titania's awakening in 4.1, for example (see illustration 1), Bottom is shown asleep and ringed by evil spirits, a nightmare riding across his forehead, and three witches, with their brood, hovering by him to the right of the picture. This sense of something more disturbing in the

[1] According to the review in *The Times*, 29 April 1932, cited by Styan, *Shakespeare Revolution*, p. 136.
[2] Richard David, 'Plays pleasant and plays unpleasant', *S.Sur.* 8 (1955), 136–8.

6   The persistence of the balletic tradition: Michael Benthall's production at the Shakespeare Memorial
Theatre, 1949: Kathleen Michael as Titania, attended by nine fairies, whose costumes strikingly resemble
those of the productions of 1856 and 1938 (illustrations 3 and 5 above)

magic world of *A Midsummer Night's Dream* surfaced occasionally in illustrations by
other artists, such as Richard Dadd, but it emerged in the theatre only in the twentieth
century, in such productions as that by Michael Langham at the Old Vic in 1960.

A year earlier, in 1959, Peter Hall had directed the play in a production revived,
with some cuts restored, in 1962. This was a different kind of attempt to escape from
stage tradition, by making the lovers 'young, foolish and clumsy', and much given
to crude horseplay, with their verse 'absurdly guyed'. To John Russell Brown it
seemed simply another form of adaptation, 'too narrowly concerned with being
brightly amusing'.[1] To many, the most successful adaptation of the play during this
period was Benjamin Britten's opera, first performed in 1960 at Aldeburgh. The
settings by John Piper were disconcerting, with suggestions of forests that had 'at
once the frightening clarity of a nightmare and the blurred edges of a dream'; and
the fairies were played by boys with 'metallic' voices, whose hardness gave them an
edge, a 'sharpness' in Britten's words, quite different from the traditional innocent
charm. These features, together with the coherent drive of the opera towards the final
reconciliation, led Moelwyn Merchant to claim that this version was 'the richest and

---

[1] John Russell Brown, 'Three adaptations', *S.Sur.* 13 (1960), 142–5; see also his 'Acting Shakespeare
today', *S.Sur.* 16 (1963), 144.

7   George Devine's production at the Shakespeare Memorial Theatre, 1954: Oberon (Powys Thomas) and Puck (David O'Brien) take on harsher tones as birdlike figures

8   Peter Hall's production at the Shakespeare Memorial Theatre, 1959: the final scene, with Oberon (Robert Hardy) and Titania (Mary Ure) on the staircase to the right, with four male and six female attendants

most faithful interpretation of Shakespeare's intentions in *A Midsummer Night's Dream* that the stage has seen in our generation'.[1]

A new generation was even then in process of taking over; from 1955 London audiences were becoming familiar with the plays of Samuel Beckett and Bertolt Brecht, and with the work of a new wave of British dramatists, beginning with John Osborne's *Look Back in Anger* in 1956. In 1959, Peter Hall, who had staged *Waiting for Godot* at the Arts Theatre in 1955, became Director of the Shakespeare Memorial Theatre at Stratford. As noted above, his own version of *A Midsummer Night's Dream* in 1959 turned out to be an unsatisfactory attempt to haul the play into the twentieth century; indeed, its heavy set and elaborate costumes now look older than their time (see illustration 8). The reason for this is that in 1970 the revolutionary implications of Granville-Barker's 1914 production were taken further in the brilliant treatment of the play by Peter Brook with the Royal Shakespeare Company. From its first night, when the audience rose to its feet to applaud at the interval, this production dazzled and delighted audiences by its freshness and inventiveness, and continued to do so on tours around the world for several years. In part this success was achieved by Brook's radical approach to rehearsals, in which, instead of imposing a concept in the

[1]   Moelwyn Merchant, '*A Midsummer Night's Dream*: a visual recreation', in John Russell Brown and Bernard Harris (ed.), *Early Shakespeare*, 1961, pp. 182–3.

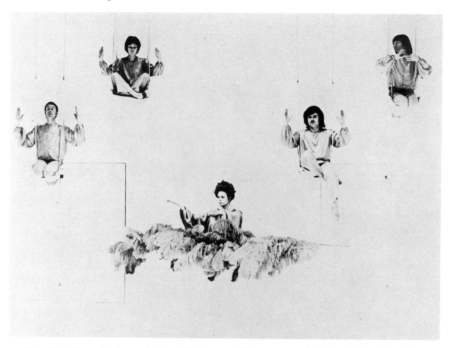

9 Peter Brook's production at the Royal Shakespeare Theatre, 1970, with Titania (Sarah Kestelman) on a trapeze among feathers at the centre, attended by Moth, Cobweb and Mustardseed, all played by male actors, and Peaseblossom

manner of what had become established in recent decades as 'director's theatre', he urged his actors to let the play work through them. So John Kane, who doubled as Puck and Philostrate, said, 'I think one of the strangest things about working for Peter for the first time is the realization that – and this is very true of the way we work at Stratford – we *do something* with the play. What was novel in working with Peter was that he wanted the play to *do things* with us.'[1] However, Brook certainly 'did things' with the play, notably in the startling originality of his staging, which employed a three-sided, brilliantly-lit white box, within which the magic of the play was translated into circus terms. The players became athletes, jugglers and trapeze-artists, running, tumbling and swinging in a white space, with Bottom as a button-nosed circus clown. Audiences responded to the sense of fun the actors conveyed, embodying Brook's vision of the play as a celebration: 'It's a celebration of the theme of theatre: the play-within-the-play-within-the-play-within-the-play.'[2]

The effect of what Brook called a 'collective creation'[3] was certainly to liberate the play at once from 'the oppression of *bad* tradition',[4] and to give the actors an exciting sense of fresh imaginative engagement with the text, as if they were encountering it

[1] *Peter Brook's Production of William Shakespeare's A Midsummer Night's Dream for The Royal Shakespeare Company: The Complete and Authorized Acting Edition*, 1974, p. 26.
[2] *Ibid.*, p. 24.   [3] *Ibid.*, p. 27.   [4] *Ibid.*, p. 30.

for the first time.[1] Yet, paradoxically, some critics found in this production a 'self-indulgent display of directorial gimmickry',[2] or the fettering of the play within an 'eccentric, single-minded (and rather simple-minded)' director's interpretation.[3] Inevitably, Brook was pressed to talk about the production, and did so; in what he said about it the notion of 'collective creation' seemed to be contradicted by his firm and peculiar interpretation of some aspects of the play. In an interview recorded late in 1970, he was asked to comment on a striking feature of his production, the doubling of Theseus with Oberon, and Hippolyta with Titania, and in explanation said that the couples were closely related because Theseus and Hippolyta are trying to 'discover what constitutes the true union of a couple', and that they go through quarrels as Oberon and Titania in order to make their marriage 'complete'. This idea is related to Brook's reading of the play as written for adults, and hence a 'very powerful sexual play'. He acknowledged the influence on him of Jan Kott in *Shakespeare Our Contemporary*, who suggested the 'dark and powerful currents of sensuality'[4] Brook exploited in his presentation, for example, of Titania and Bottom at the end of 3.1, where Bottom was carried off, to a parody of Mendelssohn's wedding march, with a phallus 'crudely mimed' by a fist thrust up between his legs.[5] This striking exit for the interval was explained by Brook's idea that 'Oberon's deliberate cool intention is to degrade Titania as a woman' by exposing her to an ass, famous in legend for the size of its genital organs.[6]

For John Russell Brown, crying for Shakespeare to be presented 'freely', this showed the director ignoring the text, bringing out his own and the actors' fantasies, and forcing the play into 'one particular interpretation'.[7] Others thought that sex was emphasised more wittily, and carnality seen with 'affectionate tolerance'.[8] Whether responding with outrage or enthusiasm, critics agreed that this was an adult reading of the play; it presented a 'magic playground of lost innocence and hidden fears',[9] and its large, beefy fairies possessed a streak of cruelty; there were hints of the jungle in the forest scenes, and a sense of disenchantment as Oberon and Titania put on robes on stage to become Theseus and Hippolyta and join the lovers in watching 'Pyramus and Thisbe'. At the same time, the production 'declared its confidence and delight in the art of performance',[10] exposing its stage-devices, and inviting the audience 'to participate as omniscient observers'.[11] It broke away completely in visual and stage

---

[1] See Alan Howard's comments in *ibid.*, pp. 25–6 (he played Theseus/Oberon), and Beauman, *Royal Shakespeare Company*, pp. 305–6.

[2] Kenneth Hurren, in *The Spectator*, 5 September 1970.

[3] John Russell Brown, 'Free Shakespeare', *S.Sur.* 24 (1971), 127–35, p. 134.

[4] *Peter Brook's Production*, pp. 31–2. See Jan Kott; *Shakespeare Our Contemporary*, 1964.

[5] This is Benedict Nightingale's description, in the *New Statesman*, 4 September 1970.

[6] 'Peter Brook talks to Peter Ansorge', *Plays and Players*, October 1970. David Selbourne, who attended rehearsals of Brook's production and kept a diary while doing so, notes that Brook thought of the play as concerned with sex, and records that here Bottom and Titania were 'amid a lascivious clutch of fairies, who seem to hang upon every sexual impulse and erotic gesture'; see Selbourne, *The Making of A Midsummer Night's Dream*, 1982, p. 237.

[7] 'Free Shakespeare', pp. 133, 134; see also his book *Free Shakespeare*, 1974, esp. pp. 40–6.

[8] Clive Barnes, in the *New York Times*, 28 August 1970.   [9] *Ibid.*

[10] Peter Thomson, 'A necessary theatre: the Royal Shakespeare season 1970 reviewed', *S.Sur.* 24 (1971), 117–26, p. 126.   [11] Styan, *Shakespeare Revolution*, p. 229.

terms from all previous presentations, and seemed altogether original, and yet was very much of its time in emphasising sensuality and cruelty in the action, and in seeing the play as part of what James Calderwood had some years previously called Shakespeare's 'exploration of the nature, function, and value of art',[1] or, in Brook's words, 'a celebration of the theme of theatre'.[2]

In retrospect we are able to see that all productions fix the play in a style, an image, appropriate to their age, and for all its originality, Peter Brook's did so. What the stage history of *A Midsummer Night's Dream* shows is the remarkable strength of a theatrical tradition of treating the play as opera and as spectacular entertainment for children. As a play about fairies and magic, it needed exceptionally gifted and imaginative directors to perceive its deeper resonances, and the productions by Granville-Barker and Peter Brook were landmarks in exposing as worn-out clichés most of the traditional decorativeness in staging the play. Even those later productions, like John Barton's (with Gillian Lynne) in 1977, which have consciously returned to orthodoxy, have done so with a difference, with a much stronger sense of potentially sinister and destructive undercurrents in the play.[3] In all this the stage history has strong connections with the critical history of *A Midsummer Night's Dream*. In the face of the operatic spectacles into which the play was transformed in his time, it was natural for Hazlitt to react by arguing that, when acted, it was 'converted from a delightful fiction into a dull pantomime. All that is finest in the play is lost in the representation.'[4] This view, echoed by Henry Morley in 1853 in his comment that every reader thinks of *A Midsummer Night's Dream* as 'the most essentially unactable'[5] of all Shakespeare's plays, reflects their experience of seeing the heavily-cut, musical versions staged in the nineteenth century; in fact they never had the experience of witnessing or hearing Shakespeare's text acted. This was first made possible by Granville-Barker, and serious critical exploration of the play for the most part also began in the twentieth century, and in the wake of his production.

The play in the mind

Converting the play into an operatic spectacular was the theatre's way of coping with fairies, an inadequate way, as Hazlitt long ago observed in his complaint: 'That which is merely an airy shape, a dream, a passing thought, immediately becomes an

---

[1] '*A Midsummer Night's Dream*: the illusion of drama', *MLQ* 26 (1965), 506–22; the quotation is from p. 507.   [2] *Peter Brook's Production*, p. 24.

[3] See, for example, the reviews of the 1977 production by John Elsom, *The Listener*, 19 May 1977, and of the 1981 production (by Ron Daniels for the Royal Shakespeare Company) by Michael Coveney, the *Financial Times*, 17 July 1981, and by Michael Billington, in the *Guardian* on the same day. Some welcomed these productions as returning to sound ways of staging the play; so Gareth Lloyd Evans in the *Stratford-on-Avon Herald*, 13 May 1977, hailed John Barton's production as one which 'blessedly returns the play from its clever callisthenics in Brook's gymnasium to its rightful place as a poetic drama'.

[4] William Hazlitt, *Characters of Shakespeare's Plays*, 1817, in *The Complete Works of William Hazlitt*, ed. P. P. Howe, 21 vols., 1930–4, IV, 247.

[5] In his review of Samuel Phelps's 1853 production of the play, reprinted in Morley, *The Journal of a London Playgoer*, 1891, and in George Rowell (ed.), *Victorian Dramatic Criticism*, 1971, p. 102.

10   Peter Brook's production, 1970, showing David Waller as Bottom being carried offstage by fairies, with Titania looking on, and other actors showering petals on them from the gallery running round the top of the white box set

unmanageable reality.'[1] The adequacy of Hazlitt's own critical assumptions is another matter; like Coleridge, who thought Helena's betrayal of Hermia in revealing to Demetrius her plan to flee from Athens (1.1.246) a false note ('however just, the representation is not poetical; we shrink from it and cannot harmonize it with the ideal'),[2] Hazlitt regarded the play as 'ideal', as belonging to 'the regions of fancy'. He was responding to the play in a particular way, at once elevating it (even Bottom became 'the most romantic of mechanics'), and emphasising its remoteness from everyday realities. It is good now, long after the Second World War, when criticism would persuade us that there are no innocent works of literature, to have reminders of the potency of *A Midsummer Night's Dream* as a delightful vision, embodying 'innocence, lyricism, poetic beauty, universal love', the happiest among those Dover Wilson grouped as the happy comedies.[3] Such an emphasis can come near to reducing the play to gossamer thinness, opening the way for those who are in any case inclined to think of comedy as trivial to treat it as an early farce;[4] and a loftier view would see a profundity within the delight, noting the changes brought about by love as embodying 'the power to confer grace', as lovers are brought through their discords to a harmony of spiritual health.[5]

In the most vigorous recent presentation of the play in these terms, as an 'extended arabesque of hope and joy', Thomas McFarland properly associates it with a pastoral tradition but overemphasises the sense of moonlight as a symbol 'of soft and benign exhilaration',[6] and cannot take seriously the lovers scrambling about for a night in an enchanted forest. The vitality of *A Midsummer Night's Dream* he finds in the play within the play, and this, like the other elements of parody in it, flaunts its general 'hermetic security from mortality's threat'.[7] McFarland was reacting strongly against Jan Kott's extraordinary sense of the lovers' quarrels as 'brutal and violent', and of Shakespeare's 'fantasies' in the scenes of Bottom and Titania as penetrating 'the dark sphere of bestiality'.[8] Kott took the play within the play literally as cruel, and his account concludes, not with a vision of grace and harmony, but with the conviction that everything is deranged: 'The world is mad and love is mad. In this universal madness of Nature and History, brief are the moments of happiness.'[9] In associating the play not with the tradition of pastoral, but with Goya's *Caprichos* and the beasts

---

[1] William Hazlitt, reviewing the production by Frederick Reynolds in *The Examiner*, 21 January 1816; see Hazlitt, *Complete Works*, ed. P. P. Howe, 21 vols., 1930–4, V, 276.
[2] *Coleridge's Shakespearean Criticism*, ed. T. M. Raysor, rev. edn, 2 vols., 1960, I, 90.
[3] The quotation is from William J. Martz, *Shakespeare's Universe of Comedy*, 1977, p. 63. John Dover Wilson's *Shakespeare's Happy Comedies* appeared in 1962. See also Thomas McFarland's essay on the play in *Shakespeare's Pastoral Comedy*, 1972, which begins (p. 78), '*A Midsummer Night's Dream* is the happiest of Shakespeare's plays...'
[4] Sometimes with an emphasis on its dry, gossamer lyricism, and sometimes seeing it as 'brawny and brawling farce', to cite E. W. Talbert, *Elizabethan Drama and Shakespeare's Early Plays*, 1963, p. 252.
[5] John Arthos, *Shakespeare's Use of Dream and Vision*, 1977, p. 89: 'All goes to show that the power in change in the world of this play at least, and in this way of looking at the most wretched entanglements of humans, is the power to confer grace'; and compare Frank Kermode, 'The mature comedies', in Brown and Harris, *Early Shakespeare*, p. 219: 'Bottom is there to tell us that the blindness of love, the dominance of the mind over the eye, can be interpreted as a means to grace.'
[6] *Shakespeare's Pastoral Comedy*, pp. 97, 79.   [7] *Ibid.*, p. 87.
[8] *Shakespeare Our Contemporary*, pp. 76, 83.   [9] *Ibid.*, p. 88.

that recur in Freud's theory of dreams, Kott was seeking to locate it firmly in the modern world, and he was interpreting it through his own experiences, in the wake of the devastation of central Europe by war, and the gas-chambers of Auschwitz.

Such contradictory interpretations of the play would seem to be irreconcilable, but are no more startling than the contrast between, say, the Bridges-Adams production of 1932, with its moving oak tree in a 'real' wood, and Peter Brook's 1970 production in a white space. Recent critical theorising has taught us the extent to which 'It is the world of words that creates the world of things',[1] and, as signs, words take their capacity for significance not from their 'truth' or expression of 'reality', but from their difference from one another within a system of signs; thus the critic '*creates* the finished work by his reading of it, and does not remain simply the inert *consumer* of a "ready-made" product'.[2] The Marxist would qualify such a view by claiming that there is no innocent work of literature, that the work 'is always determined by the existence of other works, which can belong to different areas of production. There is no first book, independent and absolutely innocent: novelty and originality, in literature as in other fields, are always defined by relationships.' To know a work we must, in consequence, 'move outside it'; the work is conditioned by the historical circumstances in which it was produced, but cannot be reduced simply to its historical relationships; what this implies, however, is that it has no intrinsic meaning, but generates meanings which the critic investigates: 'The book is not the extension of a meaning; it is generated from the incompatibility of several meanings, the strongest bond by which it is attached to reality, in a tense and ever-renewed confrontation.'[3]

It is not necessary to accept these theories in order to appreciate their significance in relation to the contradictory interpretations of *A Midsummer Night's Dream* outlined above. What current theorising shows is that the act of reading (or listening), and the critical response to a work, are not passively related to a fixed object, the book or play, but rather that the reader (viewer or critic) generates meanings through a kind of exchange, projecting and completing images in accordance with his own participation in an active entanglement with the work.[4] The critic produces meanings, in an 'ever-renewed confrontation' with the work which results in a changing sense of its historical relationships and of its significance for the moment in time at which the critic encounters it. Hence it is inevitable that there should be multiple and opposed readings of a work; each reader or viewer 'completes' the play in a different way. *A Midsummer Night's Dream* is properly to be described as a happy comedy, a genial festive work possibly written for a wedding celebration, and related to the pastoral tradition, but this way of regarding it hardly accounts for its fullness. It is, after all, Shakespeare's first sure masterwork in comedy, finely articulated, and complex in its resonances; as I remarked earlier, it stands to the comedies as *Hamlet*

---

[1] Jacques Lacan, *Écrits*, trans Alan Sheridan, 1977, p. 65; cited in Catherine Belsey, *Critical Practice*, 1980, p. 136.
[2] Terence Hawkes, *Structuralism and Semiotics*, 1977, p. 157.
[3] Pierre Macherey, *A Theory of Literary Production*, trans. Geoffrey Wall, 1978, pp. 100, 90, 80.
[4] See Wolfgang Iser, *The Act of Reading*, 1976, trans. 1978, p. 127, and E. H. Gombrich, *Art and Illusion*, 2nd edn, 1962, pp. 188–90.

does to the tragedies, and both plays, interestingly, incorporate a troupe of players into the action, as though Shakespeare was especially conscious in these works of the nature of what he was doing.

Jan Kott's reading is instructive because it accounts for some of the deeper resonances of the play, however crudely. It had a considerable effect on Peter Brook's 1970 production, in which, as noted above, the sexuality of Bottom as an ass was emphasised by giving him an enormous phallus in 3.1. Some critics found in Kott's account and Brook's production a stimulus to notice the 'serious and at times somber presence that the comedies contain',[1] and Hugh Richmond, for example, argued that Titania's 'grotesque passion' for the 'translated' Bottom is as perverse as the 'sadomasochistic type of sexuality' in Helena and Demetrius; even Theseus needs to be recognised as a 'predatory lover' amongst a cast of lovers who take a 'masochistic satisfaction' in soliciting difficulty, tension and separation.[2] If such a view seems on first encountering it to be verging on the absurd, it is in fact an extreme response to the energies released in the infatuation of the lovers, to the exposure of sensuality as Titania awakes consumed with 'shame and disgust' at being enamoured of an ass, and to the latent violence of the lovers' quarrels.[3] The twentieth century has brought a new awareness of such elements in the play, and inevitably, in the excitement of discovery, has overstressed them; but it is a rich play indeed that can generate a range of significances between the apparently irreconcilable poles of 'happy' and 'sadomasochistic' accounts of it. The more extreme accounts of the play, it is true, tend to ignore its poetry, and the stylistic controls Shakespeare built into it, and the best criticism, like the best stage productions, takes note of these.

A Midsummer Night's Dream has traditionally been associated with music, not simply because of its songs, but on account of its overall lyrical quality, which led Granville-Barker, director of the innovatory first 'modern' production in 1914, to say of it: 'This is less a play, in the sense that we call "Rosmersholm" a play, than a musical symphony. The characterization will not repay very prolonged analysis.'[4] In his view, to hold an audience by the play's beauty would depend largely on 'the right changing of tune and time, and the shifting of key from scene to scene and from speech to speech'. This is an important observation, for although it is a commonplace to note the poetic virtuosity of Shakespeare's writing, and the rhetorical skills he displays, ranging from Bottom's prose to the fairies' songs, their profounder significance in articulating the structure and meanings of the play has had less attention. The normal mode for the civilised courtier in the play is blank verse, and the human action begins and ends with blank-verse speeches by Theseus; this verse carries the dignified rational discourse of rule and law, and the dramatic tensions these generate, as in the clash between Hermia and her father in the opening scene. It is also the ordinary mode of Oberon and Titania, as in their quarrel in 2.1, reflecting the extent to which they parallel Theseus and Hippolyta as rulers in their world.

[1] Ralph Berry, *Shakespeare's Comedies: Explorations in Form*, 1972, p. 22.
[2] *Shakespeare's Sexual Comedy*, 1971, pp. 106, 111.
[3] Glynne Wickham, *Shakespeare's Dramatic Heritage*, 1969, pp. 187–8.
[4] *The Exemplary Theatre*, 1922, p. 211.

As soon as Hermia and Lysander are left on stage, in the middle of 1.1, the 'tune and time' change into a more artificial mode, heralded by the stichomythia of 1.1.135–41, their lines exactly balanced in repeating the same rhythm, and passing into rhyming couplets from line 171 to the end of the scene. These mark the quasi-hallucinatory condition induced in them by the infatuation of the lovers, whose rather absurd plan to meet in a wood seven leagues from Athens looks even sillier when Helena proposes to send Demetrius after them, and follow him herself.

> Things base and vile, holding no quantity,
> Love can transpose to form and dignity.
> Love looks not with the eyes, but with the mind,
> And therefore is winged Cupid painted blind.
> Nor hath love's mind of any judgement taste;
> Wings, and no eyes, figure unheedy haste;
> And therefore is love said to be a child
> Because in choice he is so oft beguiled.   (1.1.232–9)

So Helena argues; love's 'mind' is the fancy, not the judgement, and the blindness and 'unheedy haste' of these lovers giving the rein to their passion launch the main action of the play. At the same time, love can transform 'things base and vile', like Helena's betrayal here of her friend Hermia, to dignity, a transformation aided by the controlling artistry of Shakespeare's rhyming lines.

The 'form and dignity' of love, however childish the tantrums it provokes, are set off by the modulation into comic prose that follows in 1.2, when Quince and his company meet to rehearse, and this in turn gives way to the rhyming exchanges of the Fairy and Puck at the beginning of 2.1, the Fairy's opening speech (or song?) with its short lines marking a strong shift of 'tune and time' from the flat-footed world of Bottom and his crew to the delicacy of the spirit-world. But the entry of Oberon and Titania quarrelling returns us to blank verse, so relating them poetically to Theseus and his courtiers in the opening scene. These two figures are especially interesting stylistically, for as king and queen they speak like humans, while as fairies or spirits, they pass easily into rhyme or song, as in Oberon's spell-binding end to this scene, 'I know a bank where the wild thyme blows.' Their double nature is confirmed in their quarrel over the Indian boy. His mother was a votaress of Titania's order (2.1.123), but the boy is also a 'changeling', usually a child substituted by fairies for a stolen mortal child. Is the child's father the 'Indian king' from whom he was stolen (2.1.22), in which case he is mortal, or is the child's father conceivably Oberon, which would explain Oberon's jealousy, and make him a fairy child? As fairies or spirits Oberon and Titania cannot have children, yet Oberon is Titania's 'lord' (2.1.63), and just as she complains of his amours, so he remarks on her love for Theseus. As spirits, can they only meddle vicariously in human love affairs, or are they also, like Greek gods, capable of intercourse with humans, as Theseus takes the shape of Corin to woo Phillida? These unanswerable questions point to the ambiguities in the presentation of Oberon and Titania. She has 'forsworn his bed' (2.1.62), so that in some sense they are lovers, lord and lady, husband and wife, as well as spirits or fairies. The Indian boy, equally ambiguous, becomes a means of bridging unobtrusively their two natures, as humans and as spirits; he also provides them with a 'child' to enhance the sense that they are 'married'. This adds point to the restoration of harmony in nature brought about by their reconciliation, and to the blessing they bestow on each 'bride-bed' at the end (5.1.381). (It also adds plausibility to the doubling of the roles of Oberon and Titania with those of Theseus and Hippolyta, as in Peter Brook's 1970 production; but see also p. 4 above.)

The changes of 'tune and time' in the dialogue of Oberon and Titania relate, then, to their shifting natures, and one way in which Shakespeare neutralises the 'sensuality' Jan Kott and others have detected in the encounter between Titania and Bottom is by giving Titania rhyming lines in 3.1, very much in her character as fairy or spirit rather than queen or 'human', so emphasising a comic incongruity, not a sexual relationship. Shakespeare's stylistic control of the action is especially marked in 3.2, in which the 'fond pageant' (3.2.114) of the lovers' quarrel is played out. At first the lovers speak in rhyming couplets, which by their formality have a restraining effect upon their disagreements, but as the temperature rises, so they move, at 3.2.195, into blank verse, until their quarrel reaches a climax in the threat of physical violence. This whole sequence is watched by Oberon and Puck as stage-managers, whose control over events is marked in their spells written mainly in rhyming tetrameter, as at 3.2.100 ff.; and when Puck wears out the lovers by leading them about the wood, they collapse in turn, Lysander and Demetrius each with a speech of eight lines in couplets, Helena and Hermia each with a speech of six lines rhyming ABABCC. So the outburst of violence in the quarrel is brought under control and ritualised in the patterned speeches at the end of the scene.

Another notable instance of Shakespeare's stylistic shaping of the action occurs in 5.1, when Theseus and his court, including the now reconciled lovers, watch 'Pyramus and Thisbe'; in mocking its absurdities, the courtiers speak in prose, so that as the boors led by Quince ambitiously attempt to play a tragedy in verse, the courtiers tend to become boorish in their prose mockery of its absurdities. Their condescending wit is cruel in putting Starveling as Moonshine out of his stride, and would be humiliating if Quince's company were not so fully occupied with their performances as to be impervious to mockery. This impatience of the stage audience with what is most enjoyable for theatre audiences might be taken as suggesting the limitations of their 'courtesy' and 'reason'; for them it is beguiling the slow passage of time before they can consummate their marriages (5.1.345–6); their loves have arrived at a happy conclusion, and they are not interested in a tale of tragic love, so that their prose commentary is entirely appropriate here, and helps to give a special sweetness and enchantment to the ending, which modulates, via Theseus returning to blank verse (5.1.341), into the rhyming tetrameters and songs of Oberon, Titania and the fairies, which round off the play in harmony at the end.

Shakespeare's virtuosity in orchestrating the action of *A Midsummer Night's Dream* stylistically through the changing rhythms of blank verse, rhyme, short lines, songs, and prose, and the absence of strong or individual characterisation (except in the case of Bottom, who has in consequence received more critical attention than all the rest), encouraged for a long time an emphasis on the play's lyricism at the expense of its

31   Introduction

significances. These began to be explored seriously in two important essays by Paul
Olson and C. L. Barber.[1] Olson drew attention to the symbolism of the play, and
pointed out connections with traditional representations of and thinking about love
and marriage. So when Helena speaks of 'winged Cupid painted blind' (1.1.235), she
has in mind an earthly, sensual love: 'the bandage of blindfold Cupid...tends to retain
its specific significance wherever a lower, purely sensual and profane form of love
was contrasted with a higher, more spiritual and sacred one, whether marital, or
"Platonic", or Christian'.[2] In relation to this, Athens, in tradition a city of wisdom
and order, contrasts with the woods to which the lovers flee as a place of disorder
and licence. There the setting becomes a 'stage projection of the inner condition of
the lovers', who in Olson's view experience a kind of fall and redemption, a passage
from earthly, sensual love to rational love figured in marriage.[3] This opposition is
notably imaged in the ass-head placed on Bottom, the ass symbolising sensuality and
stupidity, the carnal as opposed to the spiritual. If Olson went too far in identifying
Oberon with reason and Titania with passion, he showed how the play is rooted in
traditions of neo-Platonic imagery and thought.

Barber's brilliant essay gave full weight to the play's links with traditional summer
festivities, both those associated with May Day, the celebration of fertility in spring
(Theseus relates the presence of the lovers in the wood to 'the rite of May' at 4.1.130),
and those of midsummer holidays. At the same time, he showed how the stylisation
and patterning of language and action complement the benevolent driving out of evil
by the fairies: 'In promoting the mastery of passion by expression, dramatic art can
provide a civilized equivalent for exorcism.'[4] The spring festival releases energies and
transforming powers that are necessary for the continuity of life, but which in the
end are given purpose and held in check within the formal bonds of marriage. A dream
has, as Freud said, something of the nature of a wish-fulfilment, as in the discovery
of the violence of passion by the lovers, the potential sexual energising for Titania
in her encounter with a beast, and in Bottom's vision of a life of luxury. Dreams open
up areas of experience repressed by the conscious mind, but can also shade into
nightmares in which the frustrations of uncontrolled passions lead to violence and
madness.

The play begins, however, from the tyranny of reason as embodied in the law that
would sentence Hermia to death or perpetual chastity for disobeying her father. The
lovers flee from Athens, the city as symbol of civilisation, to the woods outside,
symbolic of the wilderness, only to find they have escaped one form of tyranny to
encounter another, in themselves. 'Love looks not with the eyes, but with the mind'
(1.1.234), and the characters 'see' a setting that reflects their state. For the lovers,
the woods turn into a wild place, where savage beasts may be found (2.1.228), where

[1] Paul Olson, 'A Midsummer Night's Dream and the meaning of court marriage', ELH 24 (1957), 95–119;
   C. L. Barber, Shakespeare's Festive Comedy, 1959.
[2] Erwin Panofsky, Studies in Iconology, 1939, repr. 1962, pp. 125–6.
[3] Olson, 'Court marriage', p. 115; see also Wickham, Shakespeare's Dramatic Heritage, p. 183, where he
   says Shakespeare presents 'sex as a wood through which in adolescence everyone is obliged to pass. On
   the far side of the wood is marriage...'
[4] Barber, Shakespeare's Festive Comedy, p. 139.

Helena, in her unhappiness, comes to think 'I am as ugly as a bear / For beasts that meet me run away for fear' (2.2.100–1), and where Hermia dreams of being eaten by a serpent (2.2.155). What they see as savage reflects the increasing savagery of their own passions, as love and friendship turn to hatred. Demetrius 'wood within this wood' – that is, mad (wood) in a place appropriate for madness – talks already at 2.1.190 of killing Lysander, and he hates Helena (2.1.211) for following him. When Puck anoints the eyes of the wrong man, Lysander, his love for Hermia also turns to hatred as he pursues Helena: poor Hermia is now rejected, 'Of all be hated, but the most of me!' (2.2.148). Oberon's intervention at 3.2.102, transforming Demetrius into the lover of Helena instead of Hermia, exacerbates the quarrels: Helena thinks all have ganged up on her, Hermia believes Helena, a 'thief of love' (3.2.283), has stolen Lysander from her, and Lysander now quarrels with Demetrius over Helena. The upshot brings violence and the threat of death, as Hermia seeks to scratch out Helena's eyes, while Lysander and Demetrius go off, swords drawn it seems, to fight to the death (3.2.338). The lovers are wholly involved in all this, and the process we witness of love turning to hate and cruelty is real enough. As Barber put it, they 'are unreservedly *in* the passionate protestations which they rhyme at each other as they change partners'.[1]

Yet another element of discord is shown in the quarrel between Oberon and Titania, which also has its 'real' effect in the transformation of the seasons and confusion in nature:

> The spring, the summer,
> The childing autumn, angry winter change
> Their wonted liveries, and the mazèd world
> By their increase now knows not which is which. (2.1.111–14)

The passions generated by these quarrels are all part of the felt experience of the play for an audience. The stylistic control is exercised through the verse structure, the patterning of the action,[2] and through the aesthetic distancing of the lovers' quarrels into, as it were, a play within the play; this ensures the promise of a genial outcome. For Oberon and Puck, who supervise the lovers, and take care that in the end no harm is done, the woods are a different sort of place. Titania accuses Oberon of stealing away from 'Fairyland' in pursuit of amorous adventures, or more directly, from India (2.1.65, 69), but they both seem at home in the landscape of delicate English beauty created by Oberon's memorable lines

> I know a bank where the wild thyme blows,
> Where oxlips and the nodding violet grows... (2.1.249 ff.)

Titania's fairies guard her from diminutive creatures, snakes, hedgehogs, newts, spiders and beetles, all of which might be stumbled on in Warwickshire, so that Oberon's wish that Titania may wake to love a leopard, lynx, boar or bear (2.2.36–7) is unlikely to be fulfilled, though this maintains the note of wildness or savagery appropriate to the quarrels of the lovers.

---

[1] *Ibid.*, p. 128.

[2] This patterning is compared to a dance by Enid Welsford in *The Court Masque*, 1927, pp. 331–2.

Titania's vision of landscape is much more agricultural, as she lists the transformations and 'progeny of evils' (2.1.115) brought about by her quarrel with Oberon;
the ploughman's labour is wasted, and the sheepfold stands empty. The setting seen
by the 'hempen homespuns' who gather to rehearse their play is a 'green plot' with
hawthorn bushes (3.1.3) and suits the limited horizons of yokels from the English
countryside. Bottom sings of English birds, the blackbird, wren, finch, sparrow, lark
and cuckoo (3.1.103–9); the fairies he meets have associations appropriate to his
imagination (Peaseblossom, Cobweb, Moth, Mustardseed), and his transformation to
a creature as domestic as an ass also fits. The pleasantly dignified verse of the opening
establishes Athens as the civilised court of Theseus, who conquered Hippolyta by
force, and now is about to wed her in a celebration of peace and harmony; but it also
displays the tyranny of reason and the law in sentencing Hermia. The various images
different characters see in the woods establish this setting as likewise beneficent or
hostile, figuring their state of mind. Liberated from the tyranny of the law, the lovers
find 'a desert place' (2.1.218), which in its wildness reflects the tyranny of the passions
of anger and hatred unleashed by their quarrels. The woods also harbour Titania's
bower, a *locus amoenus*, an image of sweetness and beauty, and embody the liberated
imagination in a range of kindlier aspects.

The innocent images of her bower, flowers, honey-bees, butterflies, fruits of all
kinds, centre on the 'flowery bed' (4.1.1) in which she winds Bottom, or rather an
ass, in her arms, beauty throwing herself at a beast; when she wakes from this hateful
fantasy (2.1.258) it is to 'loathe' what she sees (4.1.76). The pretty images of her bower,
while generally appropriate to her as Queen of Fairies, also suit Bottom's good-
humoured, stupid innocence, as he greets what happens with an open, childlike
acceptance. The sexuality is all on Titania's side; his imagination runs to pleasures
of another kind: having his face scratched, eating 'good dry oats' (4.1.29), being
luxuriously attended by his servant fairies, and going to sleep. The comic incongruity
between the two helps to maintain the mental distance between them; it is brought
out for instance, in Titania's notion of purging his 'mortal grossness' (3.1.134) and
transforming him into an 'airy spirit'. Bottom, liberated through magic from his
self-importance and need to dominate his fellows, enters without malice or passion
into his vision, and can feel thoroughly comfortable in it. The dreams of the lovers
turn to nightmare and violence; Titania wakes to loathe what she loved, and only
Bottom has a wholly marvellous and enjoyable vision.

His experience and Titania's, like the experiences of the lovers, are placed for us
not only by the shifts of 'tune and time' in style discussed earlier (pp. 28–30 above),
but also by the structure of the play. What happens to these characters is seen as forms
of a play within the play, stage-managed and watched over by Oberon and Puck (even
if Puck's error in mistaking Lysander for Demetrius makes for confusion). It is easy
to miss, in reading the play, that the movement from Act 2, Scene 2 through to the
waking of Bottom at the end of 4.1 makes sense as a more or less continuous action,
with one area of the stage as Titania's bower, another area for the 'mechanicals' to
rehearse in 3.1, and perhaps then for the lovers to group asleep at the end of 3.2,
while Oberon and Puck can move around 'invisible' (2.1.186) to the rest. Their

11 Possible ways of staging Titania's bower (Act 2, Scene 2 and Act 3, Scene 1), by C. Walter Hodges.
11 *a* shows the bower at 2.2.91 and 11 *b* at 3.1.107. Titania's bower is described by Oberon at the end of
2.1 as canopied with flowers, and in 2.2 Titania sleeps in it. A curtained projection from the rear centre
of the stage may have been used (see 2.2.30 SD and n.). The lovers then enter, Lysander and Hermia sleep,
Demetrius and Helena quarrel, and all exit separately. There is no break in the action between Acts 2
and 3, and in 3.1, after the rehearsal of 'Pyramus and Thisbe' is interrupted by Puck, Titania wakes to
hear Bottom (see 3.1.107 and n.). The audience is aware throughout of Titania as supposedly in her bower

'magic' corresponds to the dramatist's art in controlling, shaping and distancing what happens, so that the nightmare of the lovers never erupts into tragedy, and Titania's sexual urges remain innocuous. Oberon's magic art, as a projection of the dramatist's art, makes possible imaginatively the dreams and visions seen by the lovers, Titania and Bottom, but also orders them from the perspective of a strong intelligence, making us share for the time being Puck's view, 'Lord, what fools these mortals be!' (3.2.115).

Bottom is a central figure in all this – an embodiment of earthy humanity who remains splendidly himself whatever happens to him or around him, and a character with whom an audience can readily engage; at the same time his transformation into an ass fits him as one who is, in the scale of human folly, a natural, ingrained fool, a fool positive. His experience remains at the most prosaic level, and his dream, 'past the wit of man to say what dream it was' (4.1.201), leaves him groping for words; he has no poetry in which to articulate his vision, only garbled phrases from the first sentence of 1 Corinthians 2.9–10. In the Bishops' Bible the text runs: 'The eye of man hath not seene, and the eare hath not heard, neither have entred into the heart of man, the things which God hath prepared for them that love him. But God hath revealed them unto us by his spirit; for the spirit searcheth all things, yea the deepe things of God.' This does not mean that Bottom has some access or 'means' to grace,[1] but suggests rather that the heaven revealed to Bottom corresponds to the limits of his imagination, and he is as impervious to the 'deepe things of God' as he is to Titania's attractions. He never becomes aware that he has been transformed into an ass, and if this lack of awareness marks a kind of innocence which is appealing, it also defines his limitations.

In love all mortals are foolish, true, but the lovers and Titania come to a new awareness through their experiences and visions, and this gives point to the last part of the play. As Oberon and Titania dance in celebration of harmony restored between them, and go off in 4.1, so Theseus and Hippolyta enter to the noise of horns and hounds signalling daybreak, time for the waking up of the lovers and then of Bottom. Effectively the action returns from the woods and Oberon's control to the city of Athens in the orbit of Theseus. The final act, when all the lovers, fresh from the marriage ceremony it seems, are gathered at the court of Theseus, begins with his great speech which describes the workings of imagination not unsympathetically, but from the viewpoint of 'cool reason'. Some have seen a smug or patronising rationality here,[2] but this, I think, is to misjudge these powerful lines. Shakespeare returns us here to the ordered world of a court society, and Theseus's lines establish this perspective, while at the same time notably celebrating the power of 'strong imagination'; Theseus himself, and his lines, spring from the 'shaping fantasies' of Shakespeare, the prime example of the poet he links with the lover and the lunatic. At the same time, as a character, Theseus represents the cool world of marriage rather

---

[1] See p. 26 above, n. 5.
[2] Jackson Cope, *The Theater and the Dream*, 1973, p. 224, sees Bottom's dream as a 'crucial rebuttal' of the Duke's speech on imagination; Theseus, he says, speaks from 'the smug security of his rationalism'. Sidney Homan also sees Theseus as a rationalist contemptuous of the imagination in *When the Theatre Turns to Itself: The Aesthetic Metaphor in Shakespeare*, 1981, pp. 79–103.

12   Possible ways of staging Act 4, Scene 1, by C. Walter Hodges. In this complex scene at least four areas of the stage are in use for different groups, and, until Bottom is left alone on stage at the end of the scene, there are always between ten and fifteen actors on stage. The lovers lie down separately to sleep at the end of Act 3, and 12*a* shows how the stage may have appeared at the opening of Act 4, when Titania sits with Bottom on a 'flowery bed'. 12*b* shows the entry of Theseus and Hippolyta with their 'trains' in procession at 4.1.125. (For further comment, see 4.1.0 SD and n.)

than the heated fancies of wooing, and all the happenings in the wood now grow 'to something of great constancy', as Hippolyta says, most directly in the marriages in which the couples will 'eternally be knit' (4.1.178); but she knows, too, that the 'story of the night' has more to it than mere 'tricks' of imagination, and that

> all their minds transfigured so together,
> More witnesseth than fancy's images,
> And grows to something of great constancy;
> But howsoever, strange and admirable.   (5.1.24–7)

The experiences of the lovers, their changes and illusions, have a deeper meaning in so far as their release from the restraints of the court and control of the law leads to the working out of sensual and violent impulses and a measure of self-discovery. It would not do to press such an argument too far in relation to characters as slightly drawn as Hermia, Helena, Lysander and Demetrius; but for them, as for Titania, the return to daylight, to reason, leads to a joyful acceptance or renewal of the bonds of love, and so their experiences in the wood are 'admirable', to be wondered at, for the effect they have.

Some critics have felt that the play affirms the importance of the world of dreams or fantasy, and shows that reason impoverishes the imagination;[1] others have recognised the extent to which it also exposes the absurdities of the imagination and gives approval to the voice of reason.[2] It seems to me that *A Midsummer Night's Dream* achieves a splendid balance between the two; if the imagination makes possible visions and experiences otherwise inaccessible, and liberates natural energies from the restraints of reason, those visions and experiences are only given form and meaning through the reason. Such a view fits in well with the thinking of Shakespeare's age about the relation of imagination to reason, as expressed, for instance, in Pierre de la Primaudaye's *The Second Part of the French Academie* (1594), pp. 146–7:

This virtue is called *Imagination*, or the *Imaginative* vertue, which is in the soule as the eye in the bodie, to receive the images that are offered unto it by the outward senses: and therefore it knoweth also the things that are absent, and is amongst the internal senses as it were the mouth of the vessell of memorie...Now after that the *Imagination* hath received the images of the senses, singly and particularly as they are offered unto it, then doeth it as it were prepare and digest them, eyther by joyning them together, or by separating them according as their natures require...Afterwards it is requisite, that all these things thus heaped together, should

---

[1] See, for instance, Marjorie Garber, *Dream in Shakespeare*, 1974, p. 84: 'If illusion and the imagination are not without their dangers, they are nonetheless, in the terms of this play, preferred to their radical opposite, cool reason'; and R. W. Dent, 'Imagination in *A Midsummer Night's Dream*', *SQ* 15 (1964), 115–29, who argues that the play implies a contrary view of imagination to that of Theseus. The play evidently reflects something of an important debate in the Renaissance. The imagination was widely held in disrepute and linked with the senses rather than the reason; it was held to be the source of distorted visions and a contributing factor in diseases such as melancholy; but it was also defended with vigour, especially by the poets, as able to give form to higher truths than the literal, and, under the guidance of reason, to create images that could stir the reader to virtuous courses; see William Rossky, 'Imagination in the English Renaissance: psychology and poetic', *Studies in the Renaissance* 5 (1958), 49–73.

[2] See, for example, Harriet Hawkins, *Likenesses of Truth in Elizabethan and Restoration Drama*, 1972, pp. 32–3, and Derek Traversi, *An Approach to Shakespeare*, 3rd edn, 1969, p. 148: 'we must believe that the civilizing and rational order of marriage finally prevails'.

be distributed and compared one with another, to consider how they may be conjoyned or severed, how one followeth another, and how farre asunder they are, so a man may judge what is to be retained and what to be refused. And this office belongeth to *Reason*, after which *Iudgement* followeth, whereby men chuse or refuse that which reason alloweth or disalloweth.

In psychological and social terms, as noted earlier, freedom from restraint merely replaces the tyranny of law by the tyranny of hate, and leads in the end to violence and chaos. The return to order in Act 5 fulfils the pattern of the play, which expresses the need for and exposes the limitations of both reason and imagination. The main business of the evening court is the presentation of 'Pyramus and Thisbe', a play within the play, performed for the marriage celebrations of the three couples who form the main audience on stage (even as *A Midsummer Night's Dream* itself may have been acted at a wedding feast). We see the performance by Quince and his team both for what it is, and through the distancing perspective of the stage audience. As a hilarious parody of outmoded dramatic styles and Senecan bombast, and with its misplaced accents, absurd rhymes, and comic representations of Wall, Moonshine and Lion, 'Pyramus and Thisbe' is hugely enjoyable; but part of our pleasure, albeit not consciously noticed, derives from the way it fits into the pattern of the play as a whole. For it represents a pair of lovers planning to meet by moonlight at a rendezvous which exposes them to dangerous wild beasts, and the outcome is comically tragic as both Pyramus and Thisbe 'die' extravagantly on stage. The playlet thus links with the adventures of the lovers in Acts 1 to 3, turning to comedy what might have been painful, and enabling both its audiences to triumph vicariously over the dangers latent in the passions stirred by love. 'Pyramus and Thisbe' fittingly distances through laughter and transforms to delight all the earlier threats of death, to Hermia, and to Lysander and Demetrius as they measured swords in 3.2.

In their comments on 'Pyramus and Thisbe', the stage audience speak in prose, and in spite of Theseus's initial urging to accept what is offered with generous consideration, and accept it in terms of what ability the performers have ('what poor duty cannot do, noble respect / Takes it in might, not merit' (5.1.91–2)), they point up the absurdities, and fill in with their dialogue gaps and pauses in the action of the playlet. At the same time, their remarks treat it with condescension, and poor Starveling as Moonshine is completely put out of his stride by their interruptions, so that after twice attempting his opening lines, he gives up and explains, so to speak, in his own words who he is. Hippolyta registers boredom – 'This is the silliest stuff that ever I heard' (5.1.204) – but Theseus reminds her and the others that 'in courtesy, in all reason, we must stay the time' (5.1.240). His world of reason is also one of courtesy, which demands that the court audience sit through patiently what has been offered to them in 'simpleness and duty' (5.1.83). Shakespeare cleverly plays off the reactions of the stage audience against those of the theatre audience, which is much more likely to be delighted with 'Pyramus and Thisbe'. The interaction between Quince and his players, the stage audience, and the theatre audience is complex; the court audience does not show well in its tendency to become patronising and intolerant, but at the same time their dialogue exposes the mental distance between the court and the 'rude mechanicals', who lack the wit or imagination to 'amend' their own incompetence. So Hippolyta retorts well to Theseus's famous comment:

THESEUS The best in this kind are but shadows; and the worst are no worse, if imagination amend them.
HIPPOLYTA It must be your imagination then, and not theirs.   (5.1.205–7)

Indeed, the interlude of 'Pyramus and Thisbe' makes us laugh in large part because we sense the discrepancy between the conception Quince and Bottom have of drama as realistic, holding the mirror up to nature, and their want of the imagination or skill that would enable them to achieve the dramatic illusion they aim for. Their play sets off the higher imaginative grasp of the court audience on stage; in turn the theatre audience has a more privileged perspective, and is 'given a chance to behave more astutely' than the stage audience, 'to see to it that they are not quite as condescending as Theseus, as inconsistent as Hippolyta, as oblivious, when faced with their own images, as the lovers'[1] – for the lovers do not notice the link between the play they are watching and their adventures in the wood, now forgotten like a dream. The interlude of 'Pyramus and Thisbe' also makes us more aware of Shakespeare's mastery of his art in *Midsummer Night's Dream* as a whole. So Hippolyta's lines on the experience of the lovers as growing 'to something of great constancy' take on another meaning, for in the end, as David Young says, 'The coherence and constancy are in the poet's art.'[2]

The play ends with a kind of coda, after Theseus and the lovers go off to bed, as midnight sounds and 'fairy time' (5.1.342) comes round again. Puck recalls the dangers of the night – lions, wolves, ghosts – but only to sweep them away metaphorically with his broom, for the entry of Oberon, Titania and the fairies to sing and dance hand in hand in a final celebration of harmony and blessing on the married pairs. So these triumphs of the poet's imagination at the close confirm the stability of the ordered society for which Theseus and his 'cool reason' stand, reminding us that the continuance of society depends upon marriage, as Oberon promises to ward off all blemishes that could disfigure the children of the 'couples three'. Puck is left to deliver the epilogue:

> If we shadows have offended,
> Think but this, and all is mended:
> That you have but slumbered here
> While these visions did appear;
> And this weak and idle theme,
> No more yielding but a dream,
> Gentles, do not reprehend...   (5.1.401–7)

The tone is conventionally apologetic, but Shakespeare gives Puck lines that relate both to his role as a spirit, and to the actor playing the role. 'Shadows' could refer to both, as the term was commonly used in opposition to 'substance' to mean a mere semblance or something insubstantial, and as Puck earlier called Oberon 'King of

---

[1] David P. Young, *Something of Great Constancy: The Art of A Midsummer Night's Dream*, 1966, p. 105.
[2] *Ibid.*, p. 160.

Shadows' (3.2.347), so Theseus had referred to actors as 'shadows' (5.1.205).[1] Here, as throughout a play in which we have seen Oberon and Puck stage-managing their playlets by means of magic, and Quince's company rehearsing and performing 'Pyramus and Thisbe', Shakespeare again maximises at once our sense of the artifice of the stage, our awareness of being in a theatre watching actors at work, and our ability, through our imaginations, to enter into and give assent to a magical country of the mind. In one sense the theme of the play is 'weak and idle', an 'insubstantial pageant', as Shakespeare much later makes Prospero call the masque he creates, but, as Prospero relates the dissolution of his art to the fading of all earthly things, so *A Midsummer Night's Dream*, in yielding 'but a dream', is analogous to the swift passage of love, and of life itself,

> Swift as a shadow, short as any dream. (1.1.144)

On another level we share, in Bottom's words, in a 'most rare vision', conjured up by Shakespeare's superb artistry, in which the threatened tyranny of the law, and the violence unleashed in the jealousies of love turning to hatred, are transformed in the settled harmony of marriage. It is a vision, too, which, as noted earlier, suggests the need for the release of natural instincts and energies in freedom from the restrictions of rule or reason, but also, in its overall patterning, implies that the discoveries made about themselves by the lovers lead to a reaffirmation and acceptance of the controls by which society maintains itself. So the play indeed brings concord out of discord and moves to 'something of great constancy', as the marriage vows are for eternity:

> And the issue there create
> Ever shall be fortunate.
> So shall all the couples three
> Ever true in loving be... (5.1.383-6)

The play, itself already possessing a long life of nearly four centuries, and of permanent value as a work of art, projects finally an image of harmony lasting for 'ever'. The transformations which constitute so much of the play's 'idle theme' turn out to be a means to grace, reconciliation and ordered harmony. The imagination makes possible a dramatic world in which legendary figures from Greek mythology share the stage with figures drawn from folklore in Puck and the fairies, and characters based on the actual Elizabethan peasantry of the English countryside. Shakespeare plays upon our awareness of what he is doing, our ability temporarily to believe anything while knowing it is make-believe, and enables us to enjoy the play as a delightful flight of imagination, and as an artfully structured masterpiece which gives meaning to the mysterious words Yeats used as an epigraph for *Responsibilities*, 1914: 'In dreams begins responsibility.'

This discussion is not intended as offering another reading of the play, but rather

---

[1] On this, and on the question of stage-illusion in the play, see R. A. Foakes, 'Forms to his conceit: Shakespeare and the uses of stage-illusion', *Proceedings of the British Academy* 66 (1980), 107–12.

as a way of exploring the space between extreme interpretations of the play in terms of sadomasochism as against simple innocence and charm, or in terms of the release of imagination as against the controls of reason. Inevitably, exploration of the play's content that goes beyond the superficial becomes concerned with the implications of transformations, of illusions and dreams, of disorder and order, reason and imagination, stage artifice in relation to the 'real', and the nature of theatre itself. *A Midsummer Night's Dream* is not a play which offers much depth of characterisation, though it treats with freshness and some power the staple topic of Shakespeare's romantic comedies, love and the vexations of wooing eventually resolved in marriage. The strength of the play lies in the way its delightful fictions and charming poetry, orchestrated superbly into an artistic whole, continually reverberate with profundities that are in the end as far beyond our grasp as Bottom's dream. No doubt further significances will continue to be found in it, for like other great plays by Shakespeare, it appears to be inexhaustible.

NOTE ON THE TEXT

The copy-text for this edition is the first quarto of 1600 (Q1). The second quarto (Q2), printed in 1619 with the false date 1600 on the title page, was based on Q1, and has no authority; it does, however, include corrections of some of the obvious printing errors of Q1. The First Folio text of 1623 (F) was based on Q2, but includes some important substantive changes, and adds or expands some thirty or so stage directions. The collation records substantive emendations of and additions to Q1, and also some unusual spellings in Q1 or F that could affect pronunciation or sense, like 'faining' (for 'feigning') at 1.1.31, or 'maruailes' (for 'marvellous') at 3.1.2. There are not many points of major dispute in the text of *A Midsummer Night's Dream*, and as far as editions subsequent to F are concerned, I have included only emendations generally accepted, and a selection of the most plausible suggestions relating to the few instances of real difficulty, such as 'Moon vsed' at 5.1.201. In the format of the collations, the authority for this edition's reading follows immediately after the square bracket enclosing the quotation from the text. Other readings, if any, follow in chronological order. When, as is usually the case, the variant or emendation adopted has been used or suggested by a previous editor or textual commentator, that authority is cited in the abbreviated form *Rowe* or *conj. Tyrwhitt*; see pp. ix–xii above for an explanation of the abbreviations and a list of the editions and commentaries cited. For a detailed discussion of the provenance of, and relations between, Q1, Q2 and F, see the Textual Analysis, pp. 135–43 below.

A Midsummer Night's Dream

LIST OF CHARACTERS

THESEUS, *Duke of Athens*
HIPPOLYTA, *Queen of the Amazons, betrothed to Theseus*
EGEUS, *father of Hermia*
LYSANDER, *in love with Hermia*
DEMETRIUS, *preferred by Egeus as a match for Hermia*
HERMIA, *in love with Lysander*
HELENA, *in love with Demetrius*
PHILOSTRATE, *Master of the Revels at the court of Theseus*

OBERON, *King of the Fairies*
TITANIA, *Queen of the Fairies*
PUCK *or* ROBIN GOODFELLOW, *Oberon's jester and attendant*
PEASEBLOSSOM
COBWEB
MOTH } *Fairies attending on Titania*
MUSTARDSEED
A FAIRY, *in the service of Titania*

PETER QUINCE, *carpenter (Prologue in the play of 'Pyramus and Thisbe')*
NICK BOTTOM, *weaver (Pyramus)*
FRANCIS FLUTE, *bellows-mender (Thisbe)*
TOM SNOUT, *tinker (Wall)*
ROBIN STARVELING, *tailor (Moonshine)*
SNUG, *joiner (Lion)*

'Lords and Attendants' on Theseus and Hippolyta

Notes

No list of characters appears in QQ or F; first supplied by Rowe.

PHILOSTRATE He appears twice: in 1.1, silently, and in 5.1, where he has a speaking-part. F changes the name in 5.1 to 'Egeus', and probably Shakespeare's company economised by having Egeus, whose part ends in 4.1 in Q, take over the role of Philostrate here. Possibly the actor who later played Puck doubled as Philostrate in 1.1.

PUCK Probably played by an adult actor; see p. 7 above.

FAIRY Titania has in her service four named fairies, and this one, who opens 2.1 with Puck. Oberon also appears in this scene and in 5.1 with his 'train', but his only named attendant is Puck. Titania's 'train' in 2.2 includes two fairies who sing, and one who stands 'sentinel' (2.2.32) when she sleeps. These, and the fairy in 2.1, could have been played by the same actors who later, in 3.1, appeared as Peaseblossom and the other named fairies. It would thus have been possible to perform the play with a minimum of six fairies, including Puck, and these may have been divided equally between Oberon and Titania in 2.1 to form their respective 'trains' (see notes to 2.1.59 and 4.1.0 SD). The play has three named women in the cast, plus Titania, who would have been played by boys on the Elizabethan stage. If the fairies were also played by boys, then at least eight would have been needed; but it is also possible that in the public playhouse, where such a large number of boy-actors could have been hard to provide, the four named fairies doubled as Flute, Starveling, Snout and Snug, and were played by adult actors; see p. 4 above and 2.1.59 SD.2 and n.

Lords and Attendants These, called for at 5.1.0 SD, are not essential, but whatever supernumeraries were available may have been used to grace the court of Theseus, and swell the stage audience for 'Pyramus and Thisbe'.

A MIDSUMMER NIGHT'S DREAM

1.[1] *Enter* THESEUS, HIPPOLYTA, [PHILOSTRATE,] *with others.*

THESEUS Now, fair Hippolyta, our nuptial hour
　　　　　Draws on apace; four happy days bring in
　　　　　Another moon – but O, methinks, how slow
　　　　　This old moon wanes! She lingers my desires,
　　　　　Like to a step-dame or a dowager　　　　　　　　　　5
　　　　　Long withering out a young man's revenue.
HIPPOLYTA Four days will quickly steep themselves in night;
　　　　　Four nights will quickly dream away the time;
　　　　　And then the moon, like to a silver bow
　　　　　New bent in heaven, shall behold the night　　　　　10
　　　　　Of our solemnities.
THESEUS　　　　　　　　　Go, Philostrate,
　　　　　Stir up the Athenian youth to merriments,
　　　　　Awake the pert and nimble spirit of mirth;
　　　　　Turn melancholy forth to funerals;

Act 1, Scene 1　　1] F (*Actus Primus*); *not in* Qq　　1.1] *Scene 1 / Rowe; not in* Qq, F　　0 SD PHILOSTRATE] *Theobald; not in* Qq, F　　4 wanes] Q2, F; waues Q1　　7 night] Q1; nights Q2, F　　8 nights] Q1, F; daies Q2　　10 New] *Rowe;* Now Qq, F

Act 1, Scene 1

1.1 F divides into acts, but not scenes; there are no act or scene-divisions in Qq. The problems of act and scene-divisions are considered in the Textual Analysis, pp. 135–43 below.

0 SD A processional entry would be appropriate, although the initial SD is brief, for Theseus, as Duke of Athens, appears to be holding court, and on the Elizabethan stage chairs of state may have been provided for him and Hippolyta to hear the formal complaint of Egeus (22 ff.). (Throughout the Commentary the notes on staging relate to the presentation of the play on the Elizabethan stage, as indicated in the text and stage directions of the quartos and Folio.) The name Philostrate, like those of Theseus and Hippolyta, is borrowed from Chaucer's *The Knight's Tale*: it is the alias adopted by the exiled Arcite (1, 1428).

1–19 Prompted by the opening of Chaucer's *Knight's Tale*, which describes the conquests of Theseus, his battle against the Amazons, and the feast at the wedding of Theseus and Ipolyta, their queen.

2 four happy days The action occupies two days and a night, but Shakespeare stretched the time imaginatively to enhance the impatient mood of Theseus.

4 lingers puts off.

5–6 a step-dame...revenue a stepmother or widow having little title to all or some part of her former husband's estate, and so wasting the income a young man might expect. See 157–8 and nn.

7 steep themselves be swallowed up in. Literally, soak themselves.

10 New 'Now' (Qq and F) is probably a compositor's error, due to the confusion, a common one, of 'e' and 'o', aided perhaps by a link with 'then' at 9.

11 solemnities celebrations, formal ceremonies.

13 pert cheerful, lively.

47

The pale companion is not for our pomp. 15

[*Exit Philostrate*]

Hippolyta, I wooed thee with my sword,
And won thy love doing thee injuries;
But I will wed thee in another key,
With pomp, with triumph, and with revelling.

Enter EGEUS *and his daughter* HERMIA, LYSANDER
and DEMETRIUS.

EGEUS Happy be Theseus, our renownèd Duke! 20
THESEUS Thanks, good Egeus. What's the news with thee?
EGEUS Full of vexation come I, with complaint
Against my child, my daughter Hermia.
Stand forth, Demetrius! – My noble lord,
This man hath my consent to marry her. 25
Stand forth, Lysander! – And, my gracious Duke,
This man hath bewitched the bosom of my child.
Thou, thou, Lysander, thou hast given her rhymes,
And interchanged love-tokens with my child.
Thou hast by moonlight at her window sung 30
With feigning voice verses of feigning love,
And stolen the impression of her fantasy,
With bracelets of thy hair, rings, gauds, conceits,
Knacks, trifles, nosegays, sweetmeats – messengers

---

15 SD *Exit Philostrate*] Theobald; *not in* Qq, F   19 SD LYSANDER] F; *and* Lysander *and* Helena Q1; *and* Lysander,
Helena Q2   24 Stand forth, Demetrius] *So Rowe; inset in italic as* SD *in* Qq, F   26 Stand forth, Lysander] *So Rowe;
inset in italic as* SD *in* Qq, F   27 This man] Qq, F; This F2   31 feigning ... feigning] Qq, F (faining)   32 fantasy]
Q2, F (fantasie,); phantasie: Q1

15 **companion** Used contemptuously.
15 **pomp** celebration.
16–19 In turning to Hippolyta here, Theseus
perhaps leads her to take their places in chairs of
state, in preparation for the arrival of Egeus to make
his 'complaint' in form.
19 **triumph** public festivity.
19 SD Qq and F include Helena in the entry here,
and perhaps Shakespeare's first thought was to
bring on all the rival lovers at this point; the text
requires her to enter at 179. Hermia should be short
and dark in colouring; see 3.2.257 and 295.
24, 26 **Stand forth, Demetrius!...Stand
forth, Lysander!** Printed as stage directions in
italic in Qq and F, these commands complete
blank-verse lines, which shows they should be
spoken.

27 This line has an extra syllable, and some
editors omit the word 'man', arguing that we should
expect Shakespeare's early verse to be regular, and
that the antithesis is sharpened. Neither argument
is convincing.
31 **feigning...feigning** Quibbling on a now
obsolete sense of 'feigning' (= 'singing softly') and
on the more usual meaning (= 'deceitful, sham'), as
well as on 'faining' (the spelling in Qq) from an
obsolete verb, meaning 'affectionate, wistful'.
32 i.e. impressed yourself on her imagination by
underhand means.
33 **gauds, conceits** bits of finery, fancy articles.
34 **Knacks** Trinkets, knick knacks. As in John
Dowland's well-known song, 'Fine knacks for
ladies'.

Of strong prevailment in unhardened youth;   35
With cunning hast thou filched my daughter's heart,
Turned her obedience, which is due to me,
To stubborn harshness. And, my gracious Duke,
Be it so she will not here, before your grace,
Consent to marry with Demetrius,   40
I beg the ancient privilege of Athens;
As she is mine, I may dispose of her;
Which shall be either to this gentleman
Or to her death, according to our law
Immediately provided in that case.   45
THESEUS What say you, Hermia? Be advised, fair maid.
To you your father should be as a god,
One that composed your beauties; yea, and one
To whom you are but as a form in wax
By him imprinted, and within his power   50
To leave the figure, or disfigure it.
Demetrius is a worthy gentleman.
HERMIA So is Lysander.
THESEUS   In himself he is;
But in this kind, wanting your father's voice,
The other must be held the worthier.   55
HERMIA I would my father looked but with my eyes.
THESEUS Rather your eyes must with his judgement look.
HERMIA I do entreat your grace to pardon me.
I know not by what power I am made bold,
Nor how it may concern my modesty   60
In such a presence here to plead my thoughts;
But I beseech your grace that I may know
The worst that may befall me in this case,
If I refuse to wed Demetrius.
THESEUS Either to die the death, or to abjure   65
For ever the society of men.

---

35 prevailment power to influence. This is the earliest example cited in *OED*.

39 Be it so i.e. if it turns out that.

45 Immediately Directly, with no possibility of mediation.

45 provided stipulated. A word much used in legal and formal statements (*OED* sv *pa pple* 5)

54 in this kind as is proper in this matter.

54 voice support. A Shakespearean usage, as at

Wiv. 1.4.156: 'Let me have thy voice in my behalf' (*OED* sv *sb* 10c).

56–7 The relation, or lack of it, between seeing and judging, or between what is experienced through the senses and what the mind imagines, is to be a central concern of the action; see 230–6 below and nn.

60 concern be appropriate to.

65 die the death be put to death.

Therefore, fair Hermia, question your desires,
Know of your youth, examine well your blood,
Whether, if you yield not to your father's choice,
You can endure the livery of a nun,   70
For aye to be in shady cloister mewed,
To live a barren sister all your life,
Chanting faint hymns to the cold fruitless moon.
Thrice blessèd they that master so their blood
To undergo such maiden pilgrimage;   75
But earthlier happy is the rose distilled
Than that which, withering on the virgin thorn,
Grows, lives, and dies in single blessedness.

HERMIA So will I grow, so live, so die, my lord,
Ere I will yield my virgin patent up   80
Unto his lordship, whose unwishèd yoke
My soul consents not to give sovereignty.

THESEUS Take time to pause, and by the next new moon,
The sealing-day betwixt my love and me
For everlasting bond of fellowship,   85
Upon that day either prepare to die
For disobedience to your father's will,
Or else to wed Demetrius, as he would,
Or on Diana's altar to protest
For aye austerity and single life.   90

DEMETRIUS Relent, sweet Hermia; and, Lysander, yield
Thy crazèd title to my certain right.

LYSANDER You have her father's love, Demetrius;
Let me have Hermia's – do you marry him.

EGEUS Scornful Lysander, true, he hath my love,   95
And what is mine my love shall render him;

---

72 barren] Q2, F; barraines Q1

68, 74 blood feelings, disposition. This use of the word as the 'supposed seat of emotion' is very common in Shakespeare (*OED* sv *sb* 5).

69 Whether Perhaps contracted to 'Wh'er' in delivery, to make the metre regular.

70 livery habit.

70–3 nun...moon The anachronistic Christian image of a cloistered nun coalesces with that of a pagan priestess hymning Diana, goddess of chastity, represented by the moon (see 89 below), and more appropriate to the Athens of Theseus.

71 mewed confined.

76 rose distilled rose plucked and distilled for perfume. The metaphor suggests that marriage releases the essence of the maiden's swiftly passing beauty, and transmits it to another generation.

78 single blessedness the blessedness resulting from a life of celibacy.

80 virgin patent right to my virginity.

81 his lordship, whose i.e. the dominion of someone whose. The stress is on 'his' (so Wells).

89 protest solemnly vow.

90 austerity self-restraint, abstinence.

92 crazèd title unsound claim.

And she is mine, and all my right of her
I do estate unto Demetrius.
LYSANDER I am, my lord, as well-derived as he,
As well-possessed: my love is more than his,   100
My fortunes every way as fairly ranked,
If not with vantage, as Demetrius';
And, which is more than all these boasts can be,
I am beloved of beauteous Hermia.
Why should not I then prosecute my right?   105
Demetrius, I'll avouch it to his head,
Made love to Nedar's daughter, Helena,
And won her soul; and she, sweet lady, dotes,
Devoutly dotes, dotes in idolatry,
Upon this spotted and inconstant man.   110
THESEUS I must confess that I have heard so much,
And with Demetrius thought to have spoke thereof;
But, being overfull of self-affairs,
My mind did lose it. But Demetrius, come,
And come, Egeus. You shall go with me;   115
I have some private schooling for you both.
For you, fair Hermia, look you arm yourself
To fit your fancies to your father's will;
Or else the law of Athens yields you up
(Which by no means we may extenuate)   120
To death, or to a vow of single life.
Come, my Hippolyta; what cheer, my love?
Demetrius and Egeus, go along;
I must employ you in some business

114 lose] Qq (loose Q1), F

98 **estate unto** bestow upon.
99 **as well-derived** of as good an ancestry.
100 **well-possessed** rich in possessions.
102 **with vantage** rather better.
106 **to his head** to his face, directly to him.
107 **Nedar's** The name was invented to fit the line; Helena's father makes no appearance in the play, and is mentioned again only once, at 4.1.127. T. Walter Herbert suggested that Shakespeare may have altered the name 'Tyndar', Helen's father in Golding's Ovid (VI, 400), and that Hermia may come from Hermione, Helen's daughter (*Oberon's Mazèd World*, 1977, p. 19).
110 **spotted** morally blemished (*OED* sv *a* 2b).
113 **self-affairs** my own concerns.

114 **But Demetrius, come** Theseus has presumably been sitting in his chair of state (see o SD above and n.), to hear formal complaints and charges; here the text suggests that he rises in preparation for a processional departure at 127.
117 **arm** prepare.
118 **fancies** See 155 and n.
120 **extenuate** mitigate.
122 **what cheer** how are things with you? The question may simply reflect Theseus's long neglect of her while attending to Egeus and the lovers, but Brooks thinks she is downcast at the 'ill-omen, intruding upon the joyous preparations for her wedding, of love threatened with death or a compelled celibacy'.

Against our nuptial, and confer with you   125
Of something nearly that concerns yourselves.

EGEUS With duty and desire we follow you.

Exeunt all but Lysander and Hermia

LYSANDER How now, my love? Why is your cheek so pale?
How chance the roses there do fade so fast?

HERMIA Belike for want of rain, which I could well   130
Beteem them from the tempest of my eyes.

LYSANDER Ay me! For aught that I could ever read,
Could ever hear by tale or history,
The course of true love never did run smooth;
But either it was different in blood –   135

HERMIA O cross! too high to be enthralled to low.

LYSANDER Or else misgraffèd in respect of years –

HERMIA O spite! too old to be engaged to young.

LYSANDER Or else it stood upon the choice of friends –

HERMIA O hell, to choose love by another's eyes!   140

LYSANDER Or, if there were a sympathy in choice,
War, death, or sickness did lay siege to it,
Making it momentany as a sound,
Swift as a shadow, short as any dream,
Brief as the lightning in the collied night,   145
That in a spleen unfolds both heaven and earth,
And, ere a man hath power to say 'Behold!',
The jaws of darkness do devour it up.

127 SD] F (*Exeunt Manet Lysander and Hermia*); *Exeunt.* Qq   131 my] Qq; mine F   132 Ay me!] Qq (Eigh me:);
omitted F   132 I could ever] Qq; ever I could F   136 low] *Theobald*; loue Qq, F   139 friends] Qq; merit F
140 eyes] Qq; eye F (eie)   143 momentany] Qq; momentary F

125 Against In preparation for.

127 SD Theseus sweeps off leading Hippolyta, Egeus and Demetrius, and followed by Philostrate and 'others' (0 SD); formality gives way to intimacy as Lysander and Hermia are left together on stage.

130 Belike Probably.

131 Beteem Grant.

134 This looks proverbial, but is not in Tilley.

135–41 Bernard Shaw described these lines as composing a 'duet' (*Our Theatres in the Nineties*, 3 vols., rev. edn, 1932, I, 180–1), pointing to the musical and patterning effect of such passages, where the lovers speak in alternate lines, or alternate groups of lines, and at times, as at 171 ff. or 3.2.122 ff., in rhyme. See 194–201, and pp. 28–31 above.

135 blood parentage, i.e. rank.

137 misgraffèd badly matched (misgrafted).

139 friends F substitutes 'merit', which Brooks regards as an alternative of Shakespeare's, perhaps his revised reading. It is puzzling that F printed what can hardly be an error or misreading, and therefore was probably in the MS. consulted with Q2, the main source for the text in F. If so, then it is more likely to have been Shakespeare's first thought, since 'friends' is much more appropriate in relation to the next line.

141 sympathy agreement.

143 momentany momentary. This form, now obsolete, was common in the sixteenth century.

145 collied murky. From 'colly' = soot, related to 'coal', as in the still-current term 'collier'.

146 spleen fit of temper.

So quick bright things come to confusion.

HERMIA If then true lovers have been ever crossed   150
It stands as an edict in destiny.
Then let us teach our trial patience,
Because it is a customary cross,
As due to love as thoughts, and dreams, and sighs,
Wishes, and tears – poor fancy's followers.   155

LYSANDER A good persuasion. Therefore hear me, Hermia:
I have a widow aunt, a dowager,
Of great revenue, and she hath no child.
From Athens is her house remote seven leagues;
And she respects me as her only son.   160
There, gentle Hermia, may I marry thee;
And to that place the sharp Athenian law
Cannot pursue us. If thou lov'st me, then
Steal forth thy father's house tomorrow night,
And in the wood, a league without the town   165
(Where I did meet thee once with Helena
To do observance to a morn of May),
There will I stay for thee.

HERMIA   My good Lysander,
I swear to thee by Cupid's strongest bow,
By his best arrow with the golden head,   170
By the simplicity of Venus' doves,

---

159 remote] Qq; remou'd F   167 to a] Qq; for a F

150 crossed thwarted.

155 fancy's love's. But the word was synonymous with fantasy or imagination, and more commonly meant 'capricious or arbitrary preference' (*OED* sv *sb* 5).

156 persuasion doctrine.

157 dowager See 5–6 above and n.

158 revenue This word could be accented on the first syllable, as at 6 above, or the second, as here.

160 respects regards.

165 without outside.

167 observance...May May Day festivities involving the gathering of green branches and flowers from the woods and bringing them, as symbolic of new life, into towns and villages were usual in England, if not in Athens, and Shakespeare echoes Chaucer here, in whose *Knight's Tale* Arcite rises 'to doen his observaunce to Maie' (1, 1500, and compare 1040–5).

170 best arrow...head Cupid is said in Ovid's *Metamorphoses* 1, 565 ff., to have used arrows of gold

to cause love, and arrows of lead to repel; Shakespeare knew this work well in Arthur Golding's translation, from which he derived the story of Pyramus and Thisbe for this play. In Thomas Preston's tragedy *Cambyses*, a play Shakespeare seems to echo in 'Pyramus and Thisbe' (see 1.2.9–10, 5.1.318 and nn.), Cupid is represented on stage (line 842) with a bow and two shafts 'one hedded with golde and the other hedded with lead'.

171 Hermia confirms her vow in rhyming couplets. Apart from 179, the rest of the scene is in couplets, creating a mood of lyrical intensity, and at the same time ritualising lover's quarrels, pain and hatred, colouring even these with grace and prettiness, and converting them to comic ends. See pp. 28–9 above.

171 simplicity (1) artlessness, (2) freedom from deceit, the opposite of 'duplicity'.

171 Venus' doves Doves, symbolic of tender love and fidelity, were sacred to Venus. At the end

By that which knitteth souls and prospers loves,
And by that fire which burned the Carthage queen
When the false Trojan under sail was seen,
By all the vows that ever men have broke   175
(In number more than ever women spoke),
In that same place thou hast appointed me,
Tomorrow truly will I meet with thee.

LYSANDER Keep promise, love. Look, here comes Helena.

Enter HELENA.

HERMIA God speed, fair Helena! Whither away?   180
HELENA Call you me fair? That 'fair' again unsay.
Demetrius loves your fair: O happy fair!
Your eyes are lodestars, and your tongue's sweet air
More tuneable than lark to shepherd's ear
When wheat is green, when hawthorn buds appear.   185
Sickness is catching. O, were favour so,
Yours would I catch, fair Hermia, ere I go;
My ear should catch your voice, my eye your eye,
My tongue should catch your tongue's sweet melody.
Were the world mine, Demetrius being bated,   190
The rest I'd give to be to you translated.
O, teach me how you look, and with what art
You sway the motion of Demetrius' heart.
HERMIA I frown upon him; yet he loves me still.
HELENA O that your frowns would teach my smiles such skill!   195
HERMIA I give him curses; yet he gives me love.
HELENA O that my prayers could such affection move!
HERMIA The more I hate, the more he follows me.
HELENA The more I love, the more he hateth me.

172 loves] Q1; love Q2, F   182 your] Qq; you F   187 Yours would I] *Hanmer*; Your words I Qq, F; Your words
Ide F2   191 I'd] *Hanmer*; I'll Q1 (ile), Q2, F (Ile)

of *Venus and Adonis*, Venus flies off into the skies
in a chariot drawn by 'silver doves'.
   173–4 In Virgil's *Aeneid* IV Dido sees Aeneas sail
away before consigning herself to a funeral pyre; the
'fire' is the emblem of her devotion to her love.
   175–6 Hermia's teasing anticipates the breaking
of his vows by Lysander; see 2.2.61–2 and 102–6.
   179 SD HELENA As Hermia is short and dark (see
19 SD above and n.), so Helena is tall and fair; see
3.2.187–8 and 291–3.
   182 your fair your beauty. F reads 'you fair',

which makes sense, and balances 'me fair', but
could have resulted from the accidental dropping of
a letter in the printing-house.
   183 lodestars i.e. drawing the gaze of Demetrius
as navigators fix their eyes on a guiding star.
   184 tuneable melodious.
   186 favour beauty, attractiveness.
   190 bated excepted.
   194–201 These lines constitute another formal
duet; see 135–41 above and n.

HERMIA His folly, Helena, is no fault of mine.   200
HELENA None but your beauty; would that fault were mine!
HERMIA Take comfort: he no more shall see my face;
    Lysander and myself will fly this place.
    Before the time I did Lysander see,
    Seemed Athens as a paradise to me.   205
    O then, what graces in my love do dwell,
    That he hath turned a heaven unto a hell?
LYSANDER Helen, to you our minds we will unfold:
    Tomorrow night, when Phoebe doth behold
    Her silver visage in the watery glass,   210
    Decking with liquid pearl the bladed grass
    (A time that lovers' flights doth still conceal),
    Through Athens' gates have we devised to steal.
HERMIA And in the wood, where often you and I
    Upon faint primrose beds were wont to lie,   215
    Emptying our bosoms of their counsel sweet,
    There my Lysander and myself shall meet,
    And thence from Athens turn away our eyes
    To seek new friends and stranger companies.
    Farewell, sweet playfellow; pray thou for us,   220
    And good luck grant thee thy Demetrius.
    Keep word, Lysander; we must starve our sight
    From lovers' food till morrow deep midnight.
LYSANDER I will, my Hermia.

                                        Exit Hermia

                Helena, adieu!
    As you on him, Demetrius dote on you.   *Exit Lysander*   225
HELENA How happy some o'er other some can be!
    Through Athens I am thought as fair as she.

200 no fault] Q1; none Q2, F   205 as] Q1; like Q2, F   207 unto a] Q1; into Q2, F   216 sweet] *Theobald;* sweld Qq, F   219 stranger companies] *Theobald;* strange companions Qq, F   225 dote] Qq; dotes F

204 **Lysander** At first sight, this might be thought an error for Demetrius, who has made Hermia wretched, but her paradox is that Lysander's 'graces' in his love, by provoking the jealousy of Demetrius and her father's anger, have made Athens hell for her.
207 **turned...hell?** Compare Helena's determination to 'make a heaven of hell' at 2.1.243.
209 **Phoebe** Another name for Diana, goddess of the moon; compare 73, 89 above.
212 **still** invariably.

214–20 This establishes the long intimate friendship of Hermia and Helena, the background to their quarrel in Act 3; see 3.2.198 ff.
215 **faint** pale. Referring simply to the pale yellow colour of the flowers.
219 **stranger companies** the fellowship of strangers. Theobald's emendation of 'strange companions' has been generally accepted as necessary for the rhyme.
226 **other some** i.e. some others.

But what of that? Demetrius thinks not so;
He will not know what all but he do know.
And as he errs, doting on Hermia's eyes,   230
So I, admiring of his qualities.
Things base and vile, holding no quantity,
Love can transpose to form and dignity.
Love looks not with the eyes, but with the mind,
And therefore is winged Cupid painted blind.   235
Nor hath love's mind of any judgement taste;
Wings, and no eyes, figure unheedy haste;
And therefore is love said to be a child
Because in choice he is so oft beguiled.
As waggish boys in game themselves forswear,   240
So the boy Love is perjured everywhere;
For, ere Demetrius looked on Hermia's eyne,
He hailed down oaths that he was only mine,
And when this hail some heat from Hermia felt,
So he dissolved, and showers of oaths did melt.   245
I will go tell him of fair Hermia's flight:
Then to the wood will he, tomorrow night,
Pursue her; and for this intelligence,
If I have thanks it is a dear expense;
But herein mean I to enrich my pain,   250
To have his sight thither, and back again.   *Exit*

---

229 do] Qq; doth F   **239** so oft] Q1; oft Q2; often F   **248** this] Qq; his F

232–45 Helena's lines on the power of love to transform, and the lack of connection between seeing and judgement, relate to the changes of the lovers in Act 3, and especially the infatuation of Titania with Bottom.

232 holding no quantity i.e. having no relation to the value put upon them by love.

234 Love is conventionally aroused through the eyes (see 222, 242), as Helena knows, but the lover sees beauty where others do not, and so looks with the mind, or fancy (see 155 above), but not the judgement. Compare the proverb 'Love is without reason' (Tilley L517) and see 2.2.121–4 and n.

235 Cupid...blind Cupid was generally represented as blind in medieval and Renaissance art and literature, partly because his arrows hit or miss at random, and partly with reference to the sensual nature of the love they stir, sometimes contrasted

with a clear-sighted Platonic love. By transference, the lover is 'blinded about what he loves, so that he judges wrongly of the just, the good and the honourable', as Plato said in his *Laws*; see Erwin Panofsky, *Studies in Iconology*, 1939, section IV, 'Blind Cupid', pp. 95–128.

237 figure symbolise.

240 waggish playful, mischievous.

240 game sport.

242 eyne The plural 'eyes' had begun to displace Middle English 'eyne' in the fourteenth century, so that this form was archaic in Shakespeare's time, and not much used except, as here, for rhyme.

248 intelligence information.

249 a dear expense a great sacrifice. She does not expect to be thanked, because he will begrudge doing so, just as he would a costly burden of expenditure.

1.[2] *Enter* QUINCE *the Carpenter, and* SNUG *the Joiner, and* BOTTOM
the Weaver, and FLUTE *the Bellows-mender, and* SNOUT *the Tinker and*
STARVELING *the Tailor.*

QUINCE Is all our company here?

BOTTOM You were best to call them generally, man by man, according
    to the scrip.

QUINCE Here is the scroll of every man's name which is thought fit
    through all Athens to play in our interlude before the Duke and   5
    the Duchess on his wedding day at night.

BOTTOM First, good Peter Quince, say what the play treats on; then
    read the names of the actors; and so grow to a point.

QUINCE Marry, our play is 'The most lamentable comedy and most
    cruel death of Pyramus and Thisbe'.   10

BOTTOM A very good piece of work, I assure you, and a merry. Now,
    good Peter Quince, call forth your actors by the scroll. Masters,
    spread yourselves.

QUINCE Answer as I call you. Nick Bottom, the weaver?

BOTTOM Ready. Name what part I am for, and proceed.   15

QUINCE You, Nick Bottom, are set down for Pyramus.

BOTTOM What is Pyramus? A lover or a tyrant?

QUINCE A lover that kills himself, most gallant, for love.

BOTTOM That will ask some tears in the true performing of it. If I do

---

Act 1, Scene 2   1.2] *Capell; not in* Qq, F   3 to] Q1, F; *omitted* Q2   8 grow] Qq; grow on F   18 gallant] Qq;
gallantly F

Act 1, Scene 2
    o SD This scene is to be imagined as taking place
somewhere in the 'town' (81) of Athens, though no
scenery or properties need have been used to
indicate this in Shakespeare's theatre. In contrast to
the verse of the courtly characters in 1.1, the
workmen, as is usual in Elizabethan plays, speak in
prose, and this would have sufficiently marked the
change of scene and atmosphere. The names of the
mechanicals all relate to their trade, character or
appearance: so 'Quince' suggests quoins, or wedges
used in carpentry; 'Snug' can mean close-fitting,
appropriate to a joiner; 'Bottom' suggests a bottom
of thread, or the clew or core on which the weaver's
yarn was wound; 'Flute' indicates the piping voice
of one who is to play Thisbe, and also suggests the
reedy pipes of an organ worked by bellows; 'Snout'
can mean nozzle or spout, relating to the tinker's
trade in mending kettles; and 'Starveling' points to
the proverbial image of a tailor as thin and weak
(Tilley T23), as well as being appropriate to John
Sincklo, the actor in Shakespeare's company who
played thin men's parts; see Greg, pp. 114–15 and
nn.

2 **generally** Bottom at once displays his ignorant
confidence: he means 'severally', or individually.
    3 **scrip** A scrap of paper. Bottom's mistake for
'script', meaning what is written down.
    5 **interlude** play.
    8 **grow to a point** draw to a conclusion.
    9–10 '**The most...Thisbe**'. Shakespeare was
parodying elaborate titles such as that of Thomas
Preston's *A lamentable tragedy mixed ful of pleasant
mirth, conteyning the life of Cambyses, King of Percia*
(c. 1570), or *A new Tragicall Comedie of Apius and
Virginia* (1575). See also 5.1.57 and n. The story of
Pyramus and Thisbe Shakespeare drew from Ovid's
Metamorphoses IV (see pp. 10–11 above). The
classical legend is appropriate in relation to Athens,
and comically inappropriate to the abilities of
Quince's company.
    13 **spread yourselves** This internal stage
direction suggests that the group has been huddled
around Quince, all trying to see his 'scroll'; it is not
clear whether he is simply telling his companions
to disperse and stop crowding him, or whether he
is also inviting them to recline or sit.

it, let the audience look to their eyes: I will move storms, I will   20
condole, in some measure. To the rest – yet my chief humour is
for a tyrant. I could play Ercles rarely, or a part to tear a cat in,
to make all split:

> The raging rocks
> And shivering shocks   25
> Shall break the locks
>   Of prison gates,
> And Phibbus' car
> Shall shine from far,
> And make and mar   30
>   The foolish Fates.

This was lofty. Now name the rest of the players. – This is Ercles'
vein, a tyrant's vein; a lover is more condoling.

QUINCE Francis Flute, the bellows-mender?

FLUTE Here, Peter Quince.   35

QUINCE Flute, you must take Thisbe on you.

FLUTE What is Thisbe? A wandering knight?

QUINCE It is the lady that Pyramus must love.

FLUTE Nay, faith, let not me play a woman: I have a beard coming.

QUINCE That's all one: you shall play it in a mask, and you may speak   40
as small as you will.

---

21 rest – yet] *Theobald* (rest; – yet); rest yet, Qq, F   24–31] *So Johnson; as prose* Qq, F   36 Flute, you] Q1; you Q2, F

---

21 **condole** lament, express grief.

22 **Ercles** Hercules. A two-part play called *Hercules* was performed as 'ne' (?new) by the Admiral's Men in May 1595 (*Henslowe's Diary*, pp. 28–9).

22 **tear a cat** rant and bluster. *OED* Tear *v*¹ 1d cites this as the earliest example, but the phrase became proverbial, and may have been so when Shakespeare used it.

24–31 These lines burlesque a style of verse common in the 1580s, outmoded by the time Shakespeare wrote *MND*. He seems, as Rolfe claimed, to have been prompted here by passages in John Studley's translation (1581) of Seneca's *Hercules Oetaeus*:

> O lord of ghosts, whose fiery flash
>   That forth thy hand doth shake
> Doth cause the trembling lodges twain
>   Of Phoebus' car to quake...
> The roaring rocks have quaking stirred
>   And none thereat have pushed;
> Hell gloomy gates I have brast ope
>   Where grisly ghosts all hushed
> Have stood...

28 **Phibbus' car** The chariot supposedly driven by Phoebus, god of the sun.

37 **wandering knight** knight-errant, wandering in search of adventures. Flute, as his name shows, has a piping voice quite inappropriate to the heroes of plays of this kind, such as *Sir Clyomon and Clamydes* (*c.* 1570). They were popular enough for Beaumont to burlesque in *The Knight of the Burning Pestle* (?1608).

39 The joke may have been that Flute was first played by a youth who usually took female parts; see p. 4 above.

40 **mask** A disguise for Flute, but not for Thisbe, for ladies, 'when they goe out of dores, weare upon their faces little Maskes of silk, lined with fine leather' (Fynes Moryson, *Itinerary*, III, 177, cited *OED*). Such masks, worn to protect a lady's complexion 'from the sun, or to shield her from public gaze' (Linthicum, pp. 271–2), remained fashionable until well into the seventeenth century; Autolycus carries 'Masks for faces' among his pedlar's ware in *WT* 4.4.221.

41 **small** i.e. high-pitched, like a woman. Compare *Wiv.* 1.1.48: 'speaks small like a woman', and Viola's 'shrill' small voice in *TN* 1.4.32–3.

BOTTOM And I may hide my face, let me play Thisbe too. I'll speak
in a monstrous little voice: 'Thisne, Thisne!' – 'Ah, Pyramus, my
lover dear; thy Thisbe dear, and lady dear.'

QUINCE No, no; you must play Pyramus; and Flute, you Thisbe.   45

BOTTOM Well, proceed.

QUINCE Robin Starveling, the tailor?

STARVELING Here, Peter Quince.

QUINCE Robin Starveling, you must play Thisbe's mother. Tom Snout,
the tinker?   50

SNOUT Here, Peter Quince.

QUINCE You, Pyramus' father; myself, Thisbe's father; Snug, the
joiner, you the lion's part; and I hope here is a play fitted.

SNUG Have you the lion's part written? Pray you, if it be, give it me;
for I am slow of study.   55

QUINCE You may do it extempore; for it is nothing but roaring.

BOTTOM Let me play the lion too. I will roar that I will do any man's
heart good to hear me. I will roar that I will make the Duke say
'Let him roar again, let him roar again!'

QUINCE And you should do it too terribly, you would fright the   60
Duchess and the ladies that they would shriek; and that were
enough to hang us all.

ALL That would hang us, every mother's son.

BOTTOM I grant you, friends, if you should fright the ladies out of their
wits they would have no more discretion but to hang us; but I will   65
aggravate my voice so that I will roar you as gently as any sucking
dove. I will roar you and 'twere any nightingale.

QUINCE You can play no part but Pyramus; for Pyramus is a sweet-faced

---

53 here] Qq; there F   54 if it be] Qq; if be F   60 And] Q1; If Q2, F   64 if] Qq; if that F   66 roar you] Qq;
roar F

42 And If.

43 **Thisne** Bottom, as Pyramus, calls Thisbe,
lisping her name in a 'small' voice (so Brooks, after
Sisson, I, 125), then responds as Thisbe. 'Thisne'
is italicised in Qq as a proper name, and there is no
reason to suppose with Aldis Wright that it
represents a dialectal form of 'thissen', meaning
'like this'.

49–52 **Thisbe's mother...Pyramus' father
...Thisbe's father** These parents do not appear in
the playlet as performed in Act 5, where Starveling
becomes Moonshine, Snout the Wall, and Quince
the Prologue. Such discrepancies pass unnoticed in
the theatre, but they show that Shakespeare had
probably not yet thought out how he would design
the last act.

60 And If.

65 **no more discretion** Bottom means they
would have no choice ('discretion' = the power of a
court of justice to decide a punishment), but his
confused way of putting it suggests they would have
no better judgement or discrimination than to hang
them.

66 **aggravate** He means 'moderate'; compare
2H4 2.4.162, where Mistress Quickly makes the
same error (so Wells).

66–7 **sucking dove** Another confusion, of 'sitting
dove' (as birds sit on eggs) and 'sucking lamb', both
proverbial for mildness and innocence (Tilley D573,
L34).

67 **and 'twere** as if it were.

man, a proper man as one shall see in a summer's day, a most lovely,
gentlemanlike man: therefore you must needs play Pyramus.   70

BOTTOM Well, I will undertake it. What beard were I best to play it
in?

QUINCE Why, what you will.

BOTTOM I will discharge it in either your straw-colour beard, your
orange-tawny beard, your purple-in-grain beard, or your French-   75
crown-colour beard, your perfect yellow.

QUINCE Some of your French crowns have no hair at all, and then you
will play bare-faced. But, masters, here are your parts, and I am
to entreat you, request you, and desire you to con them by
tomorrow night, and meet me in the palace wood, a mile without   80
the town, by moonlight; there will we rehearse, for if we meet in
the city we shall be dogged with company, and our devices known.
In the meantime I will draw a bill of properties, such as our play
wants. I pray you, fail me not.

BOTTOM We will meet, and there we may rehearse most obscenely and   85
courageously. Take pains, be perfect: adieu!

QUINCE At the Duke's oak we meet.

BOTTOM Enough; hold, or cut bowstrings.

Exeunt

---

76 colour] Qq; colour'd F   76, 86 perfect] F, Qq (perfit Qq)   81 will we] Q1; we will Q2, F   85 most] Q1;
more Q2, F

69 proper handsome.

74–6 Bottom's interest in colours is perhaps
appropriate to his trade as a weaver (so Martin
Wright, Wells), if irrelevant to Quince's purposes.
Bottom has to be clean-shaven, for later he acquires
an ass's beard and becomes 'hairy about the face'
(4.1.23).

75 orange-tawny tan-coloured. A common
term, occurring in a letter of Edward Alleyn and in
playhouse lists; see *Henslowe's Diary*, pp. 277, 233,
etc.

75 purple-in-grain fast-dyed crimson. 'Purple'
was still associated with red, and especially the
colour of blood, as in the 'purple blood' of *3H6*
2.5.99, and it is an absurd colour for a beard.

75–6 French-crown-colour The gold colour of
the French écu, or 'crown' as the English called it.

77 French crowns Alluding to baldness
produced by the 'French disease', syphilis; a
common joke, as at *AWW* 2.2.22.

79 con learn.

80 palace wood Associating the wood with
royalty, as it is the 'palace' of Oberon and Titania,
and contains the 'Duke's oak' (87).

80 mile Lysander planned to meet Hermia in the
wood 'a league without the town' (1.1.165).
Shakespeare does not seem to have troubled himself
about such minor discrepancies, which pass
unnoticed in performance; compare 49–52 above
and n.

83 draw a bill compile a list.

85 obscenely Bottom's error for 'seemly'? He
means 'fitly', as in Costard's misuse of the same
word in *LLL* 4.1.143: 'When it comes so smoothly
off, so obscenely, as it were, so fit'.

86 be perfect know your lines thoroughly.

88 hold…bowstrings This looks like a
proverbial expression, derived from archery, and is
close to 'Hold or cut codpiece point' (Tilley C502,
as Brooks noted; although its precise meaning
remains uncertain, it may be interpreted as 'keep
your word or else be disgraced' (so Wells).

2.[1] *Enter a* FAIRY *at one door, and* [PUCK, *or*] ROBIN GOODFELLOW
at another.

PUCK How now, spirit; whither wander you?
FAIRY   Over hill, over dale,
                Thorough bush, thorough briar,
                Over park, over pale,
                Thorough flood, thorough fire;   5
                I do wander everywhere
                Swifter than the moon's sphere;
                And I serve the Fairy Queen,
                To dew her orbs upon the green.
                The cowslips tall her pensioners be;   10
                In their gold coats spots you see –
                Those be rubies, fairy favours,
                In those freckles live their savours.
                I must go seek some dewdrops here,
                And hang a pearl in every cowslip's ear.   15

Act 2, Scene 1   2] F (*Actus Secundus*); *not in* Qq   2.1] *Scene 1* / *Rowe*; *not in* Qq, F   0 SD] Qq, F (*Enter a Fairie...
and Robin goodfellow...*)   2–9] *So Pope; as four lines in* Qq, F, *ending* brier, / ...fire: / ...sphere: / ...greene.
3, 5 Thorough...thorough] Q1; Through...through Q2, F

Act 2, Scene 1
   0 SD The action now moves to the wood (1.2.80)
in place and 'tomorrow night' (1.1.164) in time, in
relation to Act 1. The entry refers to the two doors
(one on either side of the stage), and the form is
common in plays of the period when two characters
or groups meet on stage. Here, as often in Qq and
F, and in speech headings up to line 42, Puck is
called Robin Goodfellow, which is his name (see
34); a 'puck' is a mischievous spirit or goblin, but
the character has become generally known by this
title; see also p. 7 above.
   2–59 The patterned verse of the Fairy, followed
by dialogue in rhyming couplets, makes a sharp
contrast with the prose of the previous scene. The
Fairy was presumably played by a boy but Puck was
probably a role for an adult actor; see 16 and n.
Wells notes that Robin Goodfellow or Akercock in
Grim the Collier of Croydon (?1600) is a clown figure,
a servant of Belphagor a devil, and was played by
a man.
   3 **Thorough** This archaic form of 'through'
(compare the still-current word 'thoroughfare')
remained available for poetic use.
   4 **pale** fence; i.e. enclosure or fenced-in area.

Fairies could go anywhere, unhindered by private
boundaries.
   7 **moon's sphere** Early astronomers thought
that each planet was attached to a transparent
crystal globe; these hollow 'spheres' revolved one
inside the other with the earth at their centre; the
term thus came to be used more loosely to mean
'orbit', as at 153 below.
   9 **orbs** fairy-rings. These circular bands of grass,
darker than the lawns or fields in which they appear,
were thought in Shakespeare's age to be the work
of fairies; in fact they grow where fungi have
enriched the soil.
   10 **pensioners** Gentlemen of the royal body-
guard, handsome and splendidly dressed. Queen
Elizabeth maintained a body of such pensioners,
instituted by Henry VIII in 1509.
   11 **gold coats...see** The cowslip bears drooping
umbels or sprays of yellow scented flowers, with
freckles or 'crimson drops' (*Cym* 2.2.38) in them.
   13 **savours** fragrance.
   14–15 These lines are not differentiated in
Qq, F, but they mark a transition from a basically
trochaic to iambic tetrameter, and so lead into the
iambic pentameter of 16 ff.

Farewell, thou lob of spirits; I'll be gone.
Our Queen and all her elves come here anon.
PUCK The King doth keep his revels here tonight.
Take heed the Queen come not within his sight,
For Oberon is passing fell and wrath,   20
Because that she as her attendant hath
A lovely boy stol'n from an Indian king;
She never had so sweet a changeling,
And jealous Oberon would have the child
Knight of his train, to trace the forests wild.   25
But she perforce withholds the lovèd boy,
Crowns him with flowers, and makes him all her joy.
And now they never meet in grove or green,
By fountain clear or spangled starlight sheen,
But they do square, that all their elves for fear   30
Creep into acorn cups and hide them there.
FAIRY Either I mistake your shape and making quite,
Or else you are that shrewd and knavish sprite
Called Robin Goodfellow. Are not you he
That frights the maidens of the villagery,   35
Skim milk, and sometimes labour in the quern,
And bootless make the breathless housewife churn,
And sometime make the drink to bear no barm,
Mislead night-wanderers, laughing at their harm?

---

33 sprite] Q1 ; *spirit* Q2, F   37 housewife] Qq, F (huswife)

---

16 lob bumpkin, lout. This suggests that Puck was to the Fairy a large and clumsy 'spirit'; was he played by an adult actor? Or is it simply a fairy joke?

17 elves By Shakespeare's time synonymous with fairies, and used of both sexes, though originally elves were male imps; but perhaps anticipating the male fairies, Peaseblossom and the rest, who attend on Bottom in 3.1.

20 passing...wrath bitterly vengeful and angry. 'Wrath' was a common adjectival form in Shakespeare's time, but this is his sole use of it.

22 lovely boy See pp. 29–30 above for a discussion of the significance of this Indian boy.

22 Indian king Oberon and Titania are associated with India at 69 and 124 as if it were their home.

23 changeling Usually an ugly or stupid child supposed to have been left by fairies in exchange for one they have taken by stealth, but here applied to the child stolen. The word must be pronounced here as three syllables.

25 trace range over.

26 perforce by physical force.

30 square quarrel.

33 shrewd mischievous.

34–6 Are you...Skim The verb form changes from the third person ('frights') to the second ('Skim'), as Robin is both 'he' and 'you'.

36 Skim milk i.e. steal the cream.

36 quern Hand-mill for grinding corn. Presumably Puck labours to hamper or spoil the grinding.

37 bootless uselessly. The cream will not turn to butter.

38 barm i.e. froth, or 'head' on ale or beer. Puck prevents the barm or yeast from working.

39 Mislead As later Puck leads astray Quince and his cast (3.1.88–9), and then the lovers (3.2.396 ff.).

Those that 'Hobgoblin' call you, and 'Sweet Puck',   40
You do their work, and they shall have good luck.
Are not you he?

PUCK   Thou speakest aright;
I am that merry wanderer of the night.
I jest to Oberon, and make him smile
When I a fat and bean-fed horse beguile,   45
Neighing in likeness of a filly foal;
And sometime lurk I in a gossip's bowl
In very likeness of a roasted crab,
And when she drinks, against her lips I bob,
And on her withered dewlap pour the ale.   50
The wisest aunt, telling the saddest tale,
Sometime for threefoot stool mistaketh me;
Then slip I from her bum, down topples she,
And 'Tailor' cries, and falls into a cough;
And then the whole choir hold their hips and loffe,   55
And waxen in their mirth, and neeze, and swear
A merrier hour was never wasted there.
But room, Fairy: here comes Oberon.

FAIRY And here my mistress. Would that he were gone!

Enter [OBERON,] *the King of Fairies, at one door, with his train; and*
      [TITANIA,] *the Queen, at another with hers.*

42 not you] Q1; you not Q2, F   42–3 Thou...night] *So* F; *one line in* Qq   46 filly] Q1; silly Q2, F   59 SD] Qq, F
(*Enter the King... and the Queene...*)

40 **Hobgoblin** Another name for Puck, as 'Hob' is simply a familiar by-form of 'Rob' or 'Robin'.

45 **bean-fed** well-fed. Hence, frisky.

46 **filly foal** A common expression, since 'foal', though properly meaning a colt, could be used of either sex.

48 **crab** crab-apple. Used with sugar and spice to flavour hot ale; the drink so made was known as 'lamb's-wool' (*OED* Lamb's-wool 2); compare *LLL* 5.2.925.

50 **dewlap** i.e. the loose skin of her throat, hanging like that of a cow.

51 **aunt** old woman, gossip (the only example listed in *OED*).

51 **saddest** most earnest or serious.

54 **'Tailor' cries** Dr Johnson thought he recalled hearing this said, adding 'He that slips beside his chair falls as a tailor squats upon his board.' His explanation is dubious; Hilda Hulme

thinks it probably refers to the 'tail' or backside (*Explorations in Shakespeare's Language*, 1962, pp. 99–100).

55 **choir** company. They laugh in consort like a chorus.

55–6 **loffe...waxen...neeze** Puck imitates rustic speech, using archaic forms, 'loffe' for laugh, 'waxen' for wax (= increase, grow loud), and 'neeze' for sneeze.

58 **room** give way. A stage direction within the text, equivalent to 'stand aside'.

59 SD.2 **train** Puck is already on stage, and Titania's 'train' includes the unnamed Fairy of this scene, together with Peaseblossom, Cobweb, Moth and Mustardseed. So Titania has at least five, and perhaps more, fairies waiting on her (see 4.1.0 SD). Oberon's 'train' is not seen again until 5.1.368, but if he had a matching number of attendants, a very large number of boys would have been required to

OBERON Ill met by moonlight, proud Titania!   60
TITANIA What, jealous Oberon? Fairies, skip hence.
　　　　I have forsworn his bed and company.
OBERON Tarry, rash wanton! Am not I thy lord?
TITANIA Then I must be thy lady. But I know
　　　　When thou hast stol'n away from Fairyland,   65
　　　　And in the shape of Corin sat all day
　　　　Playing on pipes of corn, and versing love
　　　　To amorous Phillida. Why art thou here
　　　　Come from the farthest step of India? –
　　　　But that, forsooth, the bouncing Amazon,   70
　　　　Your buskined mistress and your warrior love,
　　　　To Theseus must be wedded; and you come
　　　　To give their bed joy and prosperity.
OBERON How canst thou thus, for shame, Titania,
　　　　Glance at my credit with Hippolyta,   75
　　　　Knowing I know thy love to Theseus?
　　　　Didst not thou lead him through the glimmering night
　　　　From Perigenia, whom he ravishèd,
　　　　And make him with fair Aegles break his faith,

61 Fairies] *Theobald;* Fairy Qq, F   65 hast] Qq; wast F   69 step] Q1 (steppe); steepe Q2, F   79 Aegles]
Chambers; Eagles Qq, F; Ægle *Rowe*

perform in the play. Perhaps here the six 'fairies' (including Puck) who have speaking-parts were simply divided between Oberon and Titania; in any case, all but Puck must leave with Titania at 145, so that Oberon can be left alone on stage at 176. See pp. 3–4 above for further comment.

60 The entry of Oberon and Titania is marked by a change from rhyming couplets to blank verse.

61 Fairies 'Fairy' (Qq, F) may be correct if, as Wells thinks, Titania is addressing the Fairy who has been talking with Puck, but it makes more sense if she calls all her 'train' to leave. A compositor memorising a phrase might easily elide an 's' from 'Fairies, skip', which sounds virtually the same as 'Fairy, skip' (Cuningham).

63 wanton rebel. Properly, a spoiled child, someone who is unmanageable.

63–4 lord…lady i.e. husband and wife, with appropriate rights and duties.

66–8 Corin…Phillida Typical names for a shepherd and shepherdess in Arcadian pastoral verse, derived from the Corydon and Phyllis of Virgil's *Ecologues*.

67 pipes of corn i.e. made of straw. Brooks

compares *LLL* 5.2.903: 'pipe on oaten straws'.

69 step Perhaps 'utmost limit of travel or exploration' (Onions); 'steppe' (Q1) cannot mean 'plain' as in Russia, for the word was introduced into English in the late seventeenth century, but may be a variant of 'steep' (Q2, F), meaning 'mountain', if, as is possible, Shakespeare was thinking of the Himalayas.

71 buskined wearing calf- or knee-length hunting-boots. Hippolyta's prowess in hunting is touched on again in 4.1, and provides a pointer to the costume for this part.

75 Glance at Allude critically to.

78–80 Perigenia…Aegles…Ariadne…Antiopa Shakespeare probably found these names in North's translation of Plutarch's 'Life of Theseus', where 'Perigenia' is called 'Perigouna'. 'Eagles' (Qq, F) is simply a corruption of 'Aegles'. All were loved and deserted by Theseus. The legend of Ariadne, who helped Theseus to find his way through the labyrinth to destroy the Minotaur, was well known, but the other stories were not familiar. 'Antiopa' North says was an Amazon, perhaps to be identified with Hippolyta (p. 15), a connection Shakespeare omits.

With Ariadne, and Antiopa?   80
TITANIA These are the forgeries of jealousy:
And never since the middle summer's spring
Met we on hill, in dale, forest, or mead,
By pavèd fountain or by rushy brook,
Or in the beachèd margent of the sea   85
To dance our ringlets to the whistling wind,
But with thy brawls thou hast disturbed our sport.
Therefore the winds, piping to us in vain,
As in revenge have sucked up from the sea
Contagious fogs; which, falling in the land,   90
Hath every pelting river made so proud
That they have overborne their continents.
The ox hath therefore stretched his yoke in vain,
The ploughman lost his sweat, and the green corn
Hath rotted ere his youth attained a beard.   95
The fold stands empty in the drownèd field,
And crows are fatted with the murrion flock;
The nine-men's-morris is filled up with mud,
And the quaint mazes in the wanton green
For lack of tread are undistinguishable.   100

80 Antiopa] Qq; Atiopa F   91 pelting] Qq; petty F

82 **middle summer's spring** the beginning of midsummer. Compare *2H4* 4.4.35: 'the spring of day'.
84 **pavèd** flowing over stones or pebbles.
85 **margent** The usual form of 'margin' in Shakespeare's age, and the one he always used.
86 **ringlets** Circular dances, marking fairy rings. See 9 above and n.
87 **brawls** clamour. But also a dance (from the French 'bransle') which involved men and women holding hands in a ring (so Randall Cotgrave, *A Dictionarie of the French and English Tongues* (1611), cited in *OED* sv sb³ 2), and this sense no doubt prompted the link with 'ringlets'.
90 **Contagious** Pestilential, breeding disease.
91 **pelting** paltry.
92 **continents** banks. Literally, what contains the rivers. Compare *Ant.* 4.14.40: 'Heart, once be stronger than thy continent.'
95 **beard** Compare *Sonnets* 12.8: 'sheaves / Borne on the bier with white and bristly beard'.
97 **murrion** Infected with the 'murrain', a fatal sheep disease.
98 **nine-men's-morris** A game for two, each player having nine pins or stones called 'men', and

formerly played out of doors in grooves cut in turf. Three concentric squares were cut, and the midpoints of each side were joined. The 'men' could be placed at corners or midpoints, and the aim was to remove the opponent's men by forming a line of three. The word 'morris' is a corruption of 'merels', from Old French, recorded still in R. Cotgrave's *A Dictionarie of the French and English Tongues* (1611); see *Shakespeare's England*, II, 466–7.
99 **quaint mazes** A number of turf mazes still survive (see Janet Bord, *Mazes and Labyrinths of the World*, 1976, pp. 46–58), and they were numerous in Shakespeare's time. The earliest maze was traditionally the labyrinth at Knossos, associated with Theseus's rescue of Ariadne from the Minotaur. Mazes had ritual or magical associations: the penetration to the centre of a maze and the exit from it may be related to rites of initiation, and has been interpreted as analogous to death and rebirth; but their origin and full significance remain mysterious. See also W. H. Matthews, *Mazes and Labyrinths*, 1922, reprinted 1970.
99 **wanton green** lush grass.

The human mortals want their winter cheer;
No night is now with hymn or carol blessed.
Therefore the moon, the governess of floods,
Pale in her anger, washes all the air,
That rheumatic diseases do abound;   105
And thorough this distemperature we see
The seasons alter; hoary-headed frosts
Fall in the fresh lap of the crimson rose,
And on old Hiems' thin and icy crown
An odorous chaplet of sweet summer buds   110
Is, as in mockery, set. The spring, the summer,
The childing autumn, angry winter change
Their wonted liveries, and the mazèd world
By their increase now knows not which is which.
And this same progeny of evils comes   115
From our debate, from our dissension.
We are their parents and original.
OBERON Do you amend it, then: it lies in you.
Why should Titania cross her Oberon?
I do but beg a little changeling boy   120
To be my henchman.
TITANIA   Set your heart at rest.
The fairy land buys not the child of me.

---

101 cheer] *Hanmer, conj. Theobald;* heere Qq, F   106 thorough] Q1, through Q2, F   107 hoary-headed] Q1 (hoary headed); hoared headed Q2, F   109 thin] *Halliwell, conj. Tyrwhitt;* chinne Qq, F   115–16] *So* F2; *divided at* evils, / Comes *in* Qq, F

101 want...cheer Hanmer's emendation of 'heare' (Qq, F) is generally accepted as strengthening a limp phrase, and linking with the next line; 'here' makes sense, and could be correct, but a 'c' might easily have dropped out through misreading. The line leads rather abruptly into a passage on the confusion of the seasons, and implies that people have to endure unseasonable winter weather in summer, but lack the cheer, the carols and festivity, that belong to Christmas.

103 Therefore Repeating the 'Therefore' of 88 above.

103 governess of floods By extension from the association of the moon with tides.

105 rheumatic Characterised by discharge of 'rheum', or watery matter, like the common cold. Accented on the first syllable.

106 distemperature disorder, both of the weather and of the body.

109 old Hiems Winter personified, as at *LLL* 5.2.891. The image of winter as an old man with 'snowie frozen crowne' comes, as Brooks notes, from Ovid's *Metamorphoses* II, 39 (Golding's translation).

109 thin Halliwell's emendation of 'chinne' (Qq, F) is generally accepted; in Secretary hand 'c' and 't' are easily confused, and the error is a common one. Various editors have tried ingeniously to defend 'chin', but it is difficult to see how frosts could 'fall' simultaneously on chin and crown.

112 childing fruitful. Knight compares *Sonnets* 97.6: 'teeming autumn, big with rich increase'.

112 change exchange.

113 wonted usual.

113 mazèd bewildered.

114 increase produce. (See 112 above and n.)

116 debate quarrel.

His mother was a votress of my order,
And in the spicèd Indian air by night
Full often hath she gossiped by my side,   125
And sat with me on Neptune's yellow sands
Marking th'embarkèd traders on the flood,
When we have laughed to see the sails conceive
And grow big-bellied with the wanton wind;
Which she, with pretty and with swimming gait   130
Following (her womb then rich with my young squire),
Would imitate, and sail upon the land
To fetch me trifles, and return again
As from a voyage, rich with merchandise.
But she, being mortal, of that boy did die,   135
And for her sake do I rear up her boy;
And for her sake I will not part with him.

OBERON How long within this wood intend you stay?

TITANIA Perchance till after Theseus' wedding day.
If you will patiently dance in our round,   140
And see our moonlight revels, go with us:
If not, shun me, and I will spare your haunts.

OBERON Give me that boy, and I will go with thee.

TITANIA Not for thy fairy kingdom! Fairies, away.
We shall chide downright if I longer stay.   145

                Exeunt [Titania and her train]

OBERON Well, go thy way. Thou shalt not from this grove
Till I torment thee for this injury.
My gentle Puck, come hither. Thou rememberest
Since once I sat upon a promontory,
And heard a mermaid on a dolphin's back   150
Uttering such dulcet and harmonious breath

---

136 do I] Qq; I do F   145 SD] *So Theobald; Exeunt.* Qq, F   150 mermaid] Qq, F (Mearemaide Q1; Meare-maide Q2, F)

123 **votress of my order** As if she had taken vows in a religious order.

127 **traders** trading ships. The sense is unambiguous, but is first recorded in *OED* in 1712.

130 **with swimming gait** with a smooth gliding motion.

131 **Following** Resembling.

140 **round** The fairies dance in a ring; compare 'orbs' and 'ringlets', 9 and 86 above.

142 **spare** avoid (*OED* sv v^1 7b, citing this passage).

145 **chide** quarrel.

149 **Since** When. A Shakespearean usage, as at *WT* 5.1.219–20: 'Remember since you ow'd no more to time / Than I do now.'

150 **mermaid...dolphin's back** An image perhaps suggested by the legend of Arion the bard who escaped from sailors intending to murder him by leaping into the sea, where he was carried to safety on the back of a dolphin (see *TN* 1.2.15).

That the rude sea grew civil at her song,
And certain stars shot madly from their spheres
To hear the sea-maid's music?

PUCK   I remember.

OBERON That very time I saw (but thou couldst not)   155
Flying between the cold moon and the earth
Cupid all armed: a certain aim he took
At a fair vestal thronèd by the west,
And loosed his loveshaft smartly from his bow
As it should pierce a hundred thousand hearts;   160
But I might see young Cupid's fiery shaft
Quenched in the chaste beams of the watery moon;
And the imperial votress passèd on
In maiden meditation, fancy-free.
Yet marked I where the bolt of Cupid fell: 165
It fell upon a little western flower,
Before, milk-white; now purple with love's wound:
And maidens call it 'love-in-idleness'.
Fetch me that flower, the herb I showed thee once;
The juice of it on sleeping eyelids laid   170
Will make or man or woman madly dote
Upon the next live creature that it sees.
Fetch me this herb, and be thou here again
Ere the leviathan can swim a league.

PUCK I'll put a girdle round about the earth   175
In forty minutes!   [*Exit*]

---

155 saw] Q1; say Q2, F   158 by the] F; by Qq   175–6 I'll...minutes!] *So Pope; as one line in* Qq, F
175 round about] Q1; about Q2, F   176 SD] F2; *not in* Qq, F

152 **rude** rough.
153 **spheres** orbits; but see also 7 above and n.
157 **certain** unerring.
158 **fair vestal...west** This image of the fair virgin (resembling the chaste priestesses in the Temple of Vesta at Rome) throned in the west has often been interpreted as a compliment to Queen Elizabeth; it seems probable that Shakespeare had the queen in mind, but it is not necessary to assume, as Brooks does (p. lv), that she was present at the play's first performance, and that this took place at a wedding (see p. 3 above). Oberon comes from India (line 69) or the east.
158 **by** in the region of.
163 **imperial votress** This majestic figure has given vows to Diana, not, like the mother of the Indian boy, to Titania's 'order' (123 above). This sequence relates to 1.1; there the prospect of

dedicating herself to 'Diana's altar' (1.1.89) was a wretched one for Hermia, who swore by Cupid and Venus (1.1.169, 171), and was full of sighs and tears, 'poor fancy's followers' (1.1.155).
165 **bolt** arrow (the original meaning of this word).
167 **purple** The colour of blood. See 1.2.75 and n.
168 **love-in-idleness** The pansy, also called 'heart's ease'. The image may have been suggested by the account in Golding's Ovid, IV, 152, of the death of Pyramus, whose blood stains a 'darke purple colour' the berries of the mulberry tree where he was to meet Thisbe.
174 **leviathan** Sea-monster identified as the whale in the Geneva and Bishops' Bibles, as at Job 41.1, Ps. 74.15, 124.26.

OBERON   Having once this juice
             I'll watch Titania when she is asleep,
             And drop the liquor of it in her eyes:
             The next thing then she, waking, looks upon –
             Be it on lion, bear, or wolf, or bull,   180
             On meddling monkey, or on busy ape –
             She shall pursue it with the soul of love.
             And ere I take this charm from off her sight
             (As I can take it with another herb)
             I'll make her render up her page to me.   185
             But who comes here? I am invisible,
             And I will overhear their conference.

                 Enter DEMETRIUS, HELENA *following him.*

DEMETRIUS I love thee not, therefore pursue me not.
             Where is Lysander, and fair Hermia?
             The one I'll slay, the other slayeth me.   190
             Thou told'st me they were stol'n unto this wood,
             And here am I, and wood within this wood
             Because I cannot meet my Hermia.
             Hence, get thee gone, and follow me no more.
HELENA   You draw me, you hard-hearted adamant!   195
             But yet you draw not iron, for my heart
             Is true as steel. Leave you your power to draw,
             And I shall have no power to follow you.
DEMETRIUS Do I entice you? Do I speak you fair?

177 when] Q1, F; whence Q2   179 then] Q1; when Q2, F; which *Rowe*   183 from off] Q1 (from of); off from Q2,
F   190 slay...slayeth] *Theobald, conj. Thirlby;* stay...stayeth Qq, F   191 unto] Qq; into F   192 wood...wood]
Q1 (wodde...wood), Q2, F

176–87 Oberon, left alone on stage, addresses the
audience directly. His 'train' has evidently left,
absorbed into Titania's 'train' at 145; see 59 SD and
n.
    180–1 These animals suggest a jungle or wild
place rather than the pastoral countryside of
93–100; see 218 and 228–9 below, and pp. 32–3
above.
    182 soul essence, i.e. total devotion.
    186 I am invisible This probably marks some
action. The Admiral's Men in 1598 bought 'a robe
for to go invisibell' (*Henslowe's Diary*, p. 325), and
Oberon may have drawn such a 'robe' about
himself here (so Brooks). Compare the stage
directions for Prospero and Ariel to enter 'invisible'
at *Temp.*, 3.3.17 and 1.2.374.

    190 slay...slayeth 'stay...stayeth' (Qq, F)
make no sense; 't' and 'l' were readily confused in
Secretary hand, and this is a common form of
printing-error.
    192 and wood and frantic.
    195 adamant (1) loadstone or magnet, (2) the
embodiment of hardness (the diamond). Both
senses were current in the sixteenth century.
    196–7 draw not iron...steel Sliding from the
image of iron drawn by a magnet, to the notion of
her heart being soft, not iron-hard (see Tilley 196),
and so to the proverbial 'true as steel' (Tilley s840).
As Wells notes, the conceit is strained, and a
comically extravagant effect may be intended.
    197 Leave you Give up (= modern 'leave off').

Or rather do I not in plainest truth   200
Tell you I do not, nor I cannot love you?
HELENA And even for that do I love you the more.
I am your spaniel; and, Demetrius,
The more you beat me I will fawn on you.
Use me but as your spaniel: spurn me, strike me,   205
Neglect me, lose me; only give me leave,
Unworthy as I am, to follow you.
What worser place can I beg in your love
(And yet a place of high respect with me)
Than to be usèd as you use your dog?   210
DEMETRIUS Tempt not too much the hatred of my spirit;
For I am sick when I do look on thee.
HELENA And I am sick when I look not on you.
DEMETRIUS You do impeach your modesty too much,
To leave the city and commit yourself   215
Into the hands of one that loves you not;
To trust the opportunity of night,
And the ill counsel of a desert place,
With the rich worth of your virginity.
HELENA Your virtue is my privilege: for that   220
It is not night when I do see your face,
Therefore I think I am not in the night;
Nor doth this wood lack worlds of company,
For you, in my respect, are all the world.
Then how can it be said I am alone   225
When all the world is here to look on me?
DEMETRIUS I'll run from thee and hide me in the brakes,
And leave thee to the mercy of wild beasts.
HELENA The wildest hath not such a heart as you.
Run when you will: the story shall be changed;   230

---

201 not, nor] F; not, not Qq   202 you] Q1; thee Q2, F   210 use] Qq; doe F   220 privilege: for that] Qq, F;
privilege for that. *Var. 1778 (conj. Tyrwhitt)*

203–4 Proverbial (Tilley s705), and compare
TGV 4.2.14–15.
214 **impeach** call in question. The first example
recorded in *OED*.
218 **desert place** Reinforcing the images of
wildness at 180–1 above and 228–9 below; the wood
is at once a desert and a pastoral place.
220 **privilege** i.e. guarantee of immunity.
220–4 **for that...world** Because ('for that') his
face makes light the darkness, and he provides for

her a 'world' of society, she feels she is not at risk.
Helena at once rebuts Demetrius's arguments and
praises him.
224 **respect** esteem.
227 **brakes** thickets.
228–9 See 180–1, also 218 above, and nn.
230–1 **story...chase** The well-known story of
Daphne or Peneis, a shy nymph who, fleeing to
escape the embraces of Apollo, was changed into a
laurel; it is told in Ovid's *Metamorphoses* I, 581–700.

Apollo flies, and Daphne holds the chase,
The dove pursues the griffin, the mild hind
Makes speed to catch the tiger – bootless speed,
When cowardice pursues, and valour flies!
DEMETRIUS I will not stay thy questions. Let me go;   235
Or if thou follow me, do not believe
But I shall do thee mischief in the wood.
HELENA Ay, in the temple, in the town, the field,
You do me mischief. Fie, Demetrius,
Your wrongs do set a scandal on my sex!   240
We cannot fight for love, as men may do;
We should be wooed, and were not made to woo.

                                                      [*Exit Demetrius*]

I'll follow thee, and make a heaven of hell,
To die upon the hand I love so well.   *Exit*
OBERON Fare thee well, nymph. Ere he do leave this grove   245
Thou shalt fly him, and he shall seek thy love.

                              Enter Puck.

Hast thou the flower there? Welcome, wanderer.
PUCK Ay, there it is.
OBERON   I pray thee give it me.
I know a bank where the wild thyme blows,
Where oxlips and the nodding violet grows,   250
Quite overcanopied with luscious woodbine,
With sweet musk-roses, and with eglantine:

---

238 the field] Q1; and field Q2, F   242 SD] *Capell (Demetrius breaks from her, and Exit); not in* Qq, F   243 I'll]
Qq (Ile); I F   244 SD] Q2, F; *not in* Q1; *Exeunt* / *Rowe*   246 SD] Qq, F, *after* 247

232 **griffin** A fabulous beast possessing the head
and wings of an eagle, with the body of a lion;
sometimes also identified with a vulture.
232 **hind** doe, especially of the red deer.
233 **bootless** useless.
235 **stay** stay for, endure.
240 **Your wrongs...sex** The wrongs you do me
are grossly discreditable to my sex. Helena's
complaint is that she is forced to act in a way that
damages her reputation.
241 With the exception of 247–8 the rest of the
scene is in couplets, marking the intervention of
Oberon.
243 **make...hell** Echoing 1.1.207, where
Hermia complains that Demetrius has turned 'a
heaven unto a hell'.
244 **upon** by means of.
245 **nymph** Properly, semi-divine beings

imagined as beautiful maidens inhabiting woods.
The use of the term here, as at 4.1.124, playfully
absorbs the lovers into a quasi-mythological world.
249–52 These lines return us from the image of
a 'desert place' (218), or dangerous wood full of wild
animals (180–1), to a bower suggestive of Warwickshire rather than Athens. This variety of imagined
locations within a single setting is important in the
play; see pp. 32–3 above.
250 **oxlips** Flowering herbs, natural hybrids
between the cowslip (see 10 above) and the primrose
(1.1.215).
251 **woodbine** Convolvulus, or possibly honeysuckle, but see 4.1.39 and n.
252 **musk-roses** Wild rambling roses, bearing
fragrant white flowers.
252 **eglantine** Sweet-briar, a species of rose with
scented leaves and pink flowers.

There sleeps Titania sometime of the night,
Lulled in these flowers with dances and delight;
And there the snake throws her enamelled skin,   255
Weed wide enough to wrap a fairy in;
And with the juice of this I'll streak her eyes,
And make her full of hateful fantasies.
Take thou some of it, and seek through this grove:
A sweet Athenian lady is in love   260
With a disdainful youth; anoint his eyes,
But do it when the next thing he espies
May be the lady. Thou shalt know the man
By the Athenian garments he hath on.
Effect it with some care, that he may prove   265
More fond on her than she upon her love.
And look thou meet me ere the first cock crow.
PUCK Fear not, my lord; your servant shall do so.

Exeunt

2.[2] *Enter* TITANIA, *Queen of Fairies, with her train.*

TITANIA Come, now a roundel and a fairy song,
Then for the third part of a minute, hence –
Some to kill cankers in the musk-rose buds,
Some war with reremice for their leathern wings
To make my small elves coats, and some keep back   5
The clamorous owl that nightly hoots and wonders
At our quaint spirits. Sing me now asleep;
Then to your offices, and let me rest.
Fairies sing.

268 SD] Qq; *Exit* F   Act 2, Scene 2   2.2] *Capell; not in* Qq, F   0 SD *Enter* TITANIA] Q1; *Enter Queene* Q2, F

253 sometime of at some time or other during.
255 throws casts off.
256 Weed Garment. The only modern use is in the phrase 'widow's weeds'.
266 fond on infatuated with.

Act 2, Scene 2
2.2 This scene follows directly on 2.1, transporting us to the bower Oberon has just described.
0 SD *train* See 2.1.59 above and n. Two fairies have speaking-parts, and one of these could be the Fairy who spoke with Puck at the opening of 2.1; there is also a chorus of fairies, and three or four

others would be enough to make up the 'train' of five or six at most; four of these could then appear as the named fairies at 3.1.136.
1 roundel dance in a ring. See 2.1.140 and n.
2 third part of a minute Implying rapid movements by the fairies.
3 cankers canker-worms (= caterpillars).
4 reremice bats. The etymology of 'rere' is uncertain, but bats have traditionally been thought of as winged mice; compare the term 'flittermouse'.
5 elves See 2.1.17 and n.
7 quaint dainty.

[FIRST FAIRY] You spotted snakes with double tongue,
             Thorny hedgehogs, be not seen.   10
             Newts and blindworms, do no wrong,
             Come not near our Fairy Queen.
[CHORUS]   Philomel with melody
             Sing in our sweet lullaby,
           Lulla, lulla, lullaby; lulla, lulla, lullaby.   15
             Never harm
             Nor spell nor charm
             Come our lovely lady nigh.
             So good night, with lullaby.
FIRST FAIRY   Weaving spiders, come not here;   20
             Hence, you longlegged spinners, hence!
             Beetles black approach not near;
             Worm nor snail, do no offence.
[CHORUS]   Philomel with melody
             Sing in our sweet lullaby,   25
           Lulla, lulla, lullaby; lulla, lulla, lullaby.
             Never harm
             Nor spell nor charm
             Come our lovely lady nigh.
             So good night, with lullaby.   30
                  Titania sleeps.

---

9 SH FIRST FAIRY] *Capell; not in* Qq, F   13 SH CHORUS] *Capell; not in* Qq, F   14 our] Qq; your F   20 SH FIRST FAIRY] Qq (*1. Fai*); 2. *Fairy* F   24 SH CHORUS] *Capell; not in* Qq, F   24 melody] *Capell;* melody, &c Qq, F   30 SD] F (*She sleapes / after 32*); *not in* Qq

9–32 In Qq these lines are indented, with speech headings only for '1. *Fai.*' at 20 and '2. *Fai.*' at 31, but the '&c.' in 24 indicates repetition of a chorus, and the arrangement of the lines now generally accepted was first made by Capell, with 31–2 treated as dialogue rather than as part of the song. This couplet belongs metrically with the song, and perhaps should also be sung; the SD *Titania sleeps* first appeared in F, after line 32, and is not in Qq.

9 double forked.

11 Newts and blindworms Harmless creatures formerly believed to be venomous; both supply ingredients to the witches' cauldron in *Mac* 4.1.

13 Philomel The nightingale, so called after the legend of Philomela, transformed into the bird after being raped by Tereus; the story is among those told by Ovid, *Metamorphoses* VI, 542–853.

20 spiders Like newts and blindworms, thought to be poisonous, though there are no venomous

spiders in England (all the creatures mentioned in this song are common there; see 2.1.249–52 and n.).

23 offence harm.

30 SD *Titania sleeps* During the song Titania perhaps drew a curtain to display her bower, and then lay in it; she awakes at 3.1.107, and, it would seem, remains on stage asleep through the intervening action. There is no need for her to be visible to the audience all this time; as Wells notes, Oberon, going off at 40, could conveniently draw a curtain around the space where she lies, and Titania could open it when she wakes; this may well be how it was originally staged, but Qq and F give no indication, and it is equally possible that she remained in full view of the audience, but unnoticed by the lovers or the mechanicals, especially if there was no break between Acts 2 and 3 (see 3.1.0 SD n.). This indeed would fit in with the play's concern with illusion and theatricality. Titania's bower,

SECOND FAIRY
> Hence, away! Now all is well;
> One aloof stand sentinel!

[Exeunt Fairies]

Enter OBERON; [*he squeezes the juice on Titania's eyes*].

OBERON   What thou seest when thou dost wake,
               Do it for thy true love take;
               Love and languish for his sake.   35
               Be it ounce or cat or bear,
               Pard, or boar with bristled hair
               In thy eye that shall appear
               When thou wak'st, it is thy dear.
               Wake when some vile thing is near!   [*Exit*]   40

Enter LYSANDER *and* HERMIA.

LYSANDER Fair love, you faint with wandering in the wood,
               And, to speak truth, I have forgot our way.
               We'll rest us, Hermia, if you think it good,
               And tarry for the comfort of the day.
HERMIA   Be it so, Lysander; find you out a bed,   45
               For I upon this bank will rest my head.
LYSANDER One turf shall serve as pillow for us both;
               One heart, one bed, two bosoms, and one troth.
HERMIA   Nay, good Lysander, for my sake, my dear,
               Lie further off yet; do not lie so near.   50
LYSANDER O take the sense, sweet, of my innocence!
               Love takes the meaning in love's conference;
               I mean that my heart unto yours is knit,

---

31 SH SECOND FAIRY] Qq; 1. *Fairy* F   32 SD.1 *Exeunt Fairies*] Rowe; *not in* Qq, F   32 SD.2 *he…eyes*] *After Capell*; *not in* Qq, F   40 SD.1 *Exit*] Rowe; *not in* Qq, F   41 wood] Q1; woods Q2, F   42 truth] Qq, F (troth)   45 Be it] Q2, F; Bet it Q1   49 good] Q2, F; god Q1   53 is] Q2, F; it Q1

canopied with flowers, may have been suggested by hangings, and the 'bank' (2.1.249) by a property such as was listed for the Admiral's Men in 1598 as 'ij mose [i.e. moss] banckes' (*Henslowe's Diary*, p. 320).

32 aloof…sentinel No more is heard of this sentinel, and it is not clear where he was posted; if within the bower ('aloof' = at a distance), he could quietly disappear after Oberon drew the curtain, but if 'aloof' meant 'outside' or 'above', then Oberon would need to avoid being seen by him. Wells notes

that 'In stage practice, the sentinel is sometimes kidnapped by Oberon's attendants.'

36 ounce lynx.

37 Pard Leopard. The wood changes again to a desert full of 'wild beasts' (2.1.228).

48 troth truth. This variant form, once common, survives in the phrase 'to plight one's troth'.

52 Love…conference i.e. in the conversation ('conference') of lovers, the meaning is interpreted generously, and with the sympathy of love.

So that but one heart we can make of it:
Two bosoms interchainèd with an oath,   55
So then two bosoms and a single troth.
Then by your side no bed-room me deny,
For lying so, Hermia, I do not lie.
HERMIA Lysander riddles very prettily.
Now much beshrew my manners and my pride   60
If Hermia meant to say Lysander lied.
But, gentle friend, for love and courtesy
Lie further off, in human modesty;
Such separation as may well be said
Becomes a virtuous bachelor and a maid,   65
So far be distant, and good night, sweet friend;
Thy love ne'er alter till thy sweet life end!
LYSANDER Amen, amen, to that fair prayer say I,
And then end life when I end loyalty!
Here is my bed; sleep give thee all his rest.   70
HERMIA With half that wish the wisher's eyes be pressed.
They sleep.

Enter PUCK.

PUCK   Through the forest have I gone,
                But Athenian found I none
                On whose eyes I might approve
                This flower's force in stirring love.   75
                Night and silence – Who is here?
                Weeds of Athens he doth wear:
                This is he my master said
                Despisèd the Athenian maid;
                And here the maiden, sleeping sound   80
                On the dank and dirty ground.

---

54 we can] Qq; can you F   55 interchainèd] Qq; interchanged F   63 off,...modesty;] Q1 (off,...modesty:); off,
...modesty, Q2, F; off;...modesty, *Theobald*   63 human] Qq, F (humane)   71 SD.1 *They sleep*] F (*Enter Pucke. They
sleepe.*); *not in* Qq   73 found] Q1; *find* Q2, F   74 On] Qq; One F

55 **interchainèd** Perhaps Shakespeare's coinage;
the first example cited in *OED*.

58 **lie** The quibble gains some force in relation
to the 'truth' or 'troth' Lysander refers to at 42,
48 and 56.

60 **much beshrew** may evil befall, a real curse
upon.

67–9 Ironically anticipating Lysander's conver-
sion to Helena, 117 ff.

74 **approve** put to the proof.

77–9 Puck mistakes Lysander for Demetrius, as
is understandable since Puck was not present when
Oberon saw Helena being scorned by Demetrius
(2.1.188–237). The reference to 'Weeds of Athens'
suggests that the two lovers were similarly
costumed, and the confusions would be funnier if
they looked more or less alike.

Pretty soul, she durst not lie
Near this lack-love, this kill-courtesy.
Churl, upon thy eyes I throw
All the power this charm doth owe.   85
[*He squeezes the juice on Lysander's eyes.*]
When thou wak'st let love forbid
Sleep his seat on thy eyelid.
So, awake when I am gone;
For I must now to Oberon.   *Exit*

Enter DEMETRIUS *and* HELENA, *running.*

HELENA Stay, though thou kill me, sweet Demetrius!   90
DEMETRIUS I charge thee, hence, and do not haunt me thus.
HELENA O wilt thou darkling leave me? Do not so!
DEMETRIUS Stay, on thy peril; I alone will go.   *Exit*
HELENA O, I am out of breath in this fond chase!
The more my prayer, the lesser is my grace.   95
Happy is Hermia, wheresoe'er she lies,
For she hath blessèd and attractive eyes.
How came her eyes so bright? Not with salt tears –
If so, my eyes are oftener washed than hers.
No, no, I am as ugly as a bear,   100
For beasts that meet me run away for fear.
Therefore no marvel though Demetrius
Do as a monster fly my presence thus.
What wicked and dissembling glass of mine
Made me compare with Hermia's sphery eyne?   105
But who is here? – Lysander, on the ground?
Dead, or asleep? I see no blood, no wound.
Lysander, if you live, good sir, awake!

---

85 SD] *After Dyce; not in* Qq, F   93 SD] F (*Exit Demetrius*); *not in* Qq

83 This line has an extra foot. Brooks notes that it marks the climax of Puck's indignation, and breaks the flow of four-beat lines at the point where he begins his spell.

85 owe possess.

86–7 let...eyelid i.e. let love so obsess him as to banish sleep from his eyes (so Brooks).

92 darkling in the dark. This night scene (see 76 above) was played in daylight in the open-air Elizabethan theatre; the lovers see each other plainly enough in real daylight and imaginary darkness or moonlight.

94 fond foolish, or foolishly doting in love.

95 the lesser...grace i.e. the less she favours me.

101 beasts See 37 above and n.

103 as as if I were.

105 compare 'vie' or 'compare my own eyes'.

105 sphery eyne star-like eyes. On 'spheres' see 2.1.7 and 153 and nn., and on 'eyne', 1.1.242 and n.

LYSANDER [*Waking.*]
    And run through fire I will for thy sweet sake!
    Transparent Helena, nature shows art   110
    That through thy bosom makes me see thy heart.
    Where is Demetrius? O, how fit a word
    Is that vile name to perish on my sword!
HELENA Do not say so, Lysander, say not so.
    What though he love your Hermia? Lord, what though?   115
    Yet Hermia still loves you; then be content.
LYSANDER Content with Hermia? No; I do repent
    The tedious minutes I with her have spent.
    Not Hermia, but Helena I love.
    Who will not change a raven for a dove?   120
    The will of man is by his reason swayed,
    And reason says you are the worthier maid.
    Things growing are not ripe until their season;
    So I, being young, till now ripe not to reason.
    And touching now the point of human skill,   125
    Reason becomes the marshal to my will.
    And leads me to your eyes, where I o'erlook
    Love's stories written in love's richest book.
HELENA Wherefore was I to this keen mockery born?
    When at your hands did I deserve this scorn?   130
    Is't not enough, is't not enough, young man,
    That I did never, no, nor never can
    Deserve a sweet look from Demetrius' eye

---

109 SD] *Rowe; not in* Qq, F   110 shows] Qq; here shows F (her shewes), F2   119 I] Q1; now I Q2, F   125 human]
Qq, F (humane)

110 **Transparent** (1) able to be seen through, (2)
open, candid.
110 **nature shows art** A conceit based on the
traditional opposition of art – the product of human
skill – to nature; the natural body is, of course,
opaque. The line is a syllable short, and F's
correction may be authoritative.
120 **raven** Harsh, ominous and black (alluding
to Hermia's dark hair and skin; see 3.2.257, where
she is called an 'Ethiop'), in contrast to the mild
nature and whiteness of the dove; compare *Rom.*
1.5.48.
121–4 The play on 'reason' is ironic; even
Bottom knows that 'reason and love keep little
company together nowadays' (3.1.120–1), and
Egeus's 'will' (inclination or, in a stronger sense,

intent) in insisting that Hermia marry Demetrius
(1.1.87, 118) had nothing to do with reason. See
pp. 37–8 above for further comment. Tilley L517
lists 'Love is without reason' as a common proverb.
124 **ripe** ripen, mature. (The normal form of the
verb until the late sixteenth century.)
125 **point** i.e. the highest point (*OED* sv *sb*[1] A 25).
125 **skill** discrimination. (The original sense of
the word.)
127–8 **eyes...book** Love is 'first learned in a
lady's eyes', and so women's eyes become the books
in which love's 'doctrine' may be found; see *LLL*
4.3.324–50. Shakespeare frequently associates love
with books; see E. A. Armstrong, *Shakespeare's
Imagination*, rev. edn, 1963, pp. 171–3.
127 **o'erlook** read through.

But you must flout my insufficiency?
Good troth, you do me wrong, good sooth, you do,   135
In such disdainful manner me to woo!
But fare you well: perforce I must confess
I thought you lord of more true gentleness.
O, that a lady of one man refused
Should of another therefore be abused!   *Exit* 140
LYSANDER She sees not Hermia. Hermia, sleep thou there,
And never mayst thou come Lysander near.
For, as a surfeit of the sweetest things
The deepest loathing to the stomach brings,
Or as the heresies that men do leave   145
Are hated most of those they did deceive,
So thou, my surfeit and my heresy,
Of all be hated, but the most of me!
And, all my powers, address your love and might
To honour Helen, and to be her knight.   *Exit* 150
HERMIA [*Waking.*]
Help me, Lysander, help me! Do thy best
To pluck this crawling serpent from my breast!
Ay me, for pity! What a dream was here!
Lysander, look how I do quake with fear –
Methought a serpent ate my heart away,   155
And you sat smiling at his cruel prey.
Lysander! What, removed? Lysander, lord!
What, out of hearing? Gone? No sound, no word?
Alack, where are you? Speak and if you hear.
Speak, of all loves! I swoon almost with fear. 160
No? Then I well perceive you are not nigh.
Either death or you I'll find immediately.   *Exit*

146 they] Qq; that F   147 surfeit] Q2, F; surfer Q1   151 SD] *After Capell; not in* Qq, F   156 you] Qq; yet F
158 hearing? Gone?] *Capell;* hearing, gon? Qq, F

135 **good sooth** indeed, truly. ('Sooth' literally
means 'truth'.)
138 **gentleness** good breeding, courtesy.
143–4 Varying Prov. 25.27: 'It is not good to eat
too much honey' (Tilley H560); compare *Rom.*
2.6.11–12: 'The sweetest honey / Is loathsome in
his own deliciousness.'
145–6 **as...deceive** i.e. as heresies renounced
are hated most by the men once deceived by them.

148 **Of...of** By...by.
149 **address** apply.
156 **prey** 'preying' (on me), or 'act of violence'.
159 **and if** if.
160 **of all loves!** for love's sake! Formerly a
common phrase of entreaty (*OED* Love *sb* 7b.), as
at *Wiv.* 2.2.114.

3.[1] *Enter the Clowns* [, BOTTOM, QUINCE, SNOUT, STARVELING, SNUG *and* FLUTE. TITANIA *remains on stage, asleep*].

BOTTOM Are we all met?

QUINCE Pat, pat; and here's a marvellous convenient place for our rehearsal. This green plot shall be our stage, this hawthorn brake our tiring-house, and we will do it in action as we will do it before the Duke.   5

BOTTOM Peter Quince!

QUINCE What sayest thou, bully Bottom?

BOTTOM There are things in this comedy of Pyramus and Thisbe that will never please. First, Pyramus must draw a sword to kill himself, which the ladies cannot abide. How answer you that?   10

SNOUT By'r lakin, a parlous fear!

STARVELING I believe we must leave the killing out, when all is done.

BOTTOM Not a whit; I have a device to make all well. Write me a prologue, and let the prologue seem to say we will do no harm with our swords, and that Pyramus is not killed indeed; and for the more   15
better assurance, tell them that I, Pyramus, am not Pyramus, but Bottom the weaver: this will put them out of fear.

QUINCE Well, we will have such a prologue; and it shall be written in eight and six.

BOTTOM No, make it two more: let it be written in eight and eight.   20

SNOUT Will not the ladies be afeard of the lion?

STARVELING I fear it, I promise you.

BOTTOM Masters, you ought to consider with yourself, to bring in (God

---

Act 3, Scene 1   3] F (*Actus Tertius*); *not in* Qq   3.1] *Scene 1 / Rowe; not in* Qq, F   0 SD BOTTOM...*asleep*] *After Rowe; not in* Qq, F   2 marvellous] Qq, F (marvailes Q1)   11 By'r lakin] Qq, F (Berlakin)   23 yourself] Qq (your selfe); your selves F

Act 3, Scene 1

0 SD There is no break in the action; see p. 141 below on the division of the play into acts. The presence of Titania was probably suggested by curtains drawn around her bower, and there was no need for her to be visible on stage; see 2.2.30 and n.

2 Pat, pat On the dot, punctually.

3–4 green plot... tiring-house Perhaps Quince pointed to an area on the main stage and then to a stage-door leading to the dressing-rooms or tiring-house, which was behind the stage in the public theatres. A green cloth may have been used to suggest grass, and a hanging or property to suggest the 'brake' or thicket.

7 bully Implying friendly admiration, as in

Pistol's commendation of the King, 'I love the lovely bully' (*H5* 4.1.48).

11 By'r lakin By our lady (a contraction of 'ladykin'; compare 'mannekin'), a trivial oath.

11 parlous perilous.

19 eight and six Alternating lines of eight and six syllables, the usual ballad metre. Quince's prologue (5.1.126 ff.) is in fact in lines of ten syllables; the performance differs from the rehearsal, and does not include the dialogue tried out at 65 ff. This was probably calculated on Shakespeare's part; the play in Act 5 is funnier and more engaging because we have seen none of it before. But see also 1.2.49–52 and n.

23 yourself So Qq; F corrects what was probably intended as one of Bottom's solecisms.

shield us!) a lion among ladies is a most dreadful thing; for there
is not a more fearful wildfowl than your lion living; and we ought   25
to look to't.

SNOUT Therefore another prologue must tell he is not a lion.

BOTTOM Nay, you must name his name, and half his face must be seen
through the lion's neck, and he himself must speak through, saying
thus, or to the same defect: 'Ladies', or 'Fair ladies, I would wish   30
you', or 'I would request you', or 'I would entreat you, not to fear,
not to tremble: my life for yours. If you think I come hither as
a lion, it were pity of my life. No, I am no such thing; I am a man,
as other men are' – and there indeed let him name his name, and
tell them plainly he is Snug the joiner.   35

QUINCE Well, it shall be so. But there is two hard things: that is, to
bring the moonlight into a chamber; for, you know, Pyramus and
Thisbe meet by moonlight.

SNUG Doth the moon shine that night we play our play?

BOTTOM A calendar, a calendar! Look in the almanac – find out   40
moonshine, find out moonshine!

QUINCE Yes, it doth shine that night.

BOTTOM Why, then may you leave a casement of the great chamber
window, where we play, open, and the moon may shine in at the
casement.   45

QUINCE Ay; or else one must come in with a bush of thorns and a
lantern, and say he comes to disfigure, or to present the person of

---

35 them] Qq; him F   39 SH SNUG] F2; *Sn* Qq, F; *Snout* / *Cam.*   41 moonshine!] Qq (Moone-shine.); Moone-
shine. *Enter Pucke.* F   43 SH BOTTOM] Q2, F (*Bot.*); *Cet.* Q1

---

33 it were...life i.e. 'I should be sorry, by
my life', or 'my life would be to be pitied'; 'of my
life' may relate to 'pity', but it was used commonly
as a mild oath. See 5.1.218.

39 SH SNUG Qq and F have *Sn.*, expanded to
Snout in F2. This speech heading was abbreviated by
the compositor to squeeze a full measure into the
bottom line of D1ᵛ, and could refer to Snout or to
Snug, who is otherwise silent in the scene. At 96,
immediately following the entry of Snout, the
speech heading for him is abbreviated to *Sn.* in Qq,
and Brooks takes this as evidence that *Sn.* always
means Snout, assuming, what is by no means clear,
that the compositor would be consistent. See also
51 and n.

41 moonshine! F has two entries for Puck, one,
'*Enter Pucke.*' here, and another, following Qq,
'*Enter Robin.*' at 59. If that in Qq represents what
was in Shakespeare's MS., the entry here may, as

Wells suggests, reflect stage practice in bringing on
Puck to 'watch the mechanicals before he speaks'.

46 bush of thorns No one knows the origin of
the ancient and widespread legend that the moon
is inhabited by a man with a bundle of sticks on his
back. The association of the man in the moon with
thorns seems to have two sources, one the
identification of the man in the moon with Cain, the
other a legend of a man who stole a bundle of thorns
and was banished to the moon; both are found in
medieval literature, the latter, for instance, in
Robert Henryson's *Testament of Creseid*, 260–4. See
Oliver F. Emerson, 'Legends of Cain, especially in
Old and Middle English', *PMLA* 21 (1906), 840–5.
The man in the moon was also often said to have
a dog, as at 5.1.134 below.

47 disfigure Intending to say 'figure' = represent.

Moonshine. Then there is another thing: we must have a wall in
the great chamber; for Pyramus and Thisbe, says the story, did talk
through the chink of a wall.   50
SNOUT You can never bring in a wall. What say you, Bottom?
BOTTOM Some man or other must present Wall; and let him have some
plaster, or some loam, or some rough-cast about him to signify Wall;
or let him hold his fingers thus, and through that cranny shall
Pyramus and Thisbe whisper.   55
QUINCE If that may be, then all is well. Come, sit down every mother's
son, and rehearse your parts. Pyramus, you begin. When you have
spoken your speech, enter into that brake, and so everyone
according to his cue.

Enter PUCK.

PUCK What hempen homespuns have we swaggering here   60
      So near the cradle of the Fairy Queen?
      What, a play toward? I'll be an auditor,
      An actor too perhaps, if I see cause.
QUINCE Speak, Pyramus! Thisbe, stand forth!
BOTTOM (*as Pyramus*)
      Thisbe, the flowers of odious savours sweet –   65
QUINCE Odours – 'odorous'!
BOTTOM (*as Pyramus*)   ...odours savours sweet.
      So hath thy breath, my dearest Thisbe dear.
      But hark, a voice! Stay thou but here awhile,

65 SH BOTTOM (*as Pyramus*)] *Wells; Pyra.* Q1; *Pir.* Q2, F   66 Odours – 'odorous'!] Qq (*Odours, odorous*); *Odours,*
odours F; *'Odorous'! 'odorous'! Brooks, after Cuningham;* 'Odious' – odorous, *Alexander NS*   67 SH BOTTOM
(*as Pyramus*)] *Wells; Py* Q1; *Pir* Q2, F   67 odours savours] Qq, F; *Odorous savours Brooks, conj. Jenkins*

51 SH SNOUT Q2 and F have *Sn.*, and
T. W. Craik, *The Tudor Interlude*, 1958, p. 18,
points out that interludes commonly made use of
structures such as a wall, and the comedy here
would be more pointed if it is Snug, the joiner, 'the
very man who should have built the stage wall, who
sees the difficulty as insurmountable'. See also 39
above and n.
53 rough-cast A mixture of lime and gravel used
to make rough coating for walls.
60 hempen homespuns Hemp was the basis of
coarse fabrics much used for the clothing of poor
people, rustics and servants; a pointer for the
costuming of Bottom and his crew.
61 near...Queen Titania's bower, where she is
presumed to be still on stage, sleeping; 'cradle'
suggests the diminutive scale of fairies.

62 toward in preparation.
65–8 Bottom's erratic grammar and sense, and
the alteration in F of 'Odours, odorous' (Qq, line 66)
to 'Odours, odours', have combined to establish a
sense of a textual crux here, and many editors adopt
the reading of F (like Wells), or emend to
'"Odorous"! "odorous"!' (like Brooks). No
emendation turns the passage into sense, and I keep
the reading of Qq. Bottom misreads his first line, in
which 'savours' I take to be a noun (= perfumes);
Quince picks him up, demonstrating how the
correct adjective is formed, 'Odours, odorous', and
Bottom's response is to get it wrong again, in a
different way by saying 'odours', and not 'odorous'
as Quince wanted, and as Titania used it at 2.1.110
to mean 'scented'.

And by and by I will to thee appear.   *Exit*   70
PUCK A stranger Pyramus than e'er played here.   [*Exit*]
FLUTE Must I speak now?
QUINCE Ay, marry must you; for you must understand he goes but to
see a noise that he heard, and is to come again.
FLUTE (*as Thisbe*)
    Most radiant Pyramus, most lilywhite of hue,   75
        Of colour like the red rose on triumphant briar,
    Most brisky juvenal, and eke most lovely Jew,
        As true as truest horse that yet would never tire,
    I'll meet thee, Pyramus, at Ninny's tomb –
QUINCE 'Ninus' tomb', man! – Why, you must not speak that yet; that   80
you answer to Pyramus. You speak all your part at once, cues and
all. Pyramus, enter – your cue is past. It is 'never tire'.
FLUTE O –
    (*as Thisbe*)
    As true as truest horse, that yet would never tire.

Enter [Puck, and] Bottom with the ass head [on].

BOTTOM (*as Pyramus*)
    If I were fair, fair Thisbe, I were only thine.   85
QUINCE O monstrous! O strange! We are haunted! Pray, masters, fly,
masters! Help!

Exeunt Quince, Snug, Flute, Snout and Starveling

---

71 SH PUCK] F; *Quin* Qq   71 SD *Exit*] Capell; *not in* Qq, F   72 SH FLUTE] *Cam.; Thys* Qq, F   75 SH FLUTE
(*as Thisbe*)] Wells; *Thys.* Qq, F   83 SH FLUTE O – / (*as Thisbe*) *As...*] *After* Wells; *Thys.* O, *as... * Qq, F   84 SD] *After*
Capell; *not in* Qq; *Enter Piramus with the Asse head* F   85 SH BOTTOM (*as Pyramus*)] Wells; *Py* Q1; *Pir* Q2, F
87 SD] *After* F (*The Clownes all Exit*); *not in* Qq

71 The line shows that it is at this point that Puck
conceives the plan to transform Bottom. It marks
his exit.
76 **triumphant** noble, magnificent. Compare
Ant. 2.2.184–5: 'She's a most triumphant lady, if
report be square to her.' The word is, of course,
absurd in relation to the wild rose.
77 **brisky juvenal** lively youth (juvenile). This
is the only instance of 'brisky' recorded in *OED*,
suggesting how affected and 'poetical' the line is.
77 **eke** also. A conscious archaism.
77 **Jew** Sometimes explained as an abbreviation
of 'juvenal', or a 'deliberately inconsequential piece
of padding' (Wells); given the context, it could just
as well be Flute's misreading of 'jewel'.
79 **Ninny's tomb** Corrupting 'Ninus' (see
5.1.197 and n.) into 'ninny', or fool.
81–2 **You speak...all** The 'part' written out for

an actor consisted of his speeches with cues from the
lines preceding them. One such part survives, that
of Orlando in Robert Greene's *Orlando Furioso*, as
written out for Edward Alleyn to play; see
W. W. Greg, *Dramatic Documents from the Elizabethan Playhouses*, 2 vols., 1931, I, 176–87.
84 SD.2 See pp. 9–10 above for comment on this
and other examples of the transformation of human
beings into asses.
85 **fair, fair** Qq and F omit the second 'fair',
which is necessary for the metre, and could have
been omitted by a compositor taking it as repetition.
Malone thought the line as it stands in Q is misread
by Bottom, who was supposed to say, not 'If I were
fair, Thisbe', but 'If I were [i.e. true], fair Thisbe,
I were only thine', but this ingenious interpretation
can hardly be guessed from hearing the line spoken
as Q punctuates it.

PUCK   I'll follow you: I'll lead you about a round,
        Through bog, through bush, through brake, through briar;
        Sometime a horse I'll be, sometime a hound,   90
        A hog, a headless bear, sometime a fire,
        And neigh, and bark, and grunt, and roar, and burn,
        Like horse, hound, hog, bear, fire at every turn.   *Exit*
BOTTOM Why do they run away? This is a knavery of them to make
me afeard.   95

Enter Snout.

SNOUT O Bottom, thou art changed. What do I see on thee?
BOTTOM What do you see? You see an ass head of your own, do you?
                                   [Exit Snout]

Enter Quince.

QUINCE Bless thee, Bottom, bless thee! Thou art translated!   *Exit*
BOTTOM I see their knavery. This is to make an ass of me, to fright
me, if they could; but I will not stir from this place, do what they   100
can. I will walk up and down here, and will sing, that they shall
hear I am not afraid.
    [Sings.] The ousel cock so black of hue,
        With orange-tawny bill,
        The throstle with his note so true,   105
        The wren with little quill –
TITANIA *[Waking.]* What angel wakes me from my flowery bed?

97 SD.1 *Exit Snout*] *Capell; not in* Qq, F   101 and] Q1 ; and I Q2, F   103 SD *Sings*] *Pope; not in* Qq, F
103 ousel] Qq, F (Woosell)   107 SD] *Rowe; not in* Qq, F

88 round (1) roundabout way, (2) dance (as at
2.1.140).

90–3 Puck can take on the likeness of anything;
compare 2.1.46–53, and p. 7 above.

93 SD F misplaces the entry for Bottom here,
Enter Piramus with the Asse head; Qq have no entry
for him after his exit at 70, but he must return to
speak lines 94–5. It is possible, as Wells notes, that
Bottom was driven off with the other mechanicals at
87, and entered again with the ass head at 93, but
line 100 seems to imply that he has remained on
stage.

97 You see...own Proverbial ('a fool's head of
your own', Tilley F519, A388).

98 translated transformed.

101 sing Perhaps in the character of weavers, in
so far as they were thought of as psalm-singing
dissenters and refugees from Catholic Europe, as at
1H4 2.4.133.

103 ousel blackbird.

106 little quill small pipe, i.e. thin song.

107 Titania, sung to sleep by the lullaby of her
fairies (2.2.9 ff.) is woken by the raucous song of
Bottom; if she was placed in a curtained space (see
2.2.30 SD and n.), she must now draw the curtain
and appear while Bottom is singing. Her imaginary
'wood' is a place of flowers, songbirds and fruits,
not the savage desert of 2.1.228 or 2.2.36–7.

BOTTOM [*Sings.*]
> The finch, the sparrow, and the lark,
>   The plainsong cuckoo grey,
> Whose note full many a man doth mark   110
>   And dares not answer nay –

for indeed, who would set his wit to so foolish a bird? Who would
give a bird the lie, though he cry 'cuckoo' never so?

TITANIA I pray thee, gentle mortal, sing again;
> Mine ear is much enamoured of thy note.   115
> So is mine eye enthrallèd to thy shape,
> And thy fair virtue's force perforce doth move me
> On the first view to say, to swear, I love thee.

BOTTOM Methinks, mistress, you should have little reason for that. And
yet, to say the truth, reason and love keep little company together   120
nowadays; the more the pity that some honest neighbours will not
make them friends. Nay, I can gleek upon occasion.

TITANIA Thou art as wise as thou art beautiful.

BOTTOM Not so neither; but if I had wit enough to get out of this wood,
I have enough to serve mine own turn.   125

TITANIA Out of this wood do not desire to go:
> Thou shalt remain here, whether thou wilt or no.
> I am a spirit of no common rate;
> The summer still doth tend upon my state,
> And I do love thee. Therefore go with me.   130
> I'll give thee fairies to attend on thee,
> And they shall fetch thee jewels from the deep,
> And sing, while thou on pressèd flowers dost sleep;
> And I will purge thy mortal grossness so
> That thou shalt like an airy spirit go.   135
> Peaseblossom, Cobweb, Moth, and Mustardseed!

---

108 SD] *Theobald; not in* Qq, F   116–18] *As in* Q1; *118 transposed in* Q2, F *to precede 116*   136] *Names italicised in* Qq; *converted to* SD *in* F

109 plainsong i.e. with its simple theme. Alluding to the cuckoo's repeated call.

112 set...bird Varying the proverb 'Do not set your wit against a fool's' (Tilley W547).

113 'cuckoo' Associated with 'cuckold', as commonly; compare the song of Spring at the end of *LLL* (5.2.900 ff.).

117 fair virtue's force the power of your unblemished excellence (combining 'fair' = beautiful, and 'virtue' = moral superiority).

120–1 reason...nowadays See 2.2.121–4 and n., and p. 37 above.

122 gleek make a joke.

126 Titania's rhyming couplets enhance the discrepancy between her and Bottom, who speaks in prose.

128 rate estimation.

129 still...state ever waits upon (attends) my greatness. Dr Johnson defined 'state' as 'solemn pomp, appearance of greatness'.

132 jewels from the deep Like pearls and coral, 'made' in the sea (*Temp* 1.2.398–9), or scattered from wrecks, like those Clarence dreams of (*R3* 1.4.27–8).

136 Moth This was a common form of 'mote', so spelt at 5.1.301 in Q, and this may be what Shakespeare intended, a minute particle matching the mustard-seed, 'the least of all seeds' (Matt.

Enter four Fairies.

PEASEBLOSSOM Ready.

COBWEB And I.

MOTH And I.

MUSTARDSEED And I.   140

ALL Where shall we go?

TITANIA Be kind and courteous to this gentleman:
        Hop in his walks and gambol in his eyes;
        Feed him with apricocks and dewberries,
        With purple grapes, green figs, and mulberries;   145
        The honey-bags steal from the humble-bees,
        And for night-tapers crop their waxen thighs,
        And light them at the fiery glow-worms' eyes
        To have my love to bed, and to arise;
        And pluck the wings from painted butterflies   150
        To fan the moonbeams from his sleeping eyes.
        Nod to him, elves, and do him courtesies.

PEASEBLOSSOM Hail, mortal!

COBWEB Hail!

MOTH Hail!   155

MUSTARDSEED Hail!

BOTTOM I cry your worships mercy, heartily. I beseech your worship's
        name.

COBWEB Cobweb.

BOTTOM I shall desire you of more acquaintance, good Master Cobweb;   160
        if I cut my finger I shall make bold with you. Your name, honest
        gentleman?

PEASEBLOSSOM Peaseblossom.

136 SD] Qq; *Enter Pease-blossome, Cobweb, Moth, Mustard-seede, and foure Fairies.* F   137–41] *So R. G. White; one line in* Qq, F *(Fairies. Readie: and I, and I, and I. Where shall we go?)*   153–6] *So Dyce, after Capell; three lines in* Qq, F *(1. Fai. Haile mortall, haile. / 2. Fai. Haile. / 3. Fai. Haile.)*

13.32), but 'Moth' also fits, as a tiny winged creature. The two words were closer in pronunciation then than now, and both senses may be present too in the name 'Moth' for Armado's page in *LLL* (see Kökeritz, pp. 234, 320).

136 SD So Qq. The names in line 136 are italicised in Qq, and F absorbed the line into the stage direction which follows; F thus calls for eight fairies rather than four as in Qq.

137–41 Qq and F print as one line with the speech heading *Fairies* (*Fai.* in F); sometimes, as by Brooks, treated as making a verse-line, these phrases do not in fact form a pentameter, and are printed here as prose.

144 apricocks The original form of 'apricot', and Shakespeare's spelling also at *R2* 3.4.29.

144 dewberries blackberries.

148 light...eyes The female glow-worm in fact emits light from the end of the abdomen; Shakespeare may well have known this, and used 'eyes' metaphorically.

152 elves See 2.1.17 and n.

157 cry...mercy beg pardon, i.e. for asking their names.

160 desire...of ask for. A common construction in Shakespeare's time.

161 cut...bold with you Cobwebs were used to stop bleeding.

BOTTOM I pray you commend me to Mistress Squash, your mother,
and to Master Peascod, your father. Good Master Peaseblossom,   165
I shall desire you of more acquaintance, too. – Your name, I
beseech you, sir?

MUSTARDSEED Mustardseed.

BOTTOM Good Master Mustardseed, I know your patience well. That
same cowardly, giant-like ox-beef hath devoured many a gentleman   170
of your house. I promise you, your kindred hath made my eyes
water ere now. I desire you of more acquaintance, good Master
Mustardseed.

TITANIA Come, wait upon him. Lead him to my bower.
    The moon methinks looks with a watery eye,   175
    And when she weeps, weeps every little flower,
    Lamenting some enforcèd chastity.
    Tie up my lover's tongue; bring him silently.

Exeunt

3.[2] *Enter* [OBERON,] *King of Fairies.*

OBERON I wonder if Titania be awaked;
    Then what it was that next came in her eye,
    Which she must dote on, in extremity.

---

166 you of] Qq; of you F   **172** you of] *Dyce;* you Qq, F
Exit Qq, F   Act 3, Scene 2 **3.2**] *Capell; not in* Qq, F
Fairies, *and* Robin goodfellow Qq

178 lover's] Qq, F; love's *Pope*   **178** SD *Exeunt*] *Rowe;*
0 SD] F *subst.* (*Enter King of Pharies, solus.*); *Enter King of*

164 Squash An unripe peascod, which is a ripe
pea-pod. Compare *TN* 1.5.157–8: 'as a squash is
before 'tis a peascod'.

169 patience In suffering being 'devoured'.

171–2 eyes water (1) watering in sympathy, (2)
smarting because of the strength of the mustard.

172 of Not in Qq or F, but probably an accidental
omission, as Bottom is repeating what he said to the
other fairies at 160 and 166.

174 bower They presumably make their exit
through the curtained alcove or door through which
Titania emerged at 107.

176 when...flower Dew was thought to fall
from the heavens, and 'The more clere that the
mone is in the Somar tyme the more plente of dewe
is seen vpon the grasse and herbes' (Bartholomeus,
De Proprietatibus Rerum (1495), p. 326, cited in
OED).

177 enforcèd violated. A reminder that the moon
is associated with Diana, goddess of chastity; see
1.1.72–3 and 89, and 2.1.162.

178 Tie...tongue This suggests that Bottom is
'making involuntary asinine noises' (Wells).

Act 3, Scene 2

3.2 The action is more or less continuous, but a
short break in time and a shift in imagined location
away from Titania's bower (7) to 'this haunted
grove' (5; another part of the stage?) may mark an
interval; as Wells notes, the opening dialogue
between Oberon and Puck recapitulates what we
have seen in the previous scenes.

  0 SD In Qq the SD reads '*Enter King of Fairies,
and* Robin goodfellow.'; F has *Enter King of Pharies,
solus.*, followed by *Enter Pucke.* at 3. This relates
better to the text, and to stage practice.

Enter PUCK.

Here comes my messenger. How now, mad spirit?
What night-rule now about this haunted grove?   5
PUCK My mistress with a monster is in love.
Near to her close and consecrated bower,
While she was in her dull and sleeping hour,
A crew of patches, rude mechanicals,
That work for bread upon Athenian stalls,   10
Were met together to rehearse a play
Intended for great Theseus' nuptial day.
The shallowest thick-skin of that barren sort,
Who Pyramus presented, in their sport
Forsook his scene and entered in a brake,   15
When I did him at this advantage take:
An ass's nole I fixèd on his head.
Anon his Thisbe must be answerèd,
And forth my mimic comes. When they him spy –
As wild geese that the creeping fowler eye,   20
Or russet-pated choughs, many in sort,
Rising and cawing at the gun's report,
Sever themselves and madly sweep the sky –
So at his sight away his fellows fly,
And at our stamp here o'er and o'er one falls;   25
He 'Murder!' cries, and help from Athens calls.
Their sense thus weak, lost with their fears thus strong,
Made senseless things begin to do them wrong,

---

3 SD] F; *not in* Qq   6–7 love. / …bower,] *Rowe;* love, / …bower. Q; love, / …bower, Q2, F   19 mimic] F
(Mimmick); Minnick Q1; Minnock Q2

---

5 **night-rule** Probably meaning 'disorders of the night' (*OED* Rule *sb* 13c), or 'misrule' (as the day is the time for order?).

7 **close** secret, secluded. (This could also mean 'closed', 'curtained off'; Titania's bower may still be in view.)

9 **patches** clowns. See also 4.1.204 and n.

9 **rude mechanicals** rough working-men.

13 **barren sort** dull-witted crew.

17 **nole** noddle, head.

19 **mimic** comic actor.

21 **russet-pated…sort** a large group of jackdaws with heads of a neutral colour. 'Russet' seems to have been used for a range of dun colours from reddish-brown to gray, the colour of a jackdaw's head.

23 **Sever themselves** Scatter.

25 **our stamp** The royal plural is odd, and Dr Johnson conjectured a misreading here of 'a stump', noting a parallel with Drayton's *Nymphidia, The Court of Fayrie* (?1625), 452–6, which has echoes of Shakespeare's play, and in which a fairy works charms against Puck, and as he stumbles in 'Bryers and brambles', 'A Stump doth trip him in his pace.' But the text makes sense, and Reginald Scot's account of Robin Goodfellow in his *Discoverie of Witchcraft* (1584), p. 85, records his exclamation when upset at some house: 'in that case he saith; What have we here? Hemton hamten, here will I never more tread nor stampen' (cited by Brooks).

For briars and thorns at their apparel snatch,
Some sleeves, some hats; from yielders all things catch.   30
I led them on in this distracted fear,
And left sweet Pyramus translated there;
When in that moment, so it came to pass,
Titania waked, and straightway loved an ass.

OBERON This falls out better than I could devise.   35
But hast thou yet latched the Athenian's eyes
With the love juice, as I did bid thee do?

PUCK I took him sleeping – that is finished too –
And the Athenian woman by his side,
That when he waked, of force she must be eyed.   40

Enter DEMETRIUS *and* HERMIA.

OBERON Stand close: this is the same Athenian.
PUCK This is the woman, but not this the man.
DEMETRIUS O, why rebuke you him that loves you so?
Lay breath so bitter on your bitter foe.

HERMIA Now I but chide; but I should use thee worse,   45
For thou, I fear, hast given me cause to curse.
If thou hast slain Lysander in his sleep,
Being o'er shoes in blood, plunge in the deep,
And kill me too.
The sun was not so true unto the day   50
As he to me. Would he have stol'n away
From sleeping Hermia? I'll believe as soon
This whole earth may be bored, and that the moon
May through the centre creep, and so displease
Her brother's noontide with th'Antipodes.   55
It cannot be but thou hast murdered him:

48–9] *So Rowe³; one line in* Qq, F

30 **from...catch** everything snatches at those who give way to fear.

32 **translated** transformed. As at 3.1.98.

36 **latched** captured, snared. Q2 and F have 'lacht' ('latcht' Q1), which *OED* Leach *v²* 1 records as a possible rare variant of 'leached' = moistened, but no other use of the word in this sense is recorded, except in Old English.

41 **Stand close** i.e. where they will not be seen. Oberon was invisible in 2.1 when he listened to Demetrius and Helena talking (2.1.186), but here he thinks of himself as visible.

43–81 Demetrius addresses Hermia as 'you', she him as 'thou', which Furness interpreted as 'contemptuous', although Hermia also used 'thou' in speaking to Lysander at 1.1.169 ff.; 'You' seems to reflect rather Demetrius's tone of adoration, 'thou' Hermia's familiar treatment of him.

48 **Being o'er shoes** i.e. having waded in so far.

54–5 **displease...Antipodes** vex the sun's noon-tide with the people who live on the opposite side of the earth. As Wells notes, the image links with other images of cosmic disorder, notably Titania's speech at 2.1.81–114.

So should a murderer look; so dead, so grim.

DEMETRIUS So should the murdered look, and so should I,
    Pierced through the heart with your stern cruelty;
    Yet you, the murderer, look as bright, as clear,   60
    As yonder Venus in her glimmering sphere.

HERMIA What's this to my Lysander? Where is he?
    Ah, good Demetrius, wilt thou give him me?

DEMETRIUS I had rather give his carcass to my hounds.

HERMIA Out, dog! Out, cur! Thou driv'st me past the bounds   65
    Of maiden's patience. Hast thou slain him then?
    Henceforth be never numbered among men.
    O, once tell true; tell true, even for my sake:
    Durst thou have looked upon him being awake?
    And hast thou killed him sleeping? O, brave touch!   70
    Could not a worm, an adder do so much?
    An adder did it; for with doubler tongue
    Than thine, thou serpent, never adder stung.

DEMETRIUS You spend your passion on a misprised mood.
    I am not guilty of Lysander's blood,   75
    Nor is he dead, for aught that I can tell.

HERMIA I pray thee, tell me then that he is well.

DEMETRIUS And if I could, what should I get therefor?

HERMIA A privilege, never to see me more;
    And from thy hated presence part I so.   80
    See me no more, whether he be dead or no.   *Exit*

DEMETRIUS There is no following her in this fierce vein;
    Here therefore for a while I will remain.
    So sorrow's heaviness doth heavier grow

---

58 murdered] Qq (murthered); murderer F   60 look] Qq; looks F   64 I had] Q1; Ide Q2, F   65 bounds] Q1, F; bonds Q2   68 tell true; tell true] Q1; tell true, Q2, F   69 have] Qq; a F   80–1 And...more] *So Pope; one line in* Qq, F   80 I so] *Pope;* I Qq, F

---

57 **dead** deadly pale.

61 **Venus...sphere** For 'sphere' = orbit, see 2.1.7 and n. Venus is the evening star and goddess of love; compare 107 below and 1.1.171.

62 **to** to do with.

68 **once** once for all.

70 **brave touch!** courageous stroke! Compare 157 below.

71–3 Compare 2.2.152–6, where Hermia dreamed she was attacked by a serpent, and 2.2.9–11, where the fairies protect Titania against snakes.

71 **worm** snake.

72 **doubler** (1) more forked (as at 2.2.9), (2) more deceitful.

74 The sense is not clear; either 'you waste your passion in a mistaken anger', or 'you pour out your anger on me, misunderstanding my disposition'; both senses of the word 'mood' were current.

78 **therefor** for that.

81 **whether** As often, reduced in speech to one syllable, 'whe'er'.

84 **heaviness...heavier** Playing on 'heavy' = sad or burdensome, and 'heavy' = weary.

For debt that bankrupt sleep doth sorrow owe,   85
Which now in some slight measure it will pay,
If for his tender here I make some stay.
                    [He] lies down [and sleeps].
OBERON What hast thou done? Thou hast mistaken quite,
And laid the love juice on some true love's sight.
Of thy misprision must perforce ensue   90
Some true love turned, and not a false turned true.
PUCK Then fate o'errules, that, one man holding troth,
A million fail, confounding oath on oath.
OBERON About the wood go swifter than the wind,
And Helena of Athens look thou find.   95
All fancy-sick she is and pale of cheer
With sighs of love, that costs the fresh blood dear.
By some illusion see thou bring her here;
I'll charm his eyes against she do appear.
PUCK I go, I go, look how I go!   100
Swifter than arrow from the Tartar's bow.   *Exit*
OBERON   *[Squeezing the juice on Demetrius's eyes.]*
Flower of this purple dye,
Hit with Cupid's archery,
Sink in apple of his eye.
When his love he doth espy,   105
Let her shine as gloriously
As the Venus of the sky.
When thou wak'st, if she be by,
Beg of her for remedy.

---

85 sleep] *Rowe;* Qq (slippe), F (slip)   87 SD] *Dyce subst.; Lie downe* Qq, F (*Ly doune* Q1)   99 do] Qq; *doth* F
101 SD *Exit*] Q2, F; *not in* Q1   102 SD] *After Dyce; not in* Qq, F

---

85 sleep Q has 'slippe' (Q2 and F 'slip'); did the compositor spell the word as he pronounced it?

87 tender i.e. the offer made by sleep. This is the correct legal term for an offer in discharge of a debt (*OED* sv *sb²* 1b).

87 SD Q has *Ly doune*, F *Lie downe*. Compare 418 SD and n.

90 misprision mistake.

92–3 i.e. if so, fate has taken charge, since, for each man who is true in love, a million fail, breaking oath after oath. On 'troth', see 2.2.48 and n.

96 fancy-sick love-sick. But see 1.1.155 and n.

96 cheer face. The original meaning of the word.

97 A sigh was thought to cause the loss of a drop of blood, hence the 'blood-sucking sighs' of *3H6* 4.4.22.

99 against ready for when (Wells).

101 Tartar's bow Noted for its power; the image was probably derived from Golding's Ovid, *Metamorphoses* x, 687, where Atalanta runs 'as swift as arrow from a Turkye bowe'. The word 'Tartar' was used vaguely to signify anyone from central Asia, including Turkey.

102 Recalling 2.1.167–8.

104 apple pupil.

107 Venus See 61 above and n.

Enter Puck.

PUCK   Captain of our fairy band,   110
            Helena is here at hand,
            And the youth mistook by me,
            Pleading for a lover's fee.
            Shall we their fond pageant see?
            Lord, what fools these mortals be!   115
OBERON   Stand aside. The noise they make
            Will cause Demetrius to awake.
PUCK   Then will two at once woo one –
            That must needs be sport alone;
            And those things do best please me   120
            That befall prepost'rously.

                Enter LYSANDER *and* HELENA.

LYSANDER Why should you think that I should woo in scorn?
            Scorn and derision never come in tears.
            Look when I vow, I weep; and vows so born,
            In their nativity all truth appears.   125
            How can these things in me seem scorn to you,
            Bearing the badge of faith to prove them true?
HELENA You do advance your cunning more and more.
            When truth kills truth, O devilish-holy fray!
            These vows are Hermia's. Will you give her o'er?   130
            Weigh oath with oath, and you will nothing weigh;
            Your vows to her and me, put in two scales,
            Will even weigh, and both as light as tales.
LYSANDER I had no judgement when to her I swore.

123 come] Qq; comes F

113 **fee** reward.
114 **fond pageant** foolish scene or spectacle. This reminds us that Oberon and Puck here make an audience for a kind of play within the play.
119 **alone** 'by itself', or perhaps more strongly 'of a unique kind' (*OED* sv 5).
121 SD Lysander and Helena do not see Oberon and Puck (who are 'invisible', as Puck has to be at 402 ff.), or notice the sleeping Demetrius; it adds to the comedy, of course, if he is right under their noses. The lovers speak in rhyme to 194, when the mood changes as their quarrel becomes bitter.
124 **Look when** Whenever. Common usage in Shakespeare's time.

124–5 **vows...appears** i.e. when vows are born so (in weeping), nothing but truth appears in their nativity.
127 **badge of faith** i.e. his tears.
129 **truth...fray** The 'truth' Lysander now tells Helena destroys the 'truth' of his vows to Hermia, in a clash that is 'holy' as involving vows of devotion, and devilish since one vow must be false.
131 **nothing weigh** i.e. because the oaths cancel each other, and both, as idle 'tales', have no weight.
133 **tales** fictions, falsehoods.
134–5 See 2.2.121–4 and n., and pp. 31–2 above.

HELENA Nor none, in my mind, now you give her o'er.   135
LYSANDER Demetrius loves her, and he loves not you.
DEMETRIUS (*Waking.*)
    O Helen, goddess, nymph, perfect, divine!
    To what, my love, shall I compare thine eyne?
    Crystal is muddy! O, how ripe in show
    Thy lips, those kissing cherries, tempting grow!   140
    That pure congealèd white, high Taurus' snow,
    Fanned with the eastern wind, turns to a crow
    When thou hold'st up thy hand. O, let me kiss
    This princess of pure white, this seal of bliss!
HELENA O spite! O Hell! I see you all are bent   145
    To set against me for your merriment.
    If you were civil, and knew courtesy,
    You would not do me thus much injury.
    Can you not hate me, as I know you do,
    But you must join in souls to mock me too?   150
    If you were men, as men you are in show,
    You would not use a gentle lady so,
    To vow, and swear, and superpraise my parts,
    When I am sure you hate me with your hearts.
    You both are rivals, and love Hermia;   155
    And now both rivals to mock Helena.
    A trim exploit, a manly enterprise,
    To conjure tears up in a poor maid's eyes
    With your derision! None of noble sort
    Would so offend a virgin, and extort   160
    A poor soul's patience, all to make you sport.

---

137 SD *Waking*] F (*Awa.*); *not in* Qq   141 congealèd] Q2, F; concealed Q1   145 all are] Qq; are all F
151 were] Qq; are F   159 derision! None] *Theobald;* derision None Q; derision, none Q2; derision; none F

136 **loves not you** The flow of rhyme is momentarily broken as Demetrius intervenes.
  138 **eyne** See 1.1.242 and n.
  141 **Taurus'** A chain of mountains in Turkey. Brooks notes that Taurus is twice referred to in Seneca's *Hippolytus*, which he believes Shakespeare used as a source for this play (see pp. 144–5 below); in John Studley's translation, in Thomas Newton's edition (1581), Act 2, line 382, the 'watry snowes' melt on the 'toppe of Taurus hill'. Taurus is also mentioned in Golding's Ovid, II, 275.
  143 As E. W. Talbert noted in *Elizabethan Drama and Shakespeare's Early Plays*, 1963, pp. 252–3, the line suggests an action; Helena

presumably holds up one or both hands in a 'No, no, don't touch me' gesture, quite misunderstood by Demetrius.
  143–4 The inflated protestations of Demetrius culminate in the comic exaggeration of this final image. A white skin was highly prized; compare *Oth.* 5.2.4: 'that whiter skin of hers than snow'.
  146 **set against** attack (*OED* Set v 128a).
  150 **in souls** with all your beings. (Compare the phrase 'heart and soul'.)
  153 **parts** qualities.
  159 **sort** character.
  160–1 **extort...patience** i.e. force her by their torture to endure suffering.

LYSANDER You are unkind, Demetrius: be not so,
          For you love Hermia – this you know I know –
          And here with all good will, with all my heart,
          In Hermia's love I yield you up my part;   165
          And yours of Helena to me bequeath,
          Whom I do love, and will do till my death.
HELENA Never did mockers waste more idle breath.
DEMETRIUS Lysander, keep thy Hermia; I will none.
          If e'er I loved her, all that love is gone.   170
          My heart to her but as guest-wise sojourned,
          And now to Helen is it home returned,
          There to remain.
LYSANDER   Helen, it is not so.
DEMETRIUS Disparage not the faith thou dost not know,
          Lest to thy peril thou aby it dear.   175
          Look where thy love comes: yonder is thy dear.

                        Enter Hermia.

HERMIA Dark night, that from the eye his function takes,
          The ear more quick of apprehension makes;
          Wherein it doth impair the seeing sense
          It pays the hearing double recompense.   180
          Thou art not by mine eye, Lysander, found;
          Mine ear, I thank it, brought me to thy sound.
          But why unkindly didst thou leave me so?
LYSANDER Why should he stay whom love doth press to go?
HERMIA What love could press Lysander from my side?   185
LYSANDER Lysander's love, that would not let him bide,
          Fair Helena – who more engilds the night
          Than all yon fiery oes and eyes of light.
          [*To Hermia*] Why seek'st thou me? Could not this make
              thee know

167 till] Q1; to Q2, F   172 Helen is it] Q1 (*Helen,* is it); *Helen* it is Q2, F   175 aby] Q1; abide Q2, F
182 thy] Qq; that F   189 SD] *This edn; not in* Qq, F

166 bequeath assign, make over. Once normal
usage, as at *John* 1.1.149 (*OED* sv v 4a).
  169 I will none I want no part of her.
  171 to her...sojourned travelled to her. *OED*
sv 4 cites one example of this meaning from 1608,
but there are overtones here of the more usual sense
'lodged with'.

175 aby it dear pay dearly for it (= a-buy; see
426).
  177 Hermia's speech might follow directly after
her exit lines, 2.2.151–62, strengthening the sense
of a continuous action.
  188 oes and eyes stars. 'Oes' were round
spangles used to ornament dress for a glittering
effect; there is also a pun on the letters 'o' and 'i'.

        The hate I bare thee made me leave thee so?   190

HERMIA You speak not as you think; it cannot be.

HELENA Lo, she is one of this confederacy!

        Now I perceive they have conjoined all three

        To fashion this false sport in spite of me.

        Injurious Hermia, most ungrateful maid,   195

        Have you conspired, have you with these contrived

        To bait me with this foul derision?

        Is all the counsel that we two have shared,

        The sisters' vows, the hours that we have spent

        When we have chid the hasty-footed time   200

        For parting us – O, is all forgot?

        All schooldays' friendship, childhood innocence?

        We, Hermia, like two artificial gods

        Have with our needles created both one flower,

        Both on one sampler, sitting on one cushion,   205

        Both warbling of one song, both in one key,

        As if our hands, our sides, voices, and minds

        Had been incorporate. So we grew together

        Like to a double cherry, seeming parted,

        But yet an union in partition,   210

        Two lovely berries moulded on one stem;

        So with two seeming bodies but one heart,

        Two of the first, like coats in heraldry,

        Due but to one, and crownèd with one crest.

        And will you rent our ancient love asunder,   215

        To join with men in scorning your poor friend?

        It is not friendly, 'tis not maidenly.

        Our sex, as well as I, may chide you for it,

---

210 an] Qq; a F   213 first, like] *Theobald, conj. Folks;* first life Qq, F; first life, F2

---

190 hate I bare thee See 2.2.143–8 above.

194 in spite of in scorn of.

195 Rhyming couplets give way to blank verse here as the quarrel grows more serious, and the emotional temperature rises.

203 artificial highly skilled in art (*OED* sv *a* 6b).

206 in one key i.e. in perfect harmony. They were not merely singing in the same key, as would obviously be necessary, but were altogether ('voices and minds') in accord.

208 incorporate united in one body.

213–14 The 'first' is the first 'tincture' (= colour) mentioned in the elaborate process of describing a coat-of-arms; according to the rules of heraldry, it thus refers to the 'field' (i.e. the background of the coat-of-arms). Staunton noticed that the heraldic image was suggested by the word 'partition' (210), which is the correct term for the divisions of a 'parted' or a quartered shield. A 'parted' (209) shield is one divided into equal halves; so Helena's image is of a shield divided into halves of the same colour ('Two of the first'), and thus in effect not differentiated. This coat-of-arms is granted by right to one person ('Due but to one') and surmounted by a single crest (a hart or heart).

215 rent tear, rend.

       Though I alone do feel the injury.

HERMIA I am amazèd at your passionate words.   220
       I scorn you not; it seems that you scorn me.

HELENA Have you not set Lysander, as in scorn,
       To follow me, and praise my eyes and face?
       And made your other love, Demetrius,
       Who even but now did spurn me with his foot,   225
       To call me goddess, nymph, divine and rare,
       Precious, celestial? Wherefore speaks he this
       To her he hates? And wherefore doth Lysander
       Deny your love, so rich within his soul,
       And tender me, forsooth, affection,   230
       But by your setting on, by your consent?
       What though I be not so in grace as you,
       So hung upon with love, so fortunate,
       But miserable most, to love unloved:
       This you should pity rather than despise.   235

HERMIA I understand not what you mean by this.

HELENA Ay, do! Persever, counterfeit sad looks,
       Make mouths upon me when I turn my back,
       Wink each at other, hold the sweet jest up.
       This sport, well carried, shall be chronicled.   240
       If you have any pity, grace, or manners,
       You would not make me such an argument.
       But fare ye well. 'Tis partly my own fault,
       Which death or absence soon shall remedy.

LYSANDER Stay, gentle Helena: hear my excuse,   245
       My love, my life, my soul, fair Helena!

HELENA O, excellent!

HERMIA [*To Lysander*] Sweet, do not scorn her so.

DEMETRIUS If she cannot entreat, I can compel.

---

220 passionate] F; *not in* Qq   237 Ay, do!] *Rowe subst.*; I doe Q1; I, do, Q2, F (does)   243 my] Q1; mine Q2, F
247 SD] *Wells*; *not in* Qq, F

220 passionate Not in Qq; the word may have been restored in F from the prompt-book (compare 5.1.186 and n.), but NS, rejecting it as a compositor's guess, adopted J. W. Mackail's suggestion that the line began 'Her. *Helen* I am amazed...', and the compositor of Q1 dropped '*Helen*' mistaking it for a duplicated speech heading.

225 spurn...foot Recalling Helena's words to Demetrius at 2.1.204–5.
237 Persever Accented on the second syllable, as always in Shakespeare; 'persevere', accented on the first syllable, became common usage during the seventeenth century.
237 sad serious.
239 hold...up i.e. keep up, maintain.
242 argument subject of contention.

LYSANDER Thou canst compel no more than she entreat;
      Thy threats have no more strength than her weak prayers.   250
      Helen, I love thee, by my life, I do:
      I swear by that which I will lose for thee
      To prove him false that says I love thee not.

DEMETRIUS I say I love thee more than he can do.

LYSANDER If thou say so, withdraw, and prove it too.   255

DEMETRIUS Quick, come.

HERMIA   Lysander, whereto tends all this?

LYSANDER Away, you Ethiop!

DEMETRIUS   No, no, sir,
      Seem to break loose, take on as you would follow,
      But yet come not. You are a tame man, go.

LYSANDER Hang off, thou cat, thou burr! Vile thing, let loose,   260
      Or I will shake thee from me like a serpent.

HERMIA Why are you grown so rude? What change is this,
      Sweet love?

LYSANDER   Thy love? – out, tawny Tartar, out;
      Out, loathed medicine! O hated potion, hence!

HERMIA Do you not jest?

---

250 prayers] *Theobald; praise* Qq, F   257–8 DEMETRIUS No, no...follow] F *(divided at* loose; / Take*); Dem.* No, no: heele / Seeme...follow Q1; *Dem.* No, no...loose; / Take...follow Q2; *Her.* No, no; he'll – / *Dem.* Seem...follow *Chambers; Her.* No, no, he'll kill thee! / *Dem.* Seem...follow *Cuningham; Hermia.* No, no! / *Demetrius. [scoffs]* Ye'll seem...follow *NS; Dem.* No, no; he will / Seem...follow *Alexander*   257 sir] F; *not in* Qq   258 loose,...you] F; loose:...you Qq; loose:...he *Pope, Sisson;* loose – [*To Lysander*]...you *Brooks*   262–3] *So* Q1; *divided at* rude? / What *in* Q2, F   264 potion] Q1; poison Q2, F

250 prayers Theobald's emendation of 'praise' (Qq, F) is warranted by the antithesis to 'threats', and the compositor could easily have misread 'praiers'.

255 withdraw...too Lysander and Demetrius wear swords, and sometimes on stage draw them here; later they pursue one another with drawn swords; see 402, 411 below.

257 Ethiop Blackamoor. Compare the common saying 'To wash an Ethiop white' meaning 'To attempt the impossible' (Tilley E186), and Jer. 13.23.

257–8 Q has 'No, no: heele / Seeme', which is unmetrical and bad sense, since 'he'll' does not relate to 'you would follow'. F altered to 'No, no, Sir, seeme to breake loose; / Take on...', which makes better sense but not better verse. The passage is corrupt, and none of the numerous guesses editors have suggested is convincing. Possibly a line or more was omitted inadvertently in Q (not for reasons of space, as the page is not crowded), as 'No, no' would perhaps be more appropriate in Hermia's mouth. I have kept the text as in F, adjusting the line-division to make 258 a blank verse; at least this makes good sense, if Hermia clutches Lysander to prevent him fighting (she hangs on to him until 335 below), and Demetrius taunts him as if he is not really trying to 'break loose'. Demetrius addresses Lysander as 'sir' again at 322; it marks the break in their friendship.

258 take on as make a great fuss, as if.

261 serpent Compare 2.2.151–5, where Hermia cries out for Lysander to pluck a 'serpent' from her breast, and 71–3 above.

263 tawny Tartar Another reference to Hermia's dark colouring; compare 257; for 'Tartar' see 101 and n.

264 medicine...potion Referring to her 'love' with which she seeks to 'cure' his harshness. Q2 and F unnecessarily change 'potion' to 'poison'.

HELENA   Yes, sooth, and so do you.   265

LYSANDER Demetrius, I will keep my word with thee.

DEMETRIUS I would I had your bond, for I perceive
      A weak bond holds you. I'll not trust your word.

LYSANDER What? Should I hurt her, strike her, kill her dead?
      Although I hate her, I'll not harm her so.   270

HERMIA What? Can you do me greater harm than hate?
      Hate me? Wherefore? O me, what news, my love?
      Am not I Hermia? Are not you Lysander?
      I am as fair now as I was erewhile.
      Since night you loved me; yet since night you left me.   275
      Why then, you left me – O, the gods forbid! –
      In earnest, shall I say?

LYSANDER   Ay, by my life;
      And never did desire to see thee more.
      Therefore be out of hope, of question, of doubt;
      Be certain, nothing truer – 'tis no jest   280
      That I do hate thee and love Helena.

HERMIA [*To Helena*]
      O me, you juggler, you canker-blossom,
      You thief of love! What, have you come by night
      And stol'n my love's heart from him?

HELENA   Fine, i'faith!
      Have you no modesty, no maiden shame,   285
      No touch of bashfulness? What, will you tear
      Impatient answers from my gentle tongue?
      Fie, fie, you counterfeit, you puppet, you!

HERMIA 'Puppet'? Why so? – Ay, that way goes the game.
      Now I perceive that she hath made compare   290
      Between our statures; she hath urged her height,
      And with her personage, her tall personage,
      Her height, forsooth, she hath prevailed with him.

---

282 SD *To Helena*] *So Brooks, after* O me!*; not in* Qq, F   289 Why so?] Qq, F*; why, so:* Theobald*;* Why, so? *Brooks*

267–8 **bond…bond** (1) written contract, (2) tie or restraining force. Hermia still hangs on to Lysander.

282 **juggler** trickster, deceiver.

282 **canker-blossom** canker-worms (as at 2.2.3), or the flower of the dog-rose or briar (as in *Sonnets* 54.5).

284 **Fine i'faith** Helena persists in believing that Hermia is conspiring with the others to mock her.

288 **counterfeit** cheat.

288–98 The two girls differ in colouring (257, 263), in height, and in temper (301–4, 323–4), a pointed and comic sequel to Helena's image of them as a 'double cherry', 203–14 above.

289 **'Puppet'? Why so?** Hermia is taken aback by Helena's use of 'puppet', her first term of contempt.

And are you grown so high in his esteem
Because I am so dwarfish and so low? 295
How low am I, thou painted maypole? Speak!
How low am I? I am not yet so low
But that my nails can reach unto thine eyes.

HELENA I pray you, though you mock me, gentlemen,
Let her not hurt me. I was never curst; 300
I have no gift at all in shrewishness.
I am a right maid for my cowardice;
Let her not strike me. You perhaps may think
Because she is something lower than myself
That I can match her.

HERMIA   Lower? Hark, again! 305

HELENA Good Hermia, do not be so bitter with me.
I evermore did love you, Hermia,
Did ever keep your counsels, never wronged you,
Save that in love unto Demetrius
I told him of your stealth unto this wood. 310
He followed you; for love I followed him,
But he hath chid me hence, and threatened me
To strike me, spurn me, nay, to kill me too.
And now, so you will let me quiet go,
To Athens will I bear my folly back, 315
And follow you no further. Let me go;
You see how simple and how fond I am.

HERMIA Why, get you gone! Who is't that hinders you?

HELENA A foolish heart that I leave here behind.

HERMIA What, with Lysander?

HELENA   With Demetrius. 320

LYSANDER Be not afraid; she shall not harm thee, Helena.

DEMETRIUS No, sir. She shall not, though you take her part.

HELENA O, when she is angry she is keen and shrewd;
She was a vixen when she went to school,
And though she be but little, she is fierce. 325

HERMIA Little again? Nothing but low and little?
Why will you suffer her to flout me thus?
Let me come to her.

---

299 gentlemen] Q2, F; gentleman Q1   320 SH HELENA] Qq; *Her* F   323 when she is] Q1; when shee's Q2, F (when she's)

300 **curst** shrewish, fierce.
310 **stealth** stealing away.
313 **spurn** Compare 225 and 2.1.204–5 above.

317 **fond** tender, doting. Compare 2.2.94 above.
323 **keen and shrewd** harsh and malicious.

LYSANDER   Get you gone, you dwarf,
You minimus of hindering knot-grass made,
You bead, you acorn.
DEMETRIUS   You are too officious   330
In her behalf that scorns your services.
Let her alone: speak not of Helena,
Take not her part; for if thou dost intend
Never so little show of love to her,
Thou shalt aby it.
LYSANDER   Now she holds me not –   335
Now follow, if thou dur'st, to try whose right,
Of thine or mine, is most in Helena.
DEMETRIUS Follow? Nay, I'll go with thee, cheek by jowl.
                    Exeunt Lysander and Demetrius
HERMIA You, mistress, all this coil is 'long of you.
Nay, go not back.
HELENA   I will not trust you, I,   340
Nor longer stay in your curst company.
Your hands than mine are quicker for a fray;
My legs are longer, though, to run away!   *[Exit]*
HERMIA I am amazed, and know not what to say.   *Exit*
                    Oberon and Puck come forward.
OBERON This is thy negligence. Still thou mistak'st,   345
Or else committ'st thy knaveries wilfully.
PUCK Believe me, King of Shadows, I mistook.
Did not you tell me I should know the man
By the Athenian garments he had on?
And so far blameless proves my enterprise   350
That I have 'nointed an Athenian's eyes;
And so far am I glad it so did sort,

---

335 aby] Qq (abie Q2); abide F   337 Helena] Q1, F; *Helena.Exit.* Q2   338 SD] F (*Exit . . . Demetrius*.); *not in* Qq
341 Nor] Q1, F; Not Q2   343 SD *Exit*] Capell; *not in* Qq, F   344] *So* Qq; *line omitted* F   344 SD.1 *Exit*] Qq
(*Exeunt*); *not in* F   344 SD.2 *Oberon . . . forward*] Wells, *after* F (*Enter Oberon and Pucke*.); *not in* Qq   346 wilfully]
Qq; willingly F   349 had] Q1; hath Q2, F

329 minimus insignificant creature. This seems
to be Shakespeare's coinage, from 'minim' meaning
'extremely small' (compare 'minimal', which *OED*
first records in 1666).
329 knot-grass A common weed with creeping
stems. An infusion of it was supposed to stunt
growth (*OED* sv 1).
335 aby pay for. As at 175 above.
339 coil pother.

339 'long of because of, due to.
345–9 At first Oberon and Puck speak in blank
verse, marking the change in speakers and tone, as
Wells notes.
347 Shadows i.e. 'darkness' (because Oberon
rules by night), but also 'delusive appearances and
spirits', as at 381–2; see also 5.1.401 and n.
352 sort turn out.

As this their jangling I esteem a sport.

OBERON Thou seest these lovers seek a place to fight:

Hie therefore, Robin, overcast the night;   355

The starry welkin cover thou anon

With drooping fog as black as Acheron,

And lead these testy rivals so astray

As one come not within another's way.

Like to Lysander sometime frame thy tongue,   360

Then stir Demetrius up with bitter wrong,

And sometime rail thou like Demetrius;

And from each other look thou lead them thus,

Till o'er their brows death-counterfeiting sleep

With leaden legs and batty wings doth creep.   365

Then crush this herb into Lysander's eye,

Whose liquor hath this virtuous property,

To take from thence all error with his might,

And make his eyeballs roll with wonted sight.

When they next wake, all this derision   370

Shall seem a dream and fruitless vision,

And back to Athens shall the lovers wend

With league whose date till death shall never end.

Whiles I in this affair do thee employ

I'll to my Queen and beg her Indian boy;   375

And then I will her charmèd eye release

From monster's view, and all things shall be peace.

PUCK My fairy lord, this must be done with haste,

For night's swift dragons cut the clouds full fast,

And yonder shines Aurora's harbinger,   380

At whose approach ghosts wandering here and there

Troop home to churchyards. Damnèd spirits all,

That in crossways and floods have burial,

---

374 employ] Q1 (imploy); apply Q2; imply F

356 welkin sky.

357 Acheron One of the four rivers of the underworld or Hades, and so standing for the infernal regions.

359 As That.

361 wrong unjust accusations.

365 batty bat-like. The only example in Shakespeare's works, and perhaps coined by him.

368 his i.e. the liquor's.

371 fruitless vision Contrasting with Bottom's 'most rare vision' (4.1.200), and see also 5.1.401–4 and n.

355 Hie Hasten.

373 date duration.

379 dragons The chariot of Cynthia, goddess of the moon, was supposed to be drawn across the sky by dragons; compare *Cym.* 2.2.48.

380 Aurora's harbinger Forerunner of the dawn, Venus, the morning star.

382–3 Damnèd spirits...burial Suicides were buried at cross-roads, or carried away by water if they drowned themselves; these ghosts of the damned disappear each morning before the ghosts of those accorded Christian burial in churchyards.

Already to their wormy beds are gone.
For fear lest day should look their shames upon,   385
They wilfully themselves exile from light,
And must for aye consort with black-browed night.
OBERON But we are spirits of another sort.
I with the morning's love have oft made sport,
And like a forester the groves may tread   390
Even till the eastern gate, all fiery-red,
Opening on Neptune with fair blessèd beams,
Turns into yellow gold his salt green streams.
But notwithstanding, haste, make no delay;
We may effect this business yet ere day.   [*Exit*]   395
PUCK   Up and down, up and down,
I will lead them up and down;
I am feared in field and town.
Goblin, lead them up and down.
Here comes one.   400

                    Enter Lysander.

LYSANDER Where art thou, proud Demetrius? Speak thou now.
PUCK Here, villain, drawn and ready! Where art thou?
LYSANDER I will be with thee straight.
PUCK   Follow me then
To plainer ground.

                         [*Exit Lysander*]

384–5 gone:…upon,] Qq, F *(subst.)*; gone,…upon; *Alexander, Brooks* (upon:)   386 exile] Qq, F *(dxile)*; exil'd
Alexander, conj. Thirlby   395 SD] *Rowe; not in* Qq, F   396–9] *So Pope; Up…down. / I am…downe.* Q1; *as
prose* Q2, F   403–4 Follow…ground] *So Theobald; one line in* Qq, F   404 SD.I *Exit Lysander] Theobald (Lys, goes
out, as following Dem.); not in* Qq, F

386 **exile** The emendation to 'exil'd' adopted by
Brooks may be correct, as 'e' and 'd' confusion was
common in Secretary hand, but the sense is clear
anyway, and all other verbs in these lines are in the
present tense. It has been conjectured (Thirlby,
Harold Jenkins) that 386–7 should be spoken by
Oberon, as more in character with him, and
enhancing the antithesis between 'They' and 'we';
this is plausible, and only depends upon the
supposition that a speech heading has been
misplaced.
389 **morning's love…sport** Perhaps implying
that Oberon has made love to Aurora (compare
2.1.65–73), or possibly that he has hunted with
Cephalus, beloved by Aurora (Golding's Ovid, VII,
902 ff.). Cephalus is mentioned in a different
context at 5.1.193–4.

390 **forester** One whose task was to preserve the
game in woodland, and who would keep watch at
night for poachers; see 2.1.25 and 4.1.100 and n.
392–3 Compare the image of Neptune at
2.1.126–7.
395 SD No exit is marked for Oberon in Qq or F
here, but Rowe's addition has been generally
accepted, since Oberon returns at the beginning of
the next scene.
399 **Goblin** Puck himself, or Hobgoblin; see
2.1.40.
400 **Here comes one** As Wells notes, on the
modern stage an artificial 'fog' is often created, in
accordance with Oberon's instructions at 355–9
above, but the scene can be just as effective if the
fog is imagined by characters and audience.
402 **drawn** with drawn sword. See 255 above.
404 **plainer** more open.

Enter Demetrius.

DEMETRIUS   Lysander, speak again.
Thou runaway, thou coward, art thou fled?   405
Speak! In some bush? Where dost thou hide thy head?
PUCK Thou coward, art thou bragging to the stars,
Telling the bushes that thou look'st for wars,
And wilt not come? Come, recreant, come, thou child,
I'll whip thee with a rod. He is defiled   410
That draws a sword on thee.
DEMETRIUS   Yea, art thou there?
PUCK Follow my voice. We'll try no manhood here.

Exeunt

[Enter Lysander.]

LYSANDER He goes before me, and still dares me on;
When I come where he calls, then he is gone.
The villain is much lighter-heeled than I;   415
I followed fast, but faster he did fly,
That fallen am I in dark uneven way,
And here will rest me. (*Lies down.*) Come, thou gentle day,
For if but once thou show me thy grey light
I'll find Demetrius and revenge this spite. [*Sleeps.*]   420

Enter Puck and Demetrius.

PUCK Ho, ho, ho! Coward, why com'st thou not?
DEMETRIUS Abide me if thou dar'st, for well I wot
Thou runn'st before me, shifting every place,
And dar'st not stand nor look me in the face.
Where art thou now?
PUCK   Come hither; I am here.   425
DEMETRIUS Nay then, thou mock'st me. Thou shalt buy this dear
If ever I thy face by daylight see.

406 Speak! In some bush?] *After Capell;* Speake in some bush. Qq, F (*subst.*)   412 SD.1 *Exeunt*] Qq; *Exit* F   412 SD.2
Enter Lysander] Theobald (*Lys. comes back*); *not in* Qq, F   418 SD *Lies down*] F (*lye down*); *not in* Qq   420 SD.1
Sleeps] Capell; *not in* Qq, F   426 shalt] Q2; shat Q1

416 F has the SD *shifting places.* against this line,
anticipating 'shifting every place' at 423. It may be
from the prompt-book, but if so the compositor
seems to have fitted it in where he had space; he
could not have set it against lines 418–20, and it
relates best to 421–2.
  418 SD From F (*lye down.*), not in Qq; a similar

imperative is in Qq and F at 3.2.87, but neither Q
nor F provides similar directions for Demetrius at
430 or Helena at 436.
  421 Ho, ho, ho! Puck's taunting laughter;
compare 2.1.39.
  422 Abide Face, encounter (*OED* sv v 14).
  422 wot know.
  426 buy this dear pay dearly for this.

Now, go thy way; faintness constraineth me
To measure out my length on this cold bed.
By day's approach look to be visited. [*Sleeps.*]   430

Enter Helena.

HELENA O weary night, O long and tedious night,
            Abate thy hours, shine comforts from the east,
      That I may back to Athens by daylight
            From these that my poor company detest;
      And sleep, that sometimes shuts up sorrow's eye,   435
      Steal me awhile from mine own company. (*Sleeps.*)
PUCK   Yet but three? Come one more,
            Two of both kinds makes up four.
            Here she comes, curst and sad.
            Cupid is a knavish lad   440
            Thus to make poor females mad.

Enter Hermia.

HERMIA Never so weary, never so in woe,
            Bedabbled with the dew, and torn with briars –
      I can no further crawl, no further go;
            My legs can keep no pace with my desires.   445
      Here will I rest me till the break of day.
      Heavens shield Lysander, if they mean a fray. [*Sleeps.*]
PUCK   On the ground
                  Sleep sound.
                  I'll apply   450
                  To your eye,
            Gentle lover, remedy.
            [*Squeezes the juice on Lysander's eyes.*]
                  When thou wak'st,
                  Thou tak'st
                  True delight   455
                  In the sight
                  Of thy former lady's eye;

---

430 SD.1 *Sleeps*] *After Rowe* (*Lyes down*); *not in* Qq, F   436 SD *Sleeps*] *Capell; Sleepe* Qq, F   441 SD *Enter Hermia*]
F3; *after 439* Q2, F; *not in* Q1   447 SD *Sleeps*] *After Rowe* (*Lyes down*); *not in* Qq, F   448–57] *So Warburton; four lines in* Qq, F,
ending sound: / ...remedy. / ...tak'st / ...eye: 451 To] *Rowe; not in* Qq, F   452 SD] *After Rowe; not in* Qq, F

432 **Abate** Cut short, abridge.   439 **curst** ill-tempered.

And the country proverb known,
That every man should take his own,
In your waking shall be shown.   460
Jack shall have Jill,
Naught shall go ill:
The man shall have his mare again, and all shall be well.

[Exit Puck;] the lovers remain on stage, asleep

4.[1] *Enter* [TITANIA,] *Queen of Fairies, and* BOTTOM, *and Fairies* [*including* PEASEBLOSSOM, COBWEB *and* MUSTARDSEED;] *and the King* [OBERON] *behind them.*

TITANIA Come, sit thee down upon this flowery bed
While I thy amiable cheeks do coy,
And stick musk-roses in thy sleek smooth head,
And kiss thy fair large ears, my gentle joy.
BOTTOM Where's Peaseblossom?   5
PEASEBLOSSOM Ready.

461–2] So Johnson; one line in Qq, F   463 SD Exit Puck] Rowe; not in Qq, F   463 SD the lovers...asleep] After F (They sleepe all the Act); not in Qq   Act 4, Scene 1   4] F (Actus Quartus); not in Qq   4.1] Scene 1 / Rowe; not in Qq, F   0 SD] After Qq, F (Enter Queene of Faieries, and Clowne, and Faieries: and the King behinde them)

459–63 These lines contain several related proverbs: 'Let every man have his own' (Tilley M209), 'All shall be well and Jack shall have Jill' (Tilley A164), 'All is well and the man has his mare again' (Tilley A153). For the last Tilley gives no instance before this passage, but F. P. Wilson quotes one dating from before 1548 in *Shakespearian and other Studies*, 1969, p. 159 (so Brooks).

463 F adds the SD *They sleepe all the Act*, which has commonly been taken as meaning 'in the interval between acts' and as indicating a break here in performance introduced at some revival; the action is continuous, and the absence of this direction or of act-divisions in Qq suggests that Shakespeare did not conceive an interval here. However, 'act' seems generally to have its modern sense from the early seventeenth century, and to refer to the action, not the interval, as in *H8* Epilogue 2–3: 'Some come to take their ease, / And sleep an act or two.' It is possible, then, that this SD means 'They sleep through the action', i.e. through 4.1.1–135, and is a prompter's reminder that the lovers must remain on stage when Titania enters in 4.1; if so, it should be linked with the SD at 4.1.98

in F: *Sleepers Lye still.* See Textual Analysis, pp. 141–2 below.

Act 4, Scene 1

0 SD At the end of 3.2 the lovers all lie down and sleep without noticing one another, but their sight is fogged, and they can be grouped close together; this adds to the comedy, and makes good stage sense when 'they all start up' (SD in Qq and F at 4.1.135) and kneel together before Theseus. Part of the stage is needed for Titania and her train, with Oberon watching 'behind', and on their exit Theseus and his train enter, presumably by another door. Bottom remains asleep and unnoticed by Theseus or the lovers until 196. Thus four separate areas of the stage are used in this scene for the various groupings, and until Bottom is left alone at the end there are always between ten and fifteen actors on stage, depending on the number of fairies or attendants in the trains of Titania and Theseus.

1 flowery bed This may have been indicated by stage furnishings; see 2.2.30 SD and n.

2 coy caress.

3 musk-roses Adorning Titania's bower, as suggested at 2.1.252 and 2.2.3.

BOTTOM Scratch my head, Peaseblossom. Where's Mounsieur
Cobweb?

COBWEB Ready.

BOTTOM Mounsieur Cobweb, good Mounsieur, get you your weapons   10
in your hand, and kill me a red-hipped humble-bee on the top of
a thistle; and, good Mounsieur, bring me the honey-bag. Do not
fret yourself too much in the action, Mounsieur; and, good
Mounsieur, have a care the honey-bag break not; I would be loath
to have you overflown with a honey-bag, signior. Where's Moun-   15
sieur Mustardseed?

MUSTARDSEED Ready.

BOTTOM Give me your neaf, Mounsieur Mustardseed. Pray you, leave
your courtesy, good Mounsieur.

MUSTARDSEED What's your will?   20

BOTTOM Nothing, good Mounsieur, but to help Cavalery Peaseblossom
to scratch. I must to the barber's, Mounsieur, for methinks I am
marvellous hairy about the face. And I am such a tender ass, if my
hair do but tickle me, I must scratch.

TITANIA What, wilt thou hear some music, my sweet love?   25

BOTTOM I have a reasonable good ear in music. Let's have the tongs
and the bones.

TITANIA Or say, sweet love, what thou desir'st to eat.

BOTTOM Truly, a peck of provender, I could munch your good dry oats.
Methinks I have a great desire to a bottle of hay. Good hay, sweet   30
hay hath no fellow.

---

19 courtesy] Q2, F (courtesie); curtsie Q1   21 Peaseblossom] *Rann;* Cobwebbe Qq, F (Cobweb)   23 marvellous] F;
maruailes Q1; maruailous Q2   26–7] So Qq; F *adds* SD *Musicke Tongs, Rurall; Musicke*

7 **Mounsieur** Bottom addresses the fairies as if
they were French or Italian gentlemen; compare
'Cavalery' at 21.

18 **neaf** fist.

18–19 **leave your courtesy** stop bowing. Bottom
seeks to shake his hand (neaf), but the fairy
continues to show respect, as instructed by Titania
at 3.1.152. Brooks interprets as 'put on your hat',
citing *LLL* 5.1.98, but the context is different, and
this sense is a specialised one; did fairies in any case
wear hats?

21 **Cavalery** Cavaliere, a gentleman or gallant.
Compare 7 above and n.

21 **Peaseblossom** Cobweb (Qq, F) is an error,
perhaps Shakespeare's mistake in his MS., since
Cobweb has just been dismissed, and Peaseblossom

was appointed head-scratcher at 7. Probably it was
the alliteration that attracted the dramatist.

26–7 **tongs and the bones** Crude musical
instruments, metal tongs struck with a key, and
bone clappers held between the fingers and rattled
together.

27 Here F adds the SD *Musicke Tongs, Rurall
Musicke*, which many editors since Capell first
objected to it have regarded as contrary to
Shakespeare's intention, arguing that Titania at
once heads him off with her next question; but the
players may fittingly have introduced 'rural music'
here, as appropriate to the delusion of Titania, and
as a contrast to the 'music such as charmeth sleep'
she calls for when herself again at 80.

30 **bottle** bundle, truss.

TITANIA I have a venturous fairy that shall seek
The squirrel's hoard, and fetch thee new nuts.
BOTTOM I had rather have a handful or two of dried peas. But, I pray
you, let none of your people stir me; I have an exposition of sleep   35
come upon me.
TITANIA Sleep thou, and I will wind thee in my arms.
Fairies be gone, and be all ways away.

                                          [*Exeunt Fairies*]

So doth the woodbine the sweet honeysuckle
Gently entwist; the female ivy so   40
Enrings the barky fingers of the elm.
O, how I love thee! How I dote on thee!
                   [*They sleep.*]

                   Enter PUCK.

OBERON [*Coming forward.*]
Welcome, good Robin. Seest thou this sweet sight?
Her dotage now I do begin to pity;
For, meeting her of late behind the wood   45
Seeking sweet favours for this hateful fool,
I did upbraid her and fall out with her,
For she his hairy temples then had rounded
With coronet of fresh and fragrant flowers;
And that same dew, which sometime on the buds   50
Was wont to swell like round and orient pearls,
Stood now within the pretty flowerets' eyes
Like tears that did their own disgrace bewail.
When I had at my pleasure taunted her,
And she in mild terms begged my patience,   55

32–3] *So Hanmer; in* Q1 *divided at* hoord, / And; *in* Q2, F *at* Fairy, / …hoard, / …Nuts   38 SD] *Capell; not in*
Qq, F   42 SD.1 *They sleep*] *Capell; not in* Qq, F   42 SD.2 PUCK] *Rowe; Robin goodfellow* Qq; *Robin goodfellow and*
Oberon F   43 SD *Coming forward*] *This edn, after Capell; not in* Qq, F

32–3 Incorrectly divided at 'hoard, / And' in Q1,
and further subdivided into three short lines in Q2
and F, perhaps by attraction to Bottom's prose, or
because of the metrical uncertainty of 33, sometimes
emended to read 'fetch thee thence new nuts'.
  35 exposition of Bottom's error for 'disposition
to'.
  38 all ways in every direction.
  39 woodbine Convolvulus or bindweed. This is
the older sense of the word, which came to be
applied to various climbing plants, including the

honeysuckle, as perhaps at 2.1.251, and at *Ado*
3.1.30.
  40–1 female…elm This varies the proverbial
vine (= wife) embracing the elm (= husband);
compare *Err.* 2.2.174 (Tilley v61); Shakespeare
perhaps substituted 'ivy' because this is extra-
marital. The figure is also Biblical (Ps. 128.3) and
occurs in Golding's Ovid, XIV, 755–63.
  46 favours Flowers as love-tokens, like the
'musk-roses' at 3.
  51 orient lustrous.

I then did ask of her her changeling child,
Which straight she gave me, and her fairy sent
To bear him to my bower in Fairyland.
And now I have the boy, I will undo
This hateful imperfection of her eyes.   60
And, gentle Puck, take this transformèd scalp
From off the head of this Athenian swain,
That, he awaking when the other do,
May all to Athens back again repair,
And think no more of this night's accidents   65
But as the fierce vexation of a dream.
But first I will release the Fairy Queen.
　　　　[*Squeezing a herb on Titania's eyes.*]
Be as thou wast wont to be;
See as thou wast wont to see.
Dian's bud o'er Cupid's flower   70
Hath such force and blessèd power.
Now, my Titania, wake you, my sweet Queen!

TITANIA [*Starting up.*]
My Oberon, what visions have I seen!
Methought I was enamoured of an ass.

OBERON There lies your love.

TITANIA   How came these things to pass? 75
O, how mine eyes do loathe his visage now!

OBERON Silence awhile: Robin, take off this head.
Titania, music call, and strike more dead
Than common sleep of all these five the sense.

---

63 other] Qq, F; others *Rowe*   67 SD] *After Capell; not in* Qq, F   68 Be as] Qq (Be, as); Be thou as F
70 o'er] *Theobald, conj. Thirlby;* or Qq, F   79 sleep…these five] *So Theobald;* sleepe:…these, fine Qq, F

56–60 Compare 2.1.120–45.
63 **other** others. The Old and Middle English plural remained in common use until the eighteenth century.
64 **May all** i.e. all may.
66 **vexation** affliction, annoyance. Perhaps echoing the Biblical use of the word, as in Eccles. 2.17: 'All is vanitie, & vexation of the spirit' (Geneva). The phrase relates to the play's title, and reminds us that dreams can be nightmares, as well as delightful visions like that of Bottom; see 200–10 and p. 31 above.
70 **Dian's bud** This is the 'herb' mentioned at 2.1.184 and 3.2.366, and is sometimes identified as

Artemisia or wormwood (Artemis is another name for the goddess of chastity, Diana), or linked with the 'agnus castus', a tree thought to preserve chastity, a branch of which Diana bears in her hand in *The Flower and the Leaf*, a poem included in editions of Chaucer in Shakespeare's day.
70 **Cupid's flower** The pansy or 'little western flower' of 2.1.166–8.
77–80 Oberon calls for silence while soft music plays (in contrast to Bottom's tongs and bones (26–7) and the sprightly dance of 82–3); this is to 'charm' the sleep of Bottom, and of the lovers, so that they are not woken by the dance, and to symbolise the healing of their disordered minds.

TITANIA Music, ho, music such as charmeth sleep!   80
                    [*Soft music plays.*]
PUCK [*To Bottom, removing the ass's head*]
            Now when thou wak'st, with thine own fool's eyes peep.
OBERON Sound, music! Come, my Queen, take hands with me,
            And rock the ground whereon these sleepers be.
                        [*They dance.*]
            Now thou and I are new in amity,
            And will tomorrow midnight solemnly   85
            Dance in Duke Theseus' house triumphantly,
            And bless it to all fair prosperity.
            There shall the pairs of faithful lovers be
            Wedded, with Theseus, all in jollity.
PUCK   Fairy King, attend, and mark: 90
            I do hear the morning lark.
OBERON   Then, my Queen, in silence sad,
            Trip we after night's shade;
            We the globe can compass soon,
            Swifter than the wandering moon.   95
TITANIA   Come, my lord, and in our flight
            Tell me how it came this night
            That I sleeping here was found
            With these mortals on the ground.
                            Exeunt Oberon, Titania and Puck

Wind horns. Enter THESEUS *with* HIPPOLYTA, EGEUS, *and all his*
                                train.

80 ho] Q2, F; howe Q1   80 SD] *So NS; not in* Qq; *Musick still* F; *Still music* / Theobald   81 SD] *After NS; not in* Qq, F   81 Now when] Q1; When Q2, F   83 SD] *NS; not in* Qq, F   87 prosperity] Q1; posterity Q2, F   90 Fairy] Qq; Faire F   93 night's] Q1; the nights Q2, F   98] F *adds* SD *Sleepers Lye still*   99 SD.1 *Exeunt...Puck*] *After* Qq, F (*Exeunt*)   99 SD.2 *Wind...train*] *So* F (*Theseus, Egeus, Hippolita, and...*); *Enter* Theseus *and all his* traine. Winde horne. Qq (*hornes* Q2)

80 F added the SD *Musick still*, which probably means 'music continues', and relates back to F's SD at 27 above, as a prompter's reminder that the musicians need to keep alert. Brooks interprets it, following Staunton, as meaning still, or soft, music, citing the SD for *Still Musicke* at *AYLI* 5.4.107, but this is implausible in relation to the order of the words, and to the parallel SD at 98 in F, *Sleepers Lye still*.

82–3 The dance marks the renewal of love and harmony between Oberon and Titania, 'For dancing is love's proper exercise' and the image of concord in marriage (Sir John Davies, *Orchestra*

(1596), stanzas 17, 110–11). As Wells notes, this marks a turning-point in the action.

85 **solemnly** with appropriate ceremony. Compare 1.1.11.

86 **triumphantly** See 1.1.19 and n.

87 **prosperity** As promised at 2.1.73. Q2 and F have 'posterity', which some editors have preferred as anticipating 5.1.383 ff.

92 **sad** sober.

94–5 As Puck said he could circle the earth in forty minutes, 2.1.175–6.

99 SD.2 **Wind horns** This blowing of hunting-horns marks the coming of day, with a blast of sound

THESEUS Go, one of you, find out the forester;   100
        For now our observation is performed,
        And since we have the vaward of the day,
        My love shall hear the music of my hounds.
        Uncouple in the western valley; let them go:
        Dispatch, I say, and find the forester.   105
                              [*Exit an Attendant*]
        We will, fair Queen, up to the mountain's top,
        And mark the musical confusion
        Of hounds and echo in conjunction.
HIPPOLYTA I was with Hercules and Cadmus once,
        When in a wood of Crete they bayed the bear   110
        With hounds of Sparta: never did I hear
        Such gallant chiding; for besides the groves,
        The skies, the fountains, every region near
        Seemed all one mutual cry. I never heard
        So musical a discord, such sweet thunder.   115
THESEUS My hounds are bred out of the Spartan kind,

105 SD] *Dyce; not in* Qq, F   110 bear] Qq, F; boar *Hanmer*   114 Seemed] Q1; Seeme Q2, F

very different from the music for Oberon and
Titania; heard softly here, the sound is repeated
more loudly at 135. In Chaucer's *Knight's Tale*
Theseus loves to 'ryde / With hunte and horn, and
houndes hym besyde', especially in May (1,
1677–8).
    100 forester See 3.2.390 and n.; Theseus calls for
his gamekeeper twice in this speech, but like the
'huntsmen' of 135, he remains offstage; the sense
of a hunt about to begin is created by means of
bustle, the noise of horns and the dialogue.
    101 observation i.e. of 'The rite of May' (130);
see 1.1.167 and n.
    102 vaward early part. Literally, 'vanguard'.
    103 music of my hounds This is the topic of
the next twenty lines, and reflects the Elizabethan
concern for 'sweetnesse of cry' in a kennel of
hounds, as described in Gervase Markham's
Country Contentments (1615); compare *Shakespeare's
England*, II, 347. It is also the 'music' of day and
court-life, contrasting with the fairy music of night,
which returns at 5.1.378.
    104 Uncouple Set free for the chase. Hunting-
hounds were usually fastened together in pairs.
    109 Hercules and Cadmus As Brooks notes,
Hercules was associated with Theseus in North's
Plutarch, and is said to have fought with him against
the Amazons (North, p. 14); see also 5.1.47 and n.
Cadmus was the legendary founder of Thebes, and

is supposed to have lived long before Theseus;
neither is associated in legend with Hippolyta, and
Shakespeare seems to have added here his own
classical colouring. This is his only reference to
Cadmus.
    110–11 Crete...Sparta Places famous for
hounds, as Wells notes, citing Golding's Ovid, III,
247, where the leaders of Actaeon's pack are one 'a
hound of *Crete*, the other was of *Spart*'. Crete also
relates to Theseus as the place where he killed the
Minotaur; the story is narrated in North's Plutarch,
p. 9. See also 2.1.78–80 and n.
    110 bayed the bear i.e. brought it to bay with
their barking. Hanmer emended 'bear' to 'boar',
because he doubted whether there were bears in
Crete, but this is as idle as to seek them on the
sea-coast of Bohemia (*WT* 3.3.95 ff.). Shakespeare
refers to 'the boar of Thessaly' (*Ant.* 4.13.2, and see
119, 123 below), and in North's Plutarch Theseus
is said to have helped Meleager 'to kill the wild Bore
of *Calydonia*' (North, p. 16). Shakespeare's Adonis
hunted the bear (*Venus and Adonis* 883–4), and we
may just as easily imagine Hippolyta doing so.
    112 chiding yelping.
    115 So musical a discord This passage relates
to the resolution of all discords in the 'music' of the
last act, and is echoed, as Wells notes, in Theseus's
question at 5.1.60: 'How shall we find the concord
of this discord?' See also 140 below.

So flewed, so sanded; and their heads are hung
With ears that sweep away the morning dew;
Crook-kneed, and dewlapped like Thessalian bulls;
Slow in pursuit, but matched in mouth like bells,   120
Each under each. A cry more tuneable
Was never hallooed to nor cheered with horn
In Crete, in Sparta, nor in Thessaly.
Judge when you hear. But soft, what nymphs are these?

EGEUS My lord, this is my daughter here asleep,   125
And this Lysander; this Demetrius is,
This Helena, old Nedar's Helena.
I wonder of their being here together.

THESEUS No doubt they rose up early to observe
The rite of May, and hearing our intent   130
Came here in grace of our solemnity.
But speak, Egeus; is not this the day
That Hermia should give answer of her choice?

EGEUS It is, my lord.

THESEUS Go, bid the huntsmen wake them with their horns.   135
Shout within; wind horns; [the lovers] all start up.
Good morrow, friends. Saint Valentine is past;
Begin these woodbirds but to couple now?
[The lovers kneel.]

LYSANDER Pardon, my lord.

THESEUS   I pray you all, stand up.
I know you two are rival enemies:
How comes this gentle concord in the world,   140

---

122 hallooed] *So Capell;* hollows Qq; hallowed F; holla'd *Malone*   125 this is] Q2, F, this Q1   128 their] Q1; this
Q2, F   130 rite] *Pope;* right Qq, F   135 SD] Qq (*Shoute within: they all start up. Winde hornes*); Hornes and they
wake. Shout within, they all start up F   137 SD] *After Capell; not in* Qq, F

---

117 **flewed** 'Flews' are the large hanging chaps of a hound.

117 **sanded** sandy-coloured.

120 **matched...bells** Gervase Markham describes a 'consort' of hounds, with basses, counter-tenors with 'loud ringing mouthes', and dogs with 'plaine, sweet mouthes', which together 'make your cry perfect'; see 103 above and n.

121 **tuneable** melodious.

125 **this is** Corrected in Q2 from 'this' (Q1), and required by the metre; compositors can easily omit repeated letters (such omission is called haplography).

127 **Nedar's** See 1.1.107 and n.

128 **wonder of** The usual construction, from Old English, until the seventeenth century; since replaced by 'wonder at'.

129–30 **observe...May** See 1.1.167 and n.

131 **in grace of our solemnity** to honour our marriage ceremony. Compare 1.1.11.

132–3 **day...choice** See 1.1.83–6.

136–7 **Saint...now** It was proverbial that birds chose their partners on Saint Valentine's Day, 14 February; see Tilley s66.

138 **stand up** There is no SD in Qq or F, but the lovers presumably kneel to beg pardon for fleeing from Athens; Theseus is naturally surprised to find them grouped together; see 4.1. o SD and n.

            That hatred is so far from jealousy
            To sleep by hate, and fear no enmity?
LYSANDER My lord, I shall reply amazedly,
            Half sleep, half waking; but as yet, I swear,
            I cannot truly say how I came here.   145
            But as I think (for truly would I speak)
            And now I do bethink me, so it is –
            I came with Hermia hither. Our intent
            Was to be gone from Athens, where we might
            Without the peril of the Athenian law –   150
EGEUS Enough, enough, my lord; you have enough –
            I beg the law, the law upon his head!
            They would have stol'n away, they would, Demetrius,
            Thereby to have defeated you and me,
            You of your wife, and me of my consent,   155
            Of my consent that she should be your wife.
DEMETRIUS My lord, fair Helen told me of their stealth,
            Of this their purpose hither to this wood;
            And I in fury hither followed them,
            Fair Helena in fancy following me.   160
            But, my good lord, I wot not by what power
            (But by some power it is), my love to Hermia,
            Melted as the snow, seems to me now
            As the remembrance of an idle gaud
            Which in my childhood I did dote upon;   165
            And all the faith, the virtue of my heart,
            The object and the pleasure of mine eye,
            Is only Helena. To her, my lord,
            Was I betrothed ere I saw Hermia;
            But like a sickness did I loathe this food.   170
            But, as in health come to my natural taste,

---

150 law –] *After* Q1 (law,); Law. Q2, F   160 following] Q1; *followed* Q2, F   162–4] *So Pope;* Qq, F *divide* love,
/ …snowe) / …gaude,   169 saw] *Steevens;* see Qq, F

141 jealousy mistrust.
144 sleep Probably an aphetic form = asleep.
150 Without beyond, outside.
154 defeated cheated.
160 fancy love. See 1.1.155 and n.
161 wot know.
164 idle gaud worthless plaything.
169 saw The use of 'see' (Qq, F) as a past tense has survived as a vulgarism, and possibly this is what

Shakespeare wrote; NS noted the same usage in the quarto of *LLL* 4.1.70–1: 'he came, see, and overcame'.

170–1 sickness…health Compare the proverb 'Health is not valued till sickness comes' (Tilley H290). Demetrius seems to move from 'I loathed this food like a disease', via an unstated 'and as if I were ill', to 'But now I am well again.'

Now I do wish it, love it, long for it,
And will for evermore be true to it.

THESEUS Fair lovers, you are fortunately met.
Of this discourse we more will hear anon.   175
Egeus, I will overbear your will;
For in the temple, by and by, with us
These couples shall eternally be knit.
And, for the morning now is something worn,
Our purposed hunting shall be set aside.   180
Away with us to Athens. Three and three,
We'll hold a feast in great solemnity.
Come, Hippolyta.

Exit Theseus with Hippolyta, Egeus, and his train

DEMETRIUS These things seem small and undistinguishable,
Like far-off mountains turnèd into clouds.   185

HERMIA Methinks I see these things with parted eye,
When everything seems double.

HELENA   So methinks;
And I have found Demetrius, like a jewel,
Mine own, and not mine own.

DEMETRIUS   Are you sure
That we are awake? It seems to me   190
That yet we sleep, we dream. Do not you think
The Duke was here, and bid us follow him?

HERMIA Yea, and my father.

HELENA   And Hippolyta.

LYSANDER And he did bid us follow to the temple.

DEMETRIUS Why, then, we are awake. Let's follow him,   195
And by the way let us recount our dreams.

Exeunt lovers

---

172 I do] Q1 do I Q2, F   175 more will hear] Q1 (here); will heare more Q2; shall heare more F   182–3] *So* Q2, F; *one line in* Q1   183 SD] *Capell, after* F (*Exit Duke and Lords.*); *not in* Q1; *Exit.* Q2   189–90 Are...awake] Qq; *not in* F   194 did bid] Q1; bid Q2, F   195–6] *So Rowe³; as prose* Qq, F   196 let us] Q2, F; lets Q1   196 SD] F (*Bottome wakes. Exit Louers*); *not in* Q1; *Exit* Q2

177–8 The weddings take place during the day (see 4.2.12–13), between the end of this scene and 5.1, when the lovers enter 'full of joy and mirth' (5.1.28). A whole day intervenes between the morning of this scene and evening of 5.1, its passage marked by 4.2.
182 solemnity celebration. See 85 above, 1.1.11 and n., and 5.1.347–8.
186 parted divided, i.e. with the eyes out of focus.

188–9 jewel...not mine own i.e. she seizes on the jewel she has found as her own, but is still not certain whether someone else may lay claim to it.
189–90 Are you sure...awake This phrase was omitted from F, and perhaps deliberately cut. It is metrically irregular, whereas 'Mine own and not mine own. It seems to me' makes a perfect blank-verse line.

Bottom wakes.

BOTTOM When my cue comes, call me, and I will answer. My next is
'Most fair Pyramus'. Heigh ho! Peter Quince? Flute the bellows-
mender? Snout the tinker? Starveling? God's my life! Stolen hence
and left me asleep! I have had a most rare vision. I have had a dream,   200
past the wit of man to say what dream it was. Man is but an ass
if he go about to expound this dream. Methought I was – there is
no man can tell what. Methought I was – and methought I had – but
man is but a patched fool if he will offer to say what methought
I had. The eye of man hath not heard, the ear of man hath not seen,   205
man's hand is not able to taste, his tongue to conceive, nor his heart
to report what my dream was! I will get Peter Quince to write a
ballad of this dream; it shall be called 'Bottom's Dream', because
it hath no bottom; and I will sing it in the latter end of a play, before
the Duke. Peradventure, to make it the more gracious, I shall sing   210
it at her death.   *Exit*

198–9 bellows-mender] Q2; bellowes menders Q1   200 have had] Qq; had F   202 to expound] Q2; expound Q1
204 a patched] F; patcht a Qq   208 ballad] F4; Ballet Qq, F   211 SD *Exit*] Q2; *not in* Q1

197 Bottom waking returns to the moment before
his 'translation' at 3.1.85, as if he is still rehearsing
Pyramus.

198 Heigh ho! Yawning. Wells suggests there
may also be a last vestige of the ass's 'Hee-haw!'

200 rare vision Echoing Titania's 'What visions
have I seen!' (4.1.73), and contrasting with the
'fruitless vision' suffered by the lovers (3.2.371); see
also 5.1.404.

204 a patched fool So F; Qq read 'patcht a
foole', which may be correct, meaning 'shown by
his patches to be a fool', but the construction is
awkward, and F's transposition makes for better
rhythm and sense. Fools seem to have worn
parti-coloured coats rather than patched in the sense
of patchwork (see Leslie Hotson, *Shakespeare's
Motley*, 1952), but the visual effect was similar
enough for 'Patch', the name of the famous fool of
Cardinal Wolsey, to become a common term for a
fool, probably assimilating at the same time an
anglicisation of the Italian 'pazzo', 'a foole, a patch,
a madman', as John Florio defines the word in his
Italian–English dictionary, *Queen Anna's New
World of Words* (1611).

205–7 The eye of man…dream was Bottom's
garbled reference to 1 Cor. 2.9–10 has more point
than he realises; see p. 35 above. The text in the
Bishops' Bible runs: 'The eye of man hath not
seene, and the eare hath not heard, neither have
entred into the heart of man, the things which God
hath prepared for them that love him. But God hath
revealed them unto us by his spirit; for the spirit
searcheth all things, yea the deepe things of God!'
The mechanicals are given to confounding the
different senses, of sight and hearing especially;
compare 3.1.74, 5.1.187–8 and 312–17.

208 ballad In an age without newspapers,
notable events were often commemorated in
ballads, printed and issued in the form of a
broadsheet.

209 hath no bottom (1) has no reality or
foundation, (2) is unfathomably profound.

209–11 a play…her death Bottom, like the
lovers, is confused and has double vision: he says
'a play' (not 'the play') in relation to Titania, and
'her death' with reference to Thisbe.

210 gracious graceful, appealing.

4.[2] *Enter* QUINCE, FLUTE, SNOUT *and* STARVELING.

QUINCE Have you sent to Bottom's house? Is he come home yet?

STARVELING He cannot be heard of. Out of doubt he is transported.

FLUTE If he come not, then the play is marred. It goes not forward.
    Doth it?

QUINCE It is not possible. You have not a man in all Athens able to   5
    discharge Pyramus but he.

FLUTE No, he hath simply the best wit of any handicraft man in Athens.

QUINCE Yea, and the best person, too; and he is a very paramour for
    a sweet voice.

FLUTE You must say 'paragon'. A paramour is (God bless us!) a thing   10
    of naught.

Enter SNUG *the joiner.*

SNUG Masters, the Duke is coming from the temple, and there is two
    or three lords and ladies more married. If our sport had gone
    forward, we had all been made men.

FLUTE O, sweet bully Bottom! Thus hath he lost sixpence a day during   15
    his life: he could not have 'scaped sixpence a day. And the Duke
    had not given him sixpence a day for playing Pyramus, I'll be
    hanged. He would have deserved it. Sixpence a day in Pyramus,
    or nothing.

Act 4, Scene 2   4.2] *Capell; not in* Qq, F   0 SD] F; *Enter* Quince, Flute, Thisby *and the rabble* Qq   2 SH STARVELING]
F *(Staru.)*; *Flut.* Q1; *Flute* Q2   3 SH FLUTE] *Rowe³*; *Thys.* Qq, F *(so throughout scene)*   3 forward. Doth] Q1;
forward, doth Q2, F   11 naught] F2; nought Qq, F

Act 4, Scene 2

4.2 This scene returns us to Athens, and also marks the passage of a day between 4.1, which takes place at daybreak, when 'the morning lark' is heard (4.1.91), and 5.1, which is set between supper and bedtime (5.1.34). Bottom reports that the Duke has dined (26–7), so the notional time of this scene is the afternoon.

0 SD This is from F, except that, following Q, F names Flute and Thisbe; in Qq this SD reads 'Enter Quince, Flute, Thisby *and the rabble*'. Flute of course plays Thisbe, and the confusion may be due to Shakespeare's oversight, since there are also in Qq consecutive speech headings for *Flut.* and *Thys.* at 2 and 3.

2 SH STARVELING F's correction of *Flut.* (Qq) may well be from the prompt-book; see 0 SD n. Flute is named *Thys* or *This* in speech headings throughout the scene in Qq and F.

2 transported carried away (as to another realm), and enraptured. This may be Starveling's happy error for 'translated', meaning 'transformed', as at 3.1.98.

3–4 forward. Doth it? So Q1; 'forward, doth it?' is smoother, but the punctuation in Q1 may be deliberate, reflecting Flute's uncertainty.

6 discharge perform.

7 wit intellect.

8 person presence, or personal appearance.

10–11 thing of naught something wicked or immoral. (The modern 'naughty' is a much milder term.)

14 made men i.e. our fortunes would have been made.

15 sixpence a day Corresponding roughly to the wages of a skilful craftsman at the time; see *Shakespeare's England*, I, 331.

16 And If.

Enter BOTTOM.

BOTTOM Where are these lads? Where are these hearts?   20
QUINCE Bottom! O most courageous day! O most happy hour!
BOTTOM Masters, I am to discourse wonders – but ask me not what;
        for if I tell you, I am not true Athenian. I will tell you everything,
        right as it fell out.
QUINCE Let us hear, sweet Bottom.   25
BOTTOM Not a word of me. All that I will tell you is – that the Duke
        hath dined. Get your apparel together, good strings to your beards,
        new ribbons to your pumps: meet presently at the palace, every man
        look o'er his part. For the short and the long is, our play is preferred.
        In any case, let Thisbe have clean linen; and let not him that plays   30
        the lion pare his nails, for they shall hang out for the lion's claws.
        And, most dear actors, eat no onions nor garlic; for we are to utter
        sweet breath, and I do not doubt but to hear them say it is a sweet
        comedy. No more words. Away! Go, away!
                                                              Exeunt

5.[1] *Enter* THESEUS, HIPPOLYTA, PHILOSTRATE, *Lords and Attendants.*

HIPPOLYTA 'Tis strange, my Theseus, that these lovers speak of.
THESEUS More strange than true. I never may believe

---

23 not] Qq; no F   24 right as] Qq; as F   34 Go, away!] *So Theobald;* go away. Qq, F   Act 5, Scene 1 5] F (*Actus Quintus*); *not in* Qq   5.1] *Scene 1 / Rowe; not in* Qq, F   0 SD] *After* F (*Enter Theseus, Hippolita, Egeus and his Lords*); *Enter* Theseus, Hyppolita, *and* Philostrate Qq

---

20 hearts good fellows. (Compare the phrase 'hearts of oak'.)

21 courageous Quince seems to think a long word is better than a short one, and probably means 'brave', or splendid, as in Miranda's 'O brave new world' (*Temp.* 5.1.183).

27 strings to your beards i.e. to tie on false beards with. Recalling Bottom's interest in stage-beards, 1.2.71–6.

28 pumps Light shoes, worn in masques, and associated, according to Linthicum, pp. 253–4, 'with comedy, as pantofles were associated with tragedy'; the inappropriateness of their footwear perhaps enhanced the burlesque effect of the actors in 'Pyramus and Thisbe'.

28 presently immediately.

29 preferred recommended. We are given the impression that their play is to be staged, although Theseus only makes his selection at 5.1.76.

Act 5, Scene 1

5.1 The scene takes place at night, after supper (34), and ends in moonlight (350), while 'Moonshine' is also represented on stage by Starveling. The day that intervenes between the waking of the lovers at 4.1.135 and this evening festivity is rapidly passed over in 4.2.

0 SD The play comes full circle, and Act 5 opens like Act 1, probably with a similar processional entry, and with chairs of state again provided for Theseus and Hippolyta as rulers of Athens; see 1.1.0 SD and n. Philostrate has a speaking-part here as Theseus's master of ceremonies; in F this role is assigned to Egeus, whose part in Qq ends in 4.1. The change in F suggests that on stage Egeus doubled here as Philostrate, whose only other function, that of making an exit at 1.1.15, could have been assigned to any attendant on Theseus. Shakespeare, however, seems deliberately to have kept the crusty and complaining Egeus out of the 'joy and mirth' of Act 5.

These antique fables, nor these fairy toys.
Lovers and madmen have such seething brains,
Such shaping fantasies, that apprehend   5
More than cool reason ever comprehends.
The lunatic, the lover, and the poet
Are of imagination all compact:
One sees more devils than vast hell can hold;
That is the madman. The lover, all as frantic,   10
Sees Helen's beauty in a brow of Egypt.
The poet's eye, in a fine frenzy rolling,
Doth glance from heaven to earth, from earth to heaven;
And as imagination bodies forth
The forms of things unknown, the poet's pen   15
Turns them to shapes, and gives to airy nothing
A local habitation and a name.
Such tricks hath strong imagination
That if it would but apprehend some joy,
It comprehends some bringer of that joy;   20
Or in the night, imagining some fear,
How easy is a bush supposed a bear?
HIPPOLYTA But all the story of the night told over,

---

3 antique] Q; anticke Q2, F   5–6 apprehend…than] *Theobald;* apprehend more / Then Qq, F   6–8] *As* Q2, F; *two lines in* Q1, *divided at* lunatick, / The   12–14] *As Rowe; divided in* Q1 *at* glance / From…heaven. And as / Imagination; *in* Q2, F *at* glance / From…heaven. / And as imagination   14–15] *As Rowe³;* Imagination…things Q1; And as…things Q2, F   15–18] *As Rowe³; divided in* Qq, F *at* shapes, / …habitation, / …imagination,   16 airy] Qq (ayery Q1); aire F

---

3 **antique** Perhaps quibbling on 'antic' = grotesque.

3 **fairy toys** idle tales about fairies.

5–83 In Q eight passages of verse between 5 and 83 are mislined or printed virtually as prose. These have been explained as marginal insertions by Shakespeare in his MS.; see the Textual Analysis, p. 137 below.

5 **fantasies** extravagant fancies or imaginations.

5–6 **apprehend…comprehends** i.e. fancy seizes on, conceives, more than reason understands.

7 **lunatic** The word still retained its sense of insanity brought on by changes of the moon (from Latin *luna* = moon).

8 **compact** composed.

11 **Helen's…brow of Egypt** Alluding to the legendary beauty of Helen of Troy. In the play Demetrius begins by seeing beauty in Hermia, and Lysander rejects Hermia as an 'Ethiop' in favour of the fair Helen (3.2.257); 'of Egypt' probably refers to the swarthy colouring of a gipsy; gipsies

were thought to come from Egypt, and the word originated as an aphetic form of 'Egyptian'.

12 **fine frenzy** The image of poets as divinely inspired and so out of their wits derives from Plato's *Ion* and *Phaedrus,* as Brooks notes, and passes into English as poetic rapture (Latin *furor poeticus*; *OED* Frenzy *sb* 2).

19–20 **apprehend…comprehends** See 5–6 above and n.; here 'comprehends' perhaps means 'includes in the conception'.

22 Proverbial (Tilley B737, B738). At 3.2.406–8 Demetrius supposed a bush to be Lysander.

23–6 For Hippolyta the consistency of the stories the lovers have told, and the fact that their minds were all changed together, are more convincing testimony than delusions of the imagination, and what they say grows into a certainty; the word 'constancy' also means 'fidelity' and refers to the newfound steadfastness of love confirmed in marriage.

And all their minds transfigured so together,
More witnesseth than fancy's images,   25
And grows to something of great constancy;
But howsoever, strange and admirable.

Enter the lovers: LYSANDER, DEMETRIUS, HERMIA *and* HELENA.

THESEUS Here come the lovers, full of joy and mirth.
　　　　Joy, gentle friends, joy and fresh days of love
　　　　Accompany your hearts!
LYSANDER   More than to us   30
　　　　Wait in your royal walks, your board, your bed!
THESEUS Come now: what masques, what dances shall we have
　　　　To wear away this long age of three hours
　　　　Between our after-supper and bedtime?
　　　　Where is our usual manager of mirth?   35
　　　　What revels are in hand? Is there no play
　　　　To ease the anguish of a torturing hour?
　　　　Call Philostrate.
PHILOSTRATE   Here, mighty Theseus.
THESEUS Say, what abridgement have you for this evening?
　　　　What masque, what music? How shall we beguile   40
　　　　The lazy time if not with some delight?
PHILOSTRATE [*Giving him a paper.*]
　　　　There is a brief how many sports are ripe.
　　　　Make choice of which your highness will see first.

27 SD] Qq, F (*Enter Lovers...*)   29–30] *As* F2; *divided in* Qq, F *at* daies / of   30–1] *As* F2; *prose in* Qq, F
33–6] *As* Q2; *three lines in* Q1, *divided at* betweene / Or...manager / Of   34 our] F; *or* Qq   37–8] *As* Q2;
one line in Q1   38 Call Philostrate] Qq; Call Egeus. F   38 SH PHILOSTRATE] Qq; Ege. F (*so through scene, except*
at 76)   42 SD] *Theobald; not in* Qq, F

27 **admirable** to be wondered at, marvellous.
32 **masques** Entertainments focused on masked
dancers, which Ben Jonson later developed in the
early seventeenth century into lavish spectacles with
a strong literary content.
34 **after-supper** Supper was a main meal, taken
commonly about 5.30 p.m., according to William
Harrison's *Description of England*, included in
Raphael Holinshed's *Chronicles of England* (1587),
so that even a lengthy meal would allow for three
hours more until bedtime. Some directors have
taken this line as a clue to seating Theseus,

Hippolyta and the lovers in this scene at a table,
spread with wine and dessert, from which they
watch the interlude of 'Pyramus and Thisbe'.
35–6 **manager...revels** Echoing the title of Sir
Edmund Tilney, Queen Elizabeth's Master of the
Revels, who, like Philostrate, selected plays for
court performance, and saw them in rehearsal (see
68 below).
39 **abridgement** (1) something to make the time
seem shorter, (2) shortened version of a longer work.
Both meanings are possible.
42 **brief** summary.

THESEUS [*Reading.*]

> 'The battle with the Centaurs, to be sung
> By an Athenian eunuch to the harp' –   45
> We'll none of that; that have I told my love
> In glory of my kinsman, Hercules.
> [*Reading.*] 'The riot of the tipsy Bacchanals,
> Tearing the Thracian singer in their rage' –
> That is an old device, and it was played   50
> When I from Thebes came last a conqueror.
> [*Reading.*] 'The thrice three Muses mourning for the death
> Of learning, late deceased in beggary' –
> That is some satire keen and critical,
> Not sorting with a nuptial ceremony.   55
> [*Reading.*] 'A tedious brief scene of young Pyramus
> And his love Thisbe, very tragical mirth' –
> Merry and tragical? Tedious and brief?
> That is hot ice and wondrous strange snow!
> How shall we find the concord of this discord?   60

---

44 SH THESEUS] Qq; *Lis.* F (= *Lysander*)   44 SD] *Theobald; not in* Qq, F   46 We'll] Qq (Weele); *The.* Wee'l F
48 SD] *Theobald; not in* Qq, F   48 The riot] Qq; *Lis.* The riot F   50 That] Qq; *The.* That F   52 SD] *Theobald;
not in* Qq, F   52 The] Qq; *Lis.* The F   54 That] Qq; *The.* That F   56 SD] *Theobald; not in* Qq, F   56 A] Qq;
Lis. A F   58 Merry] Qq; *The.* Merry F   58–60] *As Theobald; divided in* Q1 *at* Ise, / And...côcord / Of; *in*
Q2 *at* Ice, / And...con- / cord; *prose in* F

44 In Qq Theseus reads the list, but in F the actual reading (44–5, 48–9, 52–3 and 56–7) is assigned to Lysander. This change probably comes from the prompt-book, and may indicate the way it was performed at the Globe. It is theatrically effective, and could reflect a revision by Shakespeare, but Q shows his original conception.
44 battle with the Centaurs The story is told by Nestor in Golding's Ovid, XII, 236–599, referring to Hercules only at the end.
47 kinsman, Hercules A detail taken from North's Plutarch, p. 4; in the 'Life of Theseus', Hercules is said to have been the model for Theseus, 'the rather, because they were neere Kinsemen, being cosins removed by the mother side'. Compare 4.1.109 and n.
48–9 Bacchanals...Thracian singer Orpheus, the Thracian poet, was torn to pieces by a 'drunken rout' of women, followers of Bacchus, in their frenzy; the story is told in Golding's Ovid, XI, 1–93.
50 device show, entertainment.
51 from Thebes...conqueror In Chaucer's *Knight's Tale* Theseus returns to Athens in triumph with two Theban princes, Palamon and Arcite, as his prisoners.

52–3 Poets and scholars were proverbially poor (Tilley M1316), and complaints about the neglect of learning and the arts were common enough to make it unlikely that any specific allusion is intended here. Some believe there may be a reference to the writer and dramatist Robert Greene, who died in poverty in 1592, and that the subject may have been suggested by the title of Spenser's poem *The Teares of the Muses* (1591), which is a complaint, not a keen satire.
55 sorting with appropriate to.
57 tragical mirth See 1.2.9–10 and n. Perhaps Shakespeare was not simply mocking the 'grosse absurdities' of old plays attacked by Sidney in his *Apology for Poetry* (*Elizabethan Critical Essays*, ed. G. G. Smith, 2 vols., 1904, II, 199), but specifically thinking of *Cambyses*, a play he made fun of in *1H4* 2.4.387 (so Brooks).
60 How...discord? See 4.1.115 and n. The question relates to the whole play; the discords of Oberon and Titania and the lovers having been resolved into concord in 4.1, the play of Pyramus and Thisbe offers a new set of incongruous conjunctions reflecting as in a distorting mirror aspects of the earlier discords; see pp. 38–9 above.

PHILOSTRATE A play there is, my lord, some ten words long,
            Which is as 'brief' as I have known a play,
            But by ten words, my lord, it is too long,
            Which makes it 'tedious'. For in all the play
            There is not one word apt, one player fitted.   65
            And 'tragical', my noble lord, it is,
            For Pyramus therein doth kill himself,
            Which when I saw rehearsed, I must confess,
            Made mine eyes water; but more 'merry' tears
            The passion of loud laughter never shed.   70
THESEUS What are they that do play it?
PHILOSTRATE Hard-handed men that work in Athens here,
            Which never laboured in their minds till now;
            And now have toiled their unbreathed memories
            With this same play against your nuptial.   75
THESEUS And we will hear it.
PHILOSTRATE   No, my noble lord,
            It is not for you. I have heard it over,
            And it is nothing, nothing in the world,
            Unless you can find sport in their intents,
            Extremely stretched, and conned with cruel pain,   80
            To do you service.
THESEUS   I will hear that play;
            For never anything can be amiss
            When simpleness and duty tender it.
            Go bring them in; and take your places, ladies.
                                    [*Exit Philostrate*]
HIPPOLYTA I love not to see wretchedness o'ercharged,   85
            And duty in his service perishing.
THESEUS Why, gentle sweet, you shall see no such thing.
HIPPOLYTA He says they can do nothing in this kind.
THESEUS The kinder we, to give them thanks for nothing.

66–70] *As* F2; *five lines in* Qq, F (*Pyramus*, / *Therein…saw* / *Rehearst…water*; / *But…laughter* / *Never*)   76–8 No
…world,] *As Rowe³; two lines in* Qq, F, *divided at* heard / It   81–3 I…it] *As Rowe³; two lines in* Qq, F, *divided*
at thing / Can   84 SD] *Pope; not in* Qq, F

68 saw rehearsed See 35–6 above and n.
70 passion Used of any strong feeling; compare
John 3.3.46–7: 'merriment – / A passion hateful to
my purposes' (so Wells).
74 toiled wearied with labour.
74 unbreathed unpractised.
79–80 intents…conned 'intents' means 'en-
deavours' but slides perhaps into 'the subject or

theme to be treated in a discourse' (*OED* Intent
sb 7); 'stretched and conned' refer to the play and
its language, 'strained beyond normal limits and
pored over'.
83 simpleness artless sincerity (so Kittredge).
85 wretchedness o'ercharged the lowly (i.e. in
ability and social standing) overburdened.

Our sport shall be to take what they mistake;   90
And what poor duty cannot do, noble respect
Takes it in might, not merit.
Where I have come, great clerks have purposèd
To greet me with premeditated welcomes,
Where I have seen them shiver and look pale,   95
Make periods in the midst of sentences,
Throttle their practised accent in their fears,
And in conclusion dumbly have broke off,
Not paying me a welcome. Trust me, sweet,
Out of this silence yet I picked a welcome,   100
And in the modesty of fearful duty
I read as much as from the rattling tongue
Of saucy and audacious eloquence.
Love, therefore, and tongue-tied simplicity
In least speak most, to my capacity.   105

[Enter Philostrate.]

PHILOSTRATE So please your grace, the Prologue is addressed.
THESEUS Let him approach.
                    Flourish of trumpets.

                    Enter QUINCE *as Prologue.*

QUINCE   If we offend, it is with our good will.

105 SD] *Pope; not in* Qq, F   107 SH THESEUS] Qq, F *(Duk / or / Duke / through scene)*   107 SD.1 *Flourish of Trumpets]* F *(Flor, Trum.); not in* Qq   107 SD.2 *Enter…Prologue]* F *(Enter the Prologue. Quince); Enter the Prologue* Qq

90 **take** (1) accept, (2) understand.
91 **noble respect** magnanimous or generous consideration.
92 **Takes…merit** Receives it in terms of what they can do, rather than the worth of what is done. The phrase relates to the common proverbs 'To take the will for the deed', and 'Everything is as it is taken' (Tilley W393, T31). The short line is unusual in this play, and the irregularity has led some to suspect corruption of the text, but it seems merely to mark a pause or modulation in Theseus's speech.
93 **clerks** scholars. Brooks cites two instances of scholars feeling 'fear and disability' in addresses to Queen Elizabeth, at Warwick in 1572 and Norwich in 1578, both recorded in J. Nichols, *The Progresses and Public Processions of Queen Elizabeth*, 3 vols., 1823 edn, I, 311–12, 315–16, II, 155. There is no need to look for a specific allusion, but if Queen Elizabeth saw the play she could have taken

this passage as a compliment to her; see p. 3 above.
96 **Make periods…sentences** As Quince shortly does in delivering his prologue, 108–117.
101 **modesty** deference.
101 **fearful** timid, or frightened.
105 **to my capacity** as far as I can judge.
106 **addressed** ready. But the word carried the special sense 'made ready with the proper clothing or costume' (*OED* Address *v* 4), to the extent that it is etymologically linked to 'dress', and this may be intended here; compare *Per.* 2.3.94.
107 SD.1 *Flourish of Trumpets* From F (*Flor. Trum.*), not in Qq, this SD no doubt represents stage practice; Dekker in *The Gull's Hornbook* (1609, ch. VI) refers to the Prologue giving 'the trumpets their Cue, that hees upon point to enter' (cited by Cuningham).
108–17 Quince apparently reads from a scroll, garbling the sense by mistaking the punctuation, a

That you should think, we come not to offend,
But with good will. To show our simple skill,   110
That is the true beginning of our end.
┌Consider then, we come but in despite.
We do not come as minding to content you,
Our true intent is. All for your delight,
We are not here. That you should here repent you,   115
The actors are at hand; and by their show
You shall know all that you are like to know.

THESEUS This fellow doth not stand upon points.

LYSANDER He hath rid his prologue like a rough colt; he knows not
the stop. A good moral, my lord; it is not enough to speak, but to   120
speak true.

HIPPOLYTA Indeed, he hath played on this prologue like a child on
a recorder – a sound, but not in government.

THESEUS His speech was like a tangled chain, nothing impaired, but
all disordered. Who is next?   125

Enter with a Trumpeter before them [BOTTOM *as*] *Pyramus,*
[FLUTE *as*] *Thisbe,* [SNOUT *as*] *Wall,* [STARVELING *as*] *Moonshine and*
[SNUG *as*] *Lion.*

QUINCE (*as Prologue*)
Gentles, perchance you wonder at this show,
But wonder on, till truth make all things plain.

122 this] Qq; his F   125 SD.1 *Enter...before them*] F (*Tawyer with a Trumpet before them*); *not in* Qq   125 SD.1–3
BOTTOM *as...Lion*] Wells, *after* Qq, F (*Enter* Pyramus, *and* Thisby, *and* Wall, *and* Moonshine, *and* Lyon Q1; ...Thisby,
Wall...Q2, F)   126 SH QUINCE (*as Prologue*)] *Prologue* Qq, F

device used to comic effect previously in Nicholas
Udall's *Ralph Roister Doister* 3.4 (*c.* 1553). The
Prologue is not in 'eight and six' or in 'eight and
eight' (see 3.1.18–20) as promised, but in two
quatrains ending with a couplet, like the continua-
tion, 126–50.

109–10 Correctly read = 'That you should think
we come, not to offend, / But with good will to show
our simple skill'.

112 in despite in ill-will, to vex you.

116, 126 show This may refer merely to the
appearance of the actors, but may also, as Wells
notes, mean that the actors present a tableau, or
dumb-show miming something of the action to
come, on their entry at 125 and during the rest of
the Prologue; compare Ophelia's use of the word
'show', *Ham.* 3.2.139, 143.

118 stand upon points trouble himself about
punctuation (or trifling details). i.e. he is not
'punctilious'.

120 stop (1) sudden check in managing a horse,
(2) mark of punctuation.

123 in government under control.

125 SD.1 *Trumpeter* Not in Qq; F has *Tawyer
with a Trumpet before them*, i.e. William Tawyer
who, when he died in 1625, was listed as being in
the service of John Heminge, Shakespeare's
fellow-actor and sharer in the King's Men. This
entry presumably comes from a prompt-book, and
may relate to a revival of the play; see Textual
Analysis, p. 140 below.

127 truth...plain Varying the common proverb
'Truth will come to light' (Tilley T591).

> This man is Pyramus, if you would know;
> This beauteous lady Thisbe is, certain.
> This man with lime and rough-cast doth present   130
> Wall, that vile wall which did these lovers sunder;
> And through Wall's chink, poor souls, they are content
> To whisper – at the which let no man wonder.
> This man with lanthorn, dog, and bush of thorn,
> Presenteth Moonshine; for, if you will know,   135
> By moonshine did these lovers think no scorn
> To meet at Ninus' tomb, there, there to woo.
> This grisly beast, which Lion hight by name,
> The trusty Thisbe, coming first by night,
> Did scare away, or rather did affright;   140
> And as she fled, her mantle she did fall,
> Which Lion vile with bloody mouth did stain.
> Anon comes Pyramus, sweet youth and tall,
> And finds his trusty Thisbe's mantle slain;
> Whereat with blade, with bloody, blameful blade,   145
> He bravely broached his boiling bloody breast;
> And Thisbe, tarrying in mulberry shade,
> His dagger drew, and died. For all the rest,
> Let Lion, Moonshine, Wall, and lovers twain
> At large discourse, while here they do remain.   150

Exeunt Quince, Bottom, Flute, Snug and Starveling

THESEUS   I wonder if the lion be to speak?

DEMETRIUS   No wonder, my lord; one lion may, when many asses do.

SNOUT (*as Wall*)

> In this same interlude it doth befall
> That I, one Snout by name, present a wall;

---

144 his trusty] Qq; his F   150 SD] *So* F (*Exit all but Wall*); *Exit* Lyon, Thysby, *and* Mooneshine Qq *(after 152)*
153 SH SNOUT (*as Wall*)] *Wells; Wall* Qq, F   154 Snout] F; *Flute* Qq

129 certain Accented for comic effect on the second syllable; an archaism, like 'hight' at 138.

134 lanthorn, dog An old form of 'lantern', the spelling probably arising because lanterns were commonly made of horn (so *OED*), 'lanthorn' here links with 'thorn' (see also 228–9 and n.). Starveling could have carried a stuffed dog as well as his lantern and bush of thorn, but he may have brought on a real dog, conceivably in early performances the same one that was used to notable comic effect in *TGV* 2.3 and 4.4. See 3.1.46 and n. for the legend of the man in the moon.

138–40 This is a defective quatrain, lacking a line

to rhyme with 'name', but the sense is complete; Shakespeare might count on us taking it as Quince's oversight rather than his own, as Brooks notes.

141 fall let fall, or drop.

143 tall valiant.

146 broached The original meaning is 'stabbed', but with the comic suggestion here of tapping a cask of wine or ale. The comic alliteration exaggerates a feature of the old plays Shakespeare is mocking; see, for example, *Apius and Virginia*, sig. D3ᵛ: 'Bid him imbrue his bloudy handes, in giltles bloud of mee.'

153 interlude play. As at 1.2.5.

154 Snout So F; *Flute* in Qq is an error difficult

And such a wall as I would have you think   155
That had in it a crannied hole or chink,
Through which the lovers, Pyramus and Thisbe,
Did whisper often, very secretly.
This loam, this rough-cast, and this stone doth show
That I am that same wall; the truth is so.   160
And this the cranny is, right and sinister,
Through which the fearful lovers are to whisper.
THESEUS Would you desire lime and hair to speak better?
DEMETRIUS It is the wittiest partition that ever I heard discourse, my
lord.   165

Enter [Bottom as] Pyramus.

THESEUS Pyramus draws near the wall; silence!
BOTTOM (*as Pyramus*)
O grim-looked night, O night with hue so black,
O night which ever art when day is not!
O night, O night, alack, alack, alack,
I fear my Thisbe's promise is forgot!   170
And thou, O wall, O sweet, O lovely wall,
That stand'st between her father's ground and mine,
Thou wall, O wall, O sweet and lovely wall,
Show me thy chink, to blink through with mine eyne.
[*Wall parts his fingers.*]
Thanks, courteous wall; Jove shield thee well for this!   175
But what see I? No Thisbe do I see.
O wicked wall, through whom I see no bliss,
Cursed be thy stones for thus deceiving me!
THESEUS The wall, methinks, being sensible, should curse again.

165 SD] F (*Enter Pyramus / after 166*); *not in* Qq   167 SH BOTTOM (*as Pyramus*)] *Wells; Py / Pyr / Pyra / or / Pir*
Qq, F (*through to 275*)   171 O sweet] Qq; *thou sweet* F   172 stand'st] Q1; *stands* Q2, F   174 SD] *After Capell; not
in* Qq, F

to explain as a misreading (though not impossible
if a long 's' was read as 'f'), and may be
Shakespeare's own confusion of names; but see 186
and n. for another puzzling error in Q.
   159 **stone** Compare 186–7; stone is an addition
to the lime or loam and rough-cast mentioned at 130
and at 3.1.53; like Moonshine with his dog (134),
Wall is perhaps intentionally overburdened with his
attributes, for comic effect.
   161 **sinister** left. Accented as here on the second
syllable until the eighteenth century.

162 **whisper** This lame rhyme brings Wall's
speech to a comic ending.
   163 **hair** Another pointer to the appearance of
Wall?
   164 **wittiest** most rational, or cleverest.
   174 SD Not in Qq or F, but Capell's addition is
justified by the text, and Wall's movements add to
the fun.
   179 **sensible** capable of feeling.
   179 **again** in reply.

BOTTOM No, in truth sir, he should not. 'Deceiving me' is Thisbe's   180
cue. She is to enter now, and I am to spy her through the wall.
You shall see it will fall pat as I told you. Yonder she comes.

Enter [Flute as] Thisbe.

FLUTE (*as Thisbe*)
    O wall, full often hast thou heard my moans,
      For parting my fair Pyramus and me.
    My cherry lips have often kissed thy stones,   185
      Thy stones with lime and hair knit up in thee.
BOTTOM (*as Pyramus*)
    I see a voice; now will I to the chink,
      To spy and I can hear my Thisbe's face.
    Thisbe!
FLUTE (*as Thisbe*)
           My love! Thou art my love, I think?
BOTTOM (*as Pyramus*)
    Think what thou wilt, I am thy lover's grace,   190
    And like Limander am I trusty still.
FLUTE (*as Thisbe*)
    And I like Helen, till the Fates me kill.
BOTTOM (*as Pyramus*)
    Not Shafalus to Procrus was so true.
FLUTE (*as Thisbe*)
    As Shafalus to Procrus, I to you.
BOTTOM (*as Pyramus*)
    O, kiss me through the hole of this vile wall!   195

180–2] *As Pope; verse in* Qq, F *divided at* is / *Thisbyes*...spy / *Her*...fall / Pat   182 SD] Qq (*Enter Thisby*)*; after* fall, *at* 182, *in* F   183 SH FLUTE (*as Thisbe*)] *Wells; This* Qq, F *(through to 306)*   186 up in thee] F; *now againe* Qq   188–9 To...Thisbe!] *As Rowe³; one line in* Qq, F   189 My love! Thou art] *So Rowe;* My love thou art, Qq, F   192 And I] Qq; And F   195 vile] Q2; vilde Q1

186 knit up in thee The rhyme is required, and F looks like an authentic correction; perhaps the compositor in Q1 simply made a stab at words he found blotted or illegible.

187 see a voice See 4.1.205–7 and n.

188 and if.

190 Think...wilt A commonplace; compare Tilley T27, 'Take it as you will', and T28, 'Take it or leave it.'

190 lover's grace i.e. indeed your lover. A common complimentary circumlocution (*OED* Grace *sb* 16a).

191 Limander A mistake for Leander, who attempted to swim the Hellespont for love of Hero, but echoing Lysander, or Alisander = Alexander, another name for Paris, so linking with Thisbe's Helen (of Troy) in the next line (for Hero, but recalling also Helena). Helen was of course notoriously unfaithful in love.

193–4 Shafalus...Procrus Errors for Cephalus and Procris; Cephalus in error killed his faithful wife, Procris, with a javelin she had given him; the story is told in Golding's Ovid, VII, 874–1117.

FLUTE (*as Thisbe*)
> I kiss the wall's hole, not your lips at all.

BOTTOM (*as Pyramus*)
> Wilt thou at Ninny's tomb meet me straightway?

FLUTE (*as Thisbe*)
> Tide life, tide death, I come without delay.
>
> > *[Exeunt Bottom and Flute in different directions]*

SNOUT (*as Wall*)
> Thus have I, Wall, my part dischargèd so;
> And being done, thus Wall away doth go.   *Exit*   200

THESEUS Now is the mural down between the two neighbours.

DEMETRIUS No remedy, my lord, when walls are so wilful to hear without warning.

HIPPOLYTA This is the silliest stuff that ever I heard.

THESEUS The best in this kind are but shadows; and the worst are no   205
worse, if imagination amend them.

HIPPOLYTA It must be your imagination then, and not theirs.

THESEUS If we imagine no worse of them than they of themselves, they
may pass for excellent men. Here come two noble beasts in, a man
and a lion.   210

> *Enter [Snug as] Lion and [Starveling as] Moonshine.*

SNUG (*as Lion*)
> You ladies, you whose gentle hearts do fear
> The smallest monstrous mouse that creeps on floor,

---

198 SD] *After Brooks; not in* QQ, F   200 SD *Exit*] F (*Exit Clow*); *not in* QQ; *Exeunt Wall, Pyra and Th.* / *Capell*
201 mural down] *Pope²*; *Moon used* Q; *morall downe* F; *mure all down Hanmer*; *Moon to see Sisson*; *mure rased Brooks*
204 SH HIPPOLYTA] QQ, F (*Dutch / through scene*)   209 beasts in,] *Rowe³*; *beasts, in* QQ, F   210 SD] QQ, F (*Enter
Lyon, and* Moone-shine)   211 SH SNUG (*as Lion*)] *Wells*; *Lyon* QQ, F (*through to 248*)

---

197 **Ninny's tomb** Pyramus repeats the blunder
for which Quince castigated Flute at 3.1.79–80.

198 **Tide life, tide death** Come life or death
(tide = betide). Compare the common proverb
'Come what come may' (Tilley C529).

201 **mural down** 'Moon used' (QQ) makes no
sense, and 'morall downe' (F) is at first sight little
better, but Pope's emendation 'mural down' (or
variations like 'mure all down') have been widely
accepted. Shakespeare elsewhere uses the word
'mure', or wall, once at *2H4* 4.4.119, and 'mural'
not at all, but here 'wall' or 'walls' occurs in lines
199, 200 and 202, and the dramatist may well have
resorted to 'mural' for the sake of variety. See
Textual Analysis, p. 140 below.

202–3 Demetrius jokingly alludes to the common
proverb 'Walls have ears' (Tilley W19).

202 **wilful** ready, willing (*OED* Wilful *a*¹ 3).

205 **shadows** A word relating to dreams, visions,
illusions, echoed in Puck's epilogue, 401–6, and
recalling 3.2.347; see also pp. 39–40 above.

211–18 The entry of Lion, prepared for at
1.2.53–9 and 3.1.21–34, has been seen as related
to an event at the Scottish Court on 30 August 1594,
when, according to *A True Accompt of...the
Baptism of...Prince Henry* (in *Somers Tracts*, 1809,
II, 179), at the baptismal Feast for Prince Henry,
a chariot was brought in. The plan was to have it
drawn by a lion, but 'because his presence might
have brought some feare to the nearest', and the
lights and torches might have 'commoved his
tamenes', the chariot was pulled in by a
blackamoor. Brooks takes this as a *terminus a quo* for
dating the play, but there is no reason to suppose
Shakespeare knew of this happening, or was
influenced by it.

> May now, perchance, both quake and tremble here,
>   When Lion rough in wildest rage doth roar.
> Then know that I as Snug the joiner am   215
> A lion fell, nor else no lion's dam;
> For if I should as lion come in strife
> Into this place, 'twere pity on my life.

THESEUS A very gentle beast, and of a good conscience.

DEMETRIUS The very best at a beast, my lord, that e'er I saw.   220

LYSANDER This lion is a very fox for his valour.

THESEUS True; and a goose for his discretion.

DEMETRIUS Not so, my lord; for his valour cannot carry his discretion;
and the fox carries the goose.

THESEUS His discretion, I am sure, cannot carry his valour; for the   225
goose carries not the fox. It is well: leave it to his discretion, and
let us listen to the moon.

STARVELING (*as Moonshine*)
> This lanthorn doth the hornèd moon present –

DEMETRIUS He should have worn the horns on his head.

THESEUS He is no crescent, and his horns are invisible within the   230
circumference.

STARVELING (*as Moonshine*)
> This lanthorn doth the hornèd moon present;
>   Myself the man i'th'moon do seem to be –

THESEUS This is the greatest error of all the rest; the man should be
put into the lantern. How is it else the man i'th'moon?   235

DEMETRIUS He dares not come there, for the candle; for you see it is
already in snuff.

HIPPOLYTA I am aweary of this moon. Would he would change!

---

215 as] Qq; one F   218 on] Qq; of F   227 listen] Q1; hearken Q2, F   228 SH STARVELING (*as Moonshine*)] Wells;
Moone /or/ Moon Qq, F (through to 242)   232–3] As Qq; prose in F   238 aweary] Q1; weary Q2, F

215–16 I as Snug...dam He insists it is as Snug
that he is a cruel lion, and he is not to be thought
of as a real beast, a lion's 'dam' or female parent;
in Golding's Ovid, IV, 120 ff. a lioness causes Thisbe
to flee.

221–2 fox...goose The lion was proverbial for
valour (Tilley L308, and compare *1H4* 3.1.165), the
fox for wiliness or 'discretion' (Tilley F645, F647,
F659), and the goose for stupidity (Tilley G346,
G348). The joke is rather laboured, as Theseus
seems to realise in 225–6, but the play on
'discretion' is caught up again at 239.

228 lanthorn See 134 and n.

229 i.e. as cuckold's horns, a commonplace joke
(Tilley H625).

230 crescent the waxing or growing moon.
Starveling, as his name implies, is a spare figure.

234–5 the man...lantern The joke, as Brooks
notes, is the more pointed because of Starveling's
meagre figure.

236 for i.e. for fear of.

237 in snuff (1) in need of snuffing, (2) angry.
The second meaning puns on the common phrase
'to take in snuff', meaning 'to take offence at'
(Tilley S598, and compare *1H4* 1.3.41).

THESEUS It appears by his small light of discretion that he is in the
    wane; but yet in courtesy, in all reason, we must stay the time.   240
LYSANDER Proceed, Moon.
STARVELING All that I have to say is to tell you that the lanthorn is
    the moon, I the man i'th'moon, this thorn bush my thorn bush,
    and this dog my dog.
DEMETRIUS Why, all these should be in the lantern, for all these are   245
    in the moon. But silence: here comes Thisbe.

               Enter [Flute as] Thisbe.

FLUTE (*as Thisbe*)
    This is old Ninny's tomb. Where is my love?
SNUG (*as Lion*) O!
        Lion roars. Thisbe runs off [dropping her mantle]
DEMETRIUS Well roared, Lion!
THESEUS Well run, Thisbe!   250
HIPPOLYTA Well shone, Moon! Truly, the moon shines with a good
    grace.
THESEUS Well moused, Lion!
DEMETRIUS And then came Pyramus –
LYSANDER And so the lion vanished.   255
            [Lion worries Thisbe's mantle, and exit]

            Enter [Bottom as] Pyramus.

BOTTOM (*as Pyramus*)
    Sweet moon, I thank thee for thy sunny beams;
    I thank thee, moon, for shining now so bright;
    For by thy gracious, golden, glittering gleams
    I trust to take of truest Thisbe sight.

---

243 i'th'] Q1 (ith); in the Q2, F   245 lantern] Qq, F (Lanthorne)   246 SD] Qq, F (*Enter* Thisby)   247–8 This...O!]
So F; *one line in* Qq   248 SD.2] *Brooks, after* F (*The Lion roares, Thisby runs off*); *not in* Qq   255 SD.1 *Lion...exit*]
Brooks, after Capell; not in Qq, F   255 SD.2 *Enter...Pyramus*] Qq, F (*Enter* Pyramus)   258 gleams] *Staunton,*
conj. Knight; beames Qq, F; streams F2   259 take] Qq; *taste* F   259 Thisbe] Qq; *Thisbies* F

242–4 The gibes of his stage audience put
Starveling out of his part, and he lapses into prose
(so Wells).
247 Ninny's tomb The scene has changed from
the wall separating the lovers to the 'tomb';
sometimes a property tomb is used here, and Thisbe
can win a laugh by bringing one on, though, as Wells
notes, her words give sufficient indication of the
setting. Thisbe again gets 'Ninus' wrong; see 197
above and n.
253 Well moused Showing that Lion paws the
mantle as a cat plays with a mouse; Theseus's
comment also suggests that Lion squeaks rather

than roars, and is more pitiful than fearsome in
performance. The SD, added first by Capell, for
Lion's exit, is usually placed after 252, but the text
suggests that Lion remains until he sees Pyramus,
and then goes off at 255.
258 gleams Qq and F repeat 'beams', and it
seems likely that the compositor is responsible;
'gleams' accords with Pyramus's addiction to
alliteration, as at 259, 262, 270–1 and 278, and is
the obvious word in this context.
259 take So Qq; 'taste' (F) could be a correction,
as it adds further to Pyramus's (and Bottom's) comic
habit of confounding the senses.

> But stay – O spite! 260
> But mark, poor Knight,
> What dreadful dole is here?
> Eyes, do you see?
> How can it be?
> O dainty duck, O dear! 265
> Thy mantle good –
> What, stained with blood?
> Approach, ye Furies fell!
> O Fates, come, come,
> Cut thread and thrum, 270
> Quail, crush, conclude, and quell.

THESEUS This passion, and the death of a dear friend, would go near
to make a man look sad.

HIPPOLYTA Beshrew my heart, but I pity the man.

BOTTOM (*as Pyramus*)

> O wherefore, Nature, didst thou lions frame, 275
> Since lion vile hath here deflowered my dear?
> Which is – no, no – which was the fairest dame
> That lived, that loved, that liked, that looked with cheer.
> Come tears, confound!
> Out sword, and wound 280
> The pap of Pyramus,
> Ay, that left pap,

260–1] *So Pope; one line in* Qq, F   263–4] *So Pope; one line in* Qq, F   266–7] *So Pope; one line in* Qq, F
268 ye] Qq; you F   269–70] *So Pope; one line in* Qq, F   271–3] *So* Qq; *two lines of verse in* F, *divided at* friend, /
Would   276 vile] *Pope;* vilde Qq, F   279–80] *So Johnson; one line in* Qq, F

260–71, 279–90 Pyramus here speaks in a variant of the 'eight and six' Quince envisaged for the prologue (see 3.1.19 and n.), divided into four, four and six. Shakespeare was exaggerating for comic effect the style of I. Tomson's 'A New Sonet of Pyramus and Thisbe'; see p. 11 above.

262 dole cause for sorrow.

268 Furies The avenging goddesses sent from Tartarus to punish crime, and usually three in number (Tisiphone, Megaera, Alecto). One appears in Chaucer's *Knight's Tale* (I, 2684) to cause the death of Arcite, and they feature in Seneca's tragedies and in English tragedies influenced by Seneca.

269 Fates The three goddesses Clotho, Lachesis and Atropos, supposed in Greek mythology to spin, draw and cut the thread of human life; Atropos is named in I. Tomson's 'A New Sonet of Pyramus and Thisbe' as weaving the 'fatall death' of Pyramus; see p. 11 above.

270 thread and thrum i.e. good and bad, all together. The threads (or warp) extend lengthwise in the loom to be crossed by the weft (or cross-threads) to form the web or piece of cloth. The thrum is the tufted end of the thread where it is fastened to the loom. The thrum is left unwoven when the web is cut for removal from the loom, and is worth little in relation to the thread.

271 Quail Destroy.

271 quell kill.

272 passion (1) suffering, (2) passionate outburst (*OED* sv *sb* 6d).

278 cheer Perhaps = 'face' as at 3.2.96, but suggesting also 'cheerfulness'.

282 pap Usually referring to a woman's breast, the word is used here to comic effect, although, as Brooks notes, it was sometimes used in a serious context in relation to a man, as in Chapman's translation of Homer's *Iliad* IV, 517 (cited *OED* sv IC), and compare *LLL* 4.3.24.

Where heart doth hop:
Thus die I, thus, thus, thus! [*Stabs himself.*]
Now am I dead,   285
Now am I fled;
My soul is in the sky.
Tongue, lose thy light;
Moon, take thy flight;

                                    [*Exit Starveling*]

Now die, die, die, die, die. [*He dies.*]   290

DEMETRIUS No die, but an ace for him; for he is but one.

LYSANDER Less than an ace, man; for he is dead, he is nothing.

THESEUS With the help of a surgeon he might yet recover, and yet prove
an ass.

HIPPOLYTA How chance Moonshine is gone before Thisbe comes back   295
and finds her lover?

THESEUS She will find him by starlight.

Enter [Flute as] Thisbe.

Here she comes and her passion ends the play.

HIPPOLYTA Methinks she should not use a long one for such a
Pyramus; I hope she will be brief.   300

DEMETRIUS A mote will turn the balance, which Pyramus, which
Thisbe is the better: he for a man, God warrant us; she for a woman,
God bless us.

LYSANDER She hath spied him already, with those sweet eyes.

DEMETRIUS And thus she means, videlicet –   305

282–3] *So Johnson; one line in* Qq, F   284 SD] *Dyce; not in* Qq, F   285–7] *So Johnson; one line in* Qq, F   288–9] *So Johnson; one line in* Qq, F   289 SD] *So Capell* (Exit Moonshine / *after* 290); *not in* Qq, F   290 SD] *Theobald; not in* Qq, F   293 yet prove] Q1; *prove* Q2, F   295–6 How...before...lover?] *So Rowe;* How...before?...lover, Q1; How...before? ...Lover. Q2, F   295–6 *Prose in* Q1; *two lines of verse in* Q2, F, *divided at* before? / Thisby   297 SD] F (Enter Thisby / *after* 296); *not in* Qq   301 mote] *Steevens, conj.* Heath; *moth* Qq, F   302–3 he...us] Qq; *not in* F   302 warrant] *Collier;* warnd Qq, F

288 **Tongue** For 'eye'.

291 **No die...ace** A die is one of a pair of dice, and the ace is the die marked with a single spot; after the pun on 'die', there is a further quibble on 'ass' (294) and 'ace', which could be pronounced with a short 'a' (Kökeritz, p. 89).

298 **passion** See 272 above and n.

301 **mote** minute particle. 'Moth' (Qq, F) was a possible spelling, and may have been one Shakespeare used; compare *H5* 4.1.179: 'wash every

Moth ['moath', Q 1600] out of his conscience'; see also 3.1.136 and n.

302–3 **he...bless us** Omitted from F, presumably following the statute of 1606 forbidding profanity on the stage.

305 **means** (1) 'laments' (*OED* sv *v*² 1; the word, now obsolete, was cognate with 'moans'); (2) 'submits a formal complaint' (a Scottish legal term, now obsolete, but perhaps, as Wells notes, prompting 'videlicet', used much in legal documents); (3) simply 'intends' or 'signifies'.

FLUTE (*as Thisbe*)

      Asleep, my love?

      What, dead, my dove?

      O Pyramus, arise.

      Speak, speak! Quite dumb?

      Dead, dead? A tomb   310

      Must cover thy sweet eyes.

      These lily lips,

      This cherry nose,

      These yellow cowslip cheeks

      Are gone, are gone.   315

      Lovers, make moan;

      His eyes were green as leeks.

      O sisters three,

      Come, come to me

      With hands as pale as milk;   320

      Lay them in gore,

      Since you have shore

      With shears his thread of silk.

      Tongue, not a word!

      Come, trusty sword,   325

      Come blade, my breast imbrue! [*Stabs herself.*]

      And farewell, friends.

      Thus Thisbe ends –

      Adieu, adieu, adieu! [*Dies.*]

THESEUS Moonshine and Lion are left to bury the dead.   330

DEMETRIUS Ay, and Wall, too.

306–7] *So Pope; one line in* Qq, F   309–10] *So Pope; one line in* Qq, F   312–13] *So Pope; one line in* Qq, F
312 lips] Qq, F; brows *Theobald*   315–16] *So Pope; one line in* Qq, F   318–19] *So Pope; one line in* Qq, F
321–2] *So Pope; one line in* Qq, F   324–5] *So Pope; one line in* Qq, F   326 SD] *Dyce; not in* Qq, F   327–8] *So
Pope; one line in* Qq, F   329 SD] *Theobald; not in* Qq, F

312–17 This misapplication of colours relates to the continuous thread of comic confusions; see 3.1.75–6 and 4.1.205–7 and nn. 'lily' and 'cherry' would suit a heroine rather than a man, 'cowslip' is merely absurd (compare 2.1.10), and 'green' is the colour associated not with love but with jealousy, the 'green-eyed monster' of *Oth.* 3.3.166. 'Green as leeks' was proverbial (Tilley L176), but quite inappropriate in relation to eyes.

318 sisters three the Fates (see 269 above and n.). The phrase had become a cliché (compare *MV* 2.2.63), but Shakespeare may have had in mind the 'lamentable Tragedie' of *Cambyses* Prologue 17:

'when sisters three had wrought to shere his vitall thred'; see 1.2.9–10 and n., and 5.1.57 above.

320 as pale as milk A commonplace image for a lady's skin; compare *TGV* 3.1.252: 'the milk-white bosom of thy love' (Tilley M931).

322 shore For 'shorn', providing a comic rhyming effect.

326 imbrue pierce and stain with blood. In Edward Sharpham's play *The Fleire* (1607), written for a private theatre, there is a possible reference to comic stage-business here in the line 'Faith, like *Thisbe* in the play, 'a has almost killed himself with the scabbard' (2.434–5).

330 left i.e. remain alive.

BOTTOM [*Starting up, as Flute does also.*] No, I assure you, the wall is
down that parted their fathers. Will it please you to see the epilogue,
or to hear a Bergomask dance between two of our company?

THESEUS No epilogue, I pray you; for your play needs no excuse. Never   335
excuse; for when the players are all dead, there need none to be
blamed. Marry, if he that writ it had played Pyramus and hanged
himself in Thisbe's garter, it would have been a fine tragedy: and
so it is, truly, and very notably discharged. But come, your
Bergomask; let your epilogue alone.   340

[*The company return; two of them dance, then exeunt Bottom, Flute
and their fellows.*]

    The iron tongue of midnight hath told twelve.
    Lovers, to bed; 'tis almost fairy time.
    I fear we shall outsleep the coming morn
    As much as we this night have overwatched.
    This palpable-gross play hath well beguiled   345
    The heavy gait of night. Sweet friends, to bed.
    A fortnight hold we this solemnity
    In nightly revels and new jollity.

                                                       Exeunt

            Enter PUCK [*carrying a broom*].

PUCK   Now the hungry lion roars,
           And the wolf behowls the moon,   350

332 SH BOTTOM] F; *Lyon* Qq   332 SD *Starting up*] Capell *(following* I assure you*); not in* Qq, F   332 SD *as...also*]
After Brooks *(Flute rises / following* fathers *at 333); not in* Qq, F   337 hanged] Qq; hung F   340 SD] *This edn, after*
Brooks; *Here a dance of clowns / Rowe; not in* Qq, F   345 palpable-gross] Capell; palpable grosee Qq, F   348 SD.2
carrying a broom] *This edn; not in* Qq, F   349 lion roars] *Rowe;* Lyons roares Qq, F   350 behowls] *Theobald, conj.*
Warburton; beholds Qq, F

332 SH BOTTOM Q1's *Lyon* was perhaps caught
up from 330; the speech is very much in Bottom's
style (compare 180–2 above), and Lion (Snug)
'vanished' offstage at 255.

333–4 see...hear Bottom's final confusion of
senses; see 312–17 above and n.

334 Bergomask A rustic dance named after the
people of Bergamo in northern Italy, who were
ridiculed as clownish in their manners (*OED*, citing
this as its sole instance).

337–8 hanged...garter Varying the proverbial
phrase 'He may go hang himself in his own garters'
(Tilley G42), and compare *1H4* 2.2.43–4.

340 There is no SD here in Qq or F, so that the
'two of our company' who dance cannot be
identified. The mechanicals must make their exit

here, for Theseus's next speech assumes they have
departed.

341 iron tongue i.e. of a bell. Compare *John*
3.3.38.

344 overwatched kept watch over by staying
awake.

345 palpable-gross plainly rough and ready.

346 heavy gait sluggish passage.

348 SD.2 Puck carries a broom, as commonly;
Brooks notes an example in Jonson's masque *Love
Restored* (1612); see 367–8 below and n.

349–52 Suggesting at once a wilderness (the lion
recalls the play of Pyramus and Thisbe, too), and
a pastoral landscape; see 2.1.93–102, 180–1, 249–52
and nn.

Whilst the heavy ploughman snores,
    All with weary task foredone.
Now the wasted brands do glow,
    Whilst the screech-owl, screeching loud,
Puts the wretch that lies in woe   355
    In remembrance of a shroud.
Now it is the time of night
    That the graves, all gaping wide,
Every one lets forth his sprite
    In the church-way paths to glide.   360
And we fairies, that do run
    By the triple Hecate's team
From the presence of the sun,
    Following darkness like a dream,
Now are frolic; not a mouse   365
Shall disturb this hallowed house.
I am sent with broom before
To sweep the dust behind the door.

Enter [OBERON *and* TITANIA,] *the King and Queen of Fairies, with
all their train.*

OBERON   Through the house give glimmering light
    By the dead and drowsy fire;   370
Every elf and fairy sprite
    Hop as light as bird from briar,
And this ditty after me
Sing, and dance it trippingly.

368 SD] Qq, F (*Enter King and Queene of Fairies, with all their traine*)   373–4] *So Rowe³; one line in* Qq, F

351 **heavy** i.e. weighed down with weariness.
352 **foredone** exhausted.
353 **wasted** burnt out.
354–6 The owl was regarded as a bird of ill-omen, the 'ominous and fearful owl of death' (*1H6* 4.2.15).
357–60 At midnight ghosts wander abroad, returning at dawn; compare 3.2.380–2.
362 **triple Hecate's team** Hecate, goddess of the moon, held sway under this name or Proserpine in Hades, Diana on earth (see 1.1.89), and Cynthia or Phoebe in the heavens (see 1.1.209). The 'team' appears to refer again to the chariot of the moon, drawn across the sky by dragons; see 3.2.379 and n.
365 **frolic** frolicsome, merry.
367–8 According to Reginald Scot, *Discoverie of Witchcraft* (1584), p. 85, if maids set out a bowl of milk for Robin Goodfellow he would sweep the house at midnight, and so do them a good turn.
368 SD.2 **all their train** See 2.1.59 and n. The whole 'train' of fairies would include at least Puck, the four named fairies, and the unnamed Fairy who speaks in 2.1, a total of six in all. Stage tradition has often swollen the number who enter here into a large troop, played sometimes by women, and sometimes by children; see pp. 13–19 above.
369 **glimmering light** Probably, as NS suggests, the fairies have tapers fixed in headbands, like the 'fairies' of *Wiv.* 5.5.37 SD (bad quarto), who enter 'with waxen tapers on their heads'. The fairies must have hands free to dance 'Hand in hand' (377), probably a round dance – compare 2.1.86 and n. Puck with his broom perhaps sweeps a path for them, and presumably does not participate in the dance.

TITANIA   First rehearse your song by rote,   375
             To each word a warbling note;
             Hand in hand with fairy grace
             Will we sing and bless this place.
                           Song [and dance].
OBERON   Now until the break of day
             Through this house each fairy stray.   380
             To the best bride-bed will we,
             Which by us shall blessèd be;
             And the issue there create
             Ever shall be fortunate.
             So shall all the couples three   385
             Ever true in loving be,
             And the blots of nature's hand
             Shall not in their issue stand.
             Never mole, harelip, nor scar,
             Nor mark prodigious, such as are   390
             Despisèd in nativity,
             Shall upon their children be.
             With this field-dew consecrate,
             Every fairy take his gait,
             And each several chamber bless   395
             Through this palace with sweet peace;
             And the owner of it blessed
             Ever shall in safety rest.
             Trip away, make no stay;
             Meet me all by break of day.   400
                           Exeunt [all but Puck]

375 your] Q1; this Q2, F   378 SD] *Capell; not in* Qq; *The Song* F; *Oberon leading, the Fairies sing and dance.* / *Alexander
conj. Singer;* Ever...rest, / And...blest. Qq, F   379 SH OBERON] Qq (*Ob.*); *not in* F   379–400] *So* Qq; *italicised and inset as the song in* F   397–8] *So Staunton,
400 SD *Exeunt all but Puck*] *Alexander, after Capell (Exeunt King,
Queen and Train); Exeunt* Qq; *not in* F

379–400 In F these lines are headed *The Song*, and
set off by being indented and italicised; in Q they
are printed as ordinary dialogue, and assigned to
Oberon. It seems likely that in fact the text of the
'ditty' is missing; Oberon's 'Now' (379) suggests
a resumption of the dialogue beginning at 349, for
it is in the same metre, and Shakespeare's habit is
to differentiate his songs metrically, as at 2.2.9 ff.
   381 **best bride-bed** That of Theseus and
Hippolyta.

390 **mark prodigious** ominous birthmark.
   393 **consecrate** consecrated. Titania's fairies
'dew her orbs' at 2.1.9, and for the association of
dew with benediction, compare *Cym.* 5.5.351.
   394 **gait** way.
   395 **several** separate.
   397–8 These lines were transposed in Qq, F,
wrecking the sense; presumably this was an
accident in printing, for the lines are parallel to
385–6.

PUCK [*To the audience*]

    If we shadows have offended,
    Think but this, and all is mended:
    That you have but slumbered here
    While these visions did appear;
    And this weak and idle theme,   405
    No more yielding but a dream,
    Gentles, do not reprehend;
    If you pardon, we will mend.
    And, as I am an honest Puck,
    If we have unearnèd luck   410
    Now to 'scape the serpent's tongue
    We will make amends ere long,
    Else the Puck a liar call.
    So, good night unto you all.
    Give me your hands, if we be friends,   415
    And Robin shall restore amends.   [*Exit*]

---

401 SD *To the audience*] *Wells; not in* Qq, F   416 SD] *So Rowe; not in* Qq, F

401–4 See 5.1.205 in relation to 'shadows', and also 3.2.347 and n.; and on 'visions' see also 3.2.371 and 4.1.73 and 200. Both fairies and actors are 'shadows', delusive appearances; see also pp. 39–40 above.

406 **No more yielding** i.e. producing or yielding no more profit.

407 **Gentles** Courteously addressing the aud-

ience as gentlefolk, paralleling Quince's address to his stage audience as Prologue, 126 above.

408 **mend** improve, do better. This, like 415, seems to be addressed to a regular theatre audience, promising better plays to come; see pp. 3–4 above.

411 **serpent's tongue** i.e. hisses.

415 **Give…hands** Applaud.

416 **restore amends** give satisfaction in return.

TEXTUAL ANALYSIS

The play was entered in the Stationers' Register for Thomas Fisher, a draper turned bookseller, on 8 October 1600. This was, in fact, the first work entered for Fisher, who became a freeman of the Stationers' Company in this year, and whose involvement with publishing seems to have lasted only two or three years. John Marston's plays *Antonio and Mellida* (printed for Matthew Lownes and Fisher), and *Antonio's Revenge* (entered in the Stationers' Register 24 October 1601), were also associated with Fisher, but he is not known to have any other connection with Shakespeare or his company. The entry reads:

8. Octobr.^{is}

Tho. Fysšher   Entred for his copie vnder the hands of m^r Rodes and the Wardens.
              A book called A mydsomer nights dreame   vj^d

The first quarto (Q1), printed in the same year, probably by Richard Bradock, who printed a number of play quartos between 1598 and 1602, has a title page which reads as follows:

A / Midsommer nights / dreame.
As it hath been sundry times pub-/ *lickely acted, by the Right honoura-* / ble, the Lord Chamberlaine his / *seruants.* / *Written by William Shakespeare.* [Printer's device, McKerrow 321]
    Imprinted at London, for *Thomas Fisher*, and are to / be soulde at his shoppe, at the Signe of the White Hart, / in *Fleetestreete.* 1600.

A second quarto (Q2), reprinted from the first in 1619 by William Jaggard, was issued with the false statement on the title page that it was printed by James Roberts in 1600. This was one of a set of ten reprints of plays by Shakespeare or attributed to him printed by Jaggard, who kept his own name out of it, soon after Shakespeare's death in 1616. Shortly after Jaggard printed these for his friend Thomas Pavier, he became involved in plans for the production, sponsored by Shakespeare's fellow-actors, of a collected edition of the plays, the First Folio (F), which appeared in 1623.[1] The text of *A Midsummer Night's Dream* in F was printed from Q2, with corrections and additions, mostly stage directions, which appear to derive from the theatre.

The first quarto thus provides an authoritative text, and is the basis for the present edition. It may well have been printed from an authorial manuscript, probably his 'foul papers', or rough draft, the fair copy being handed over to the players for their use. There are several reasons for believing that Q1 originated in this way. One is the nature of the stage directions and speech headings in it, which would not have been full or consistent enough for guidance in staging the play. So, for instance, no entries

---

[1] See Greg, pp. 9–17.

135

are marked for Puck at 3.1.84, for Lysander at 3.2.412, for Philostrate at 5.1.105, or for Flute (Thisbe) at 5.1.297; and speech headings vary, as Puck is sometimes *Rob*[*in*], Titania becomes *Que*[*en*], Theseus and Hippolyta in Act 5 become *Duk*[*e*] and *Dutch*, and Bottom in 4.1 is *Clo*[*wn*]. In addition to such omissions and variations, there are some general entries, such as *Enter the Clownes* (3.1.1), *Enter Theseus and all his traine* (4.1.99) and *Enter Quince, Flute, Thisby and the rabble* (4.2.0). Such vagueness would not serve the book-holder or prompter, who would need to known exactly who was to be on stage, and it is much more likely to reflect the author's inconsistencies in the flow of composition. He might easily forget to register an entry for a character, vary speech headings, especially when he was simultaneously thinking of a character as Puck and Robin Goodfellow, or Titania and Queen of the Fairies, and adopt a shorthand such as 'train' or 'rabble' for a group of characters established in his mind's eye.

A further reason for supposing that Q1 was printed from a draft in Shakespeare's hand is the presence of a number of individual spellings which may be attributable to him. Spellings were not fixed in Shakespeare's age, and printers found this useful in setting prose, when a line could be adjusted by removing or adding letters: so 'richness' could appear as 'richnes', 'richness' or 'richnesse'. A compositor working at speed would be likely to carry over some of the unusual spellings in the manuscript, but might equally convert common spellings into his own habitual style. The evidence provided by spellings, then, is rarely conclusive, though it can sometimes be assumed that an author's spelling has survived into print, as in the curious form 'Scilens' in the name of Justice Silence, which occurs a number of times in the 1600 quarto of *2 Henry IV*. This spelling also appears in a passage in Hand D in the manuscript play *Sir Thomas More*, comprising about 150 lines often attributed to Shakespeare.[1] One striking feature of this passage is the writer's preference for 'oo' spellings, such as are found in Q1 of *A Midsummer Night's Dream* in words like 'prooue' (5 times), 'prooues', 'hoord', 'boorde', 'shooes', and 'mooue'. Hand D also shows a liking for 'ea' where modern English has 'e', 'ei' or 'ie', as in 'sealf' or 'perceaue', and Q1 of the play has such spellings as 'pearce' and 'uneauen'. A number of other possible Shakespearean spellings have been pointed out, for which analogies can be found in other good quartos, notably 'warnd' for 'warrant' (compare 'warn't', *Ham.* 1.2.242) and 'maruailes' for 'marvellous' (3.1.2) (compare 'marvaile' for 'marvel', 2.2.102).[2] Taken all together, the evidence is strong enough to suggest that Q1 gives us as near a sense of what Shakespeare wrote as a printed text is likely to get.

If so, then a notable feature of the text – the mislineations, especially in Act 5 – calls for explanation. The most noticeable mislining is found in one of the play's most memorable speeches, at the opening of 5.1, which is printed thus in Q1:

[1] This attribution has been vigorously challenged by Carol Chillington in 'Playwrights at work: Henslowe's, not Shakespeare's, *Book of Sir Thomas More*', *English Literary Renaissance* 10 (1980), 439–79, and must be regarded as doubtful.

[2] For further comment on spellings, see Brooks, pp. xxv–xxvi; Greg, pp. 147–9; and Dover Wilson in NS, pp. 79, 112, 116, 121, 148.

Louers, and mad men haue such seething braines,
Such shaping phantasies, that apprehend more,
Then coole reason euer comprehends. The lunatick,
The louer, and the Poet are of imagination all compact.
One sees more diuels, then vast hell can holde:
That is the mad man. The louer, all as frantick,
Sees *Helens* beauty in a brow of *Ægypt.*
The Poets eye, in a fine frenzy, rolling, doth glance
From heauen to earth, from earth to heauen. And as
Imagination bodies forth the formes of things
Vnknowne: the Poets penne turnes them to shapes,
And giues to ayery nothing, a locall habitation,
And a name. Such trickes hath strong imagination,
That if it would but apprehend some ioy,
It comprehends some bringer of that ioy.

John Dover Wilson showed that if the irregular lines were removed, the text would still make excellent sense, reading as follows:[1]

Lovers and madmen have such seething brains,
Such shaping fantasies that apprehend
More than cool reason ever comprehends.
One sees more devils than vast hell can hold;
That is the madman. The lover, all as frantic,
Sees Helen's beauty in a brow of Egypt.
Such tricks hath strong imagination,
That if it would but apprehend some joy,
It comprehends some bringer of that joy.

As W. W. Greg has said, 'There is no escaping the conclusion that in this we have the original writing, which was supplemented by fresh lines crowded into the margin so that their metrical structure was obscured.'[2] Dover Wilson thought that here, and in the other passages where lineation is disturbed in this scene (in 5.1.29–83), he could detect a much later layer of composition; he also found indications elsewhere in the text which he interpreted as supporting his theory that the play originated in 1592, and was twice revised, in 1594 and again in 1598.[3]

His explanation of the extensive mislineations in 5.1 has won general assent, but not his assumption that revisions took place over a number of years.[4] We do not know why some plays and not others were released by Shakespeare and his company for publication, but it was in the company's interest to retain the fair copy marked up for use in the theatre, and to supply the printer with the author's draft or foul papers. The obvious way of accounting for confusions in lineation in the quarto is to suppose that they result from alterations and reworkings made by the author in the course of composition. Later revisions would need to be made, if at all, in the copy used in the theatre, and though it is possible that Shakespeare revised his manuscript for

[1] NS, pp. 80–6.   [2] Greg, p. 242.
[3] NS, pp. 77–100; see also Robert K. Turner, Jr, 'Printing methods and textual problems in *A Midsummer Night's Dream* Q1', *Studies in Bibliography* 15 (1962), 33–55, esp. pp. 46–7.
[4] See Greg, p. 242; Brooks, pp. xli–xlii.

publication in 1600, the only serious grounds for so arguing are that the revisions show a much more mature style; this was Dover Wilson's case, but the various styles in the play now seem to most critics to reflect Shakespeare's deliberate artistry and conscious variation during a single period of composition.[1]

The additions to the speech of Theseus, cited above, are nevertheless especially interesting, because they add the figure of the poet to those of the lunatic and lover, and so complicate the argument of the speech by incorporating, as it were, the dramatist reflecting on his art. However, these revisions, if this is what they are, though certainly more extensive and noteworthy, are not necessarily different in kind from various other difficulties the printer found in the manuscript. After analysing all the instances of mislineation, Robert K. Turner came to the conclusion that the 'quarto was set largely by formes under adverse conditions caused by sections of difficult copy. In only two places (B2^r, 33 and H2^r, 35, or 1.2.46–7 and 5.1.247–8, where lines are crowded on to the page) does there seem to be any likelihood that the compositor juggled the lineation of the text in order to fit copy to a predetermined space.'[2] Difficult copy would seem, then, to be the readiest explanation for the irregular lineation, instances of prose set as verse, or verse set as prose, and other kinds of confusion that occur at various points through the text. The passage in Hand D in *Sir Thomas More* illustrates how some kinds of confusion could arise; there, perhaps to save paper, at the foot of one page four lines of blank verse are written as two, and might easily have been converted into prose by a compositor, especially as there are no capital letters to mark the beginning of a line. Elsewhere $2\frac{1}{2}$ lines are cancelled at one point, except perhaps for one word, 'why', and a phrase is interlined to complete the third line, which, however, is no longer a complete blank verse, so that a printer might well have been puzzled to know how to set it.[3]

The second quarto was printed from Q1, and follows it page for page, except for the first four pages of sheet G. The standard measure in Q1 is 35 lines of type to the page, but there are only 34 lines on the first four pages of sheet G; Q2 adheres to the 35-line measure throughout, returning to accord with Q1 on G3 by spacing the text more generously. The additional type-space in Q2 also enabled the compositor partly to restore correct lineation in 5.1, notably 5.1.32–8, lines printed as prose in Q1; but if he could recognise metrical lines (as he may have deliberately corrected 'no fault' (Q1) to 'none' at 1.1.200 for the sake of the metre), he made no consistent effort to correct the mislineations of Q1. It is easy to show the dependence of Q2 upon Q1, since it retains a great many of the variations in speech headings in Q1, repeats most of its errors, and generally spaces the text in the same way, including its eccentricities. Some of the errors in Q1 are corrected in Q2, like 'wanes' for 'waues' (1.1.4), 'is' for 'it' (2.2.54), 'surfeit' for 'surfer' (2.2.147), *Bot* for *Cet* (3.1.43), and 'to expound' for 'expound' (4.1.202), but all these are obvious mistakes or omissions for which the context suggests the correct reading. In addition, Q2 supplies a few exits not in Q1, as at 2.1.244, 3.2.101, 338, 4.1.196 and 4.1.211, and an entry for Hermia at 3.2.440;

---

[1] See pp. 28–30 above. [2] Turner, 'Printing methods', p. 55.

[3] This passage is conveniently set out, with facsimiles, in *The Riverside Shakespeare*, ed. G. Blakemore Evans, 1974, pp. 1686–1700.

again these are all points such as any reader might notice, and which common sense might provide, without reference to any authority other than the context. As against these casual and inconsistent attempts at improving what he found in Q1, the printer of Q2 introduced numerous errors of his own. These include inversions like 'we will' for 'will we' (1.2.81), omissions of words as in 'about' for 'round about' (2.1.175), or 'prove' for 'yet prove' (5.1.293), substitutions like 'poison' for 'potion' (3.2.264), 'apply' for 'employ' (3.2.374), 'posterity' for 'prosperity' (4.1.87) and 'hearken' for 'listen' (5.1.227), and simple errors such as 'silly' for 'filly' (2.1.46, a misreading of 'f' as a long 's'), and 'hoared headed' for 'hoary-headed' (2.1.107). In other words, Q2 has no independent authority, and in the present discussion is worth so much attention only because the text in the First Folio was set up from it.

It was easier to set up the Folio text from printed copy than from manuscript, but the compositors introduced a large number of new substantive errors, in addition to those carried over from Q2.[1] Most of these are trivial, and fall into typical categories of printers' mistakes, such as substitutions ('mine' for 'my', 1.1.131; 'doth' for 'do', 1.1.229; 'into' for 'unto', 2.1.191; 'murderer' for 'murdered', 3.2.58); transpositions ('I could ever' for 'ever I could', 1.1.132; 'I do' for 'do I', 2.1.136; 'are all' for 'all are', 3.2.145); misreadings ('gallantly' for 'gallant', 1.2.18; 'there' for 'here', 1.2.53; 'wast' for 'hast', 2.1.65; 'interchanged' for 'interchained', 2.2.55); expansions ('grow on' for 'grow', 1.2.8; 'if that' for 'if', 1.2.64); and omissions of words here and there, but most notably of three lines, at 3.2.344, 4.1.189–90 and 5.1.302–3. At the same time the Folio text has changes and additions that must stem from an editor's notation on the copy of Q2 used for printing it. Like most of the comedies in the Folio, A Midsummer Night's Dream is divided into five acts. In Act 5 Egeus replaces Philostrate as Theseus's master of ceremonies. The Folio text also makes some corrections, and adds or clarifies about thirty stage directions. It looks very much, therefore, as though the Folio text was somewhat carelessly set up from a copy of Q2 that had been rather haphazardly corrected and expanded by an editor who was able to compare it with a manuscript marked up for use in the theatre.[2]

It is evident that this editor had little sense of theatre, and did not always observe the relation between dialogue and stage directions. So he did add *Enter Piramus with the Asse head*, an important direction, as it suggests that Shakespeare's company used a property head, but he added it in the wrong place, at 3.1.93 instead of 3.1.84. At 5.1.150, he incorporated what was no doubt the prompter's manuscript direction, *Exit all but Wall*, but failed to cancel the equivalent stage direction as it appears in the quartos at 5.1.152, *Exit Lyon, Thisbie and Moonshine*. Furthermore, he converted a line of text into a stage direction at 3.1.136, where Titania summons her fairies by name, 'Peaseblossom, Cobweb, Moth, and Mustardseed!'; the names were italicised in Q1, and Q2 italicised the whole line, which the editor misinterpreted as a direction, *Enter Pease-blossome, Cobweb, Moth, Mustard-seede, and foure Fairies*. A glance at the text should have shown him that only four fairies were needed in the scene; eight

---

[1] For an analysis of the compositors who worked on the Folio text, see Charlton Hinman, *The Printing and Proof-Reading of the First Folio of Shakespeare*, 1963, II, 414–26.
[2] Greg, p. 246, called him 'fussy but incompetent', but this is to judge him by modern standards.

were too many, and almost certainly beyond the resources of the company.[1] For all this, it seems that, if the editor did not altogether understand what he was about, he did transcribe into his copy of Q2 what he noticed as different in the manuscript, though it is not possible to guess how much he failed to notice. The evidence of these stage directions shows that he did not read the dialogue attentively.

There is, however, no reason to doubt the authority of the few corrections he made in the dialogue, notably the insertion of 'passionate' at 3.2.220, where a word has clearly been omitted in Q1, the correction of 'Minnock' in Q2 ('Minnick', Q1) to 'Mimmick' at 3.2.19, and the alteration of 'knit now againe' to 'knit up in thee' at 5.1.186. Bearing these in mind, there is a good case also for accepting the Folio changes of 'merit' for 'friends' at 1.1.139, and of 'morall downe' (i.e. 'mural down') for 'Moon vsed' at 5.1.201. Brooks proposes an ingenious hypothesis to allow him to retain 'friends' as a preferred reading,[2] but it seems more likely that 'merit' was a revision incorporated into the prompt-copy. The word 'mural' was in use as meaning a wall by the sixteenth century, and although it does not occur elsewhere in Shakespeare's works, he did once use the equivalent 'mure' at *2 Henry IV* 4.4.119. The word 'wall' appears in 5.1.195, 196, 199, 200 and 202, and it would not be surprising if Shakespeare chose an alternative in 5.1.201. There is no need to look with Brooks for conjectural misreadings, and revise to 'mure rased'; in any case, this makes poor sense, for Wall has simply walked off, and has not been 'rased' – effaced or destroyed.[3]

The editor of the text printed in the Folio added to what he found in Q2 stage directions which must have come from a theatre manuscript, since at 5.1.125 the entry of Pyramus and Thisbe is preceded by *Tawyer with a Trumpet before them.* William Tawyer, who died in 1625, was a member of the King's Men.[4] Other added directions supply guidance omitted from the quartos, in which directions are often vague or missing; examples are the addition *Manet Lysander and Hermia* at 1.1.127, the entry for Oberon *solus* followed a few lines later by Puck in 3.2.0–4, and the identification of the Prologue as Quince at 5.1.107. The additions still leave some gaps and uncertainties, and in particular a number of exits are not marked; this might be due to carelessness on the editor's part, though exits are often obvious enough from the dialogue, and it was not perhaps essential to mark them all in the prompt-book. Some of the additions are of special interest. At 3.1.41 F adds *Enter Pucke*, duplicating the later direction, copied from Q2, at line 58; this addition Brooks attributed to the editor's negligence, as simply 'wrong',[5] but it would seem rather to be a direction from the prompt-copy, suggesting that Puck should overhear rather more of the dialogue between Quince and his crew than his entry in the quartos would permit. At 4.1.42, F adds an entry for Oberon, following on the entry at the beginning of the scene of Titania and the fairies with *the King behind them.* This parallels the similar direction at 3.2.344, *Enter Oberon and Pucke*, who have been on stage since the opening

---

[1] See William A. Ringler, Jr, 'The number of actors in Shakespeare's early plays', in G. E. Bentley (ed.), *The Seventeenth-Century Stage*, 1968, pp. 133–4.

[2] Brooks, pp. 154–5.   [3] Brooks, pp. 159–62.

[4] He was buried as 'Mr Heminges man' in June 1625 (E. K. Chambers, *Elizabethan Stage*, 4 vols., 1923, II, 345); John Heminges, a senior sharer in the King's Men, was one of the signatories of the dedicatory letter in the First Folio.   [5] Brooks, p. xxxi.

of the scene, but stood 'aside' (3.2.116) to watch and overhear the lovers quarrel. These two entries presumably stood so in the prompt-book, and may relate to the staging of the play at the Globe or Blackfriars – where did Oberon stand to be 'behind' Titania, or 'aside' and watching the lovers? The additional entries might suggest that he left the main stage, watched from the gallery or tarras behind the stage,[1] and needed to be recalled when he intervened in the action again.

The Folio text also shows some changes early in Act 5, where Philostrate is replaced by Egeus as Theseus's 'manager of mirth', at the cost of spoiling the metre of 5.1.38. Philostrate elsewhere appears only as a mute in Act 1, so that the substitution here, doing away with one speaking-part, was a natural economy for an acting company. In addition, the list of possible entertainments for the wedding night, read and commented on by Theseus in the quartos, is divided in the Folio between Lysander, who reads the titles, and Theseus as commentator on them. This was perhaps an arrangement designed to make the passage more dramatic, and to give more involvement in the action to at least one of the lovers, who otherwise stand silent through the first part of the scene; possibly it was always played in this way. Since William Tawyer died in 1625, he may not have been the musician who led in Pyramus and Thisbe in 1595 or whenever the play was first staged at the Globe, and it has been assumed that the prompt-copy used by the editor of the Folio text was marked up for a revival of the play at the Blackfriars Theatre after the King's Men began to use it as a winter house about 1609.[2]

This assumption turns on an explanation of the most puzzling additional stage direction in the Folio: *They sleepe all the Act*, at the end of Act 3. The division of a play into acts seems to have been a matter of convention, and *A Midsummer Night's Dream* appears to have been conceived by Shakespeare as a continuous action. It may be that the act-divisions were introduced into the Folio text at the time of printing, as for *The Comedy of Errors*,[3] in which the direction *Enter Antipholus and Dromio again* at 5.1.9, after they have left the stage at the end of Act 4, shows that the act-division there is arbitrary, and that Shakespeare was thinking of a continuous action. In the Folio text of *A Midsummer Night's Dream*, the transition from Act 3 to Act 4 appears as follows:

They sleepe all the Act.

Actus Quartus

Enter Queene of Fairies, and Clowne, and Fairies, and the King behinde them.

[1] This assumes that the stage and its façade at the Globe were more or less as described by Andrew Gurr in *The Shakespearean Stage*, 2nd edn, 1980, pp. 120–1.

[2] Greg, pp. 144, 244; Brooks, pp. xxxii–xxxiii. Apart from the performance of 'a play of Robin goode-fellow' on New Year's night 1604 (Chambers, *Shakespeare*, 11, 329), nothing is certainly known of the early stage history of the play, but the continuing popularity of it is suggested by the publication of a droll based on the subplot and called 'Bottom the Weaver' in 1661. If the play was revived several times, the prompt-copy could have been used and re-used over a long period.

[3] See Greg, p. 201, and R. A. Foakes (ed.), *Err.*, 1962, pp. xii–xiii.

The wide spacing visually separates the two directions, and 'the Act' has usually been taken to mean 'interval between the acts'.[1] If, however, the heading for Act 4 was inserted as a matter of general editorial policy at the time of printing, the directions could well have been much more closely related in the prompt-manuscript.

It has been argued recently by G. K. Hunter that 'the habit of thinking about plays in five acts prevailed throughout the whole period of public theater writing', and can be related to 'the customs of the Globe'.[2] The matter is not as clear-cut as this would suggest; the Horatian precept that a play should have five acts seems to have been taken over as a conventional assumption about plays, and by the late 1590s Philip Henslowe was paying authors for contributing one or more acts to a play.[3] As time went by, so the custom of dividing plays by acts, and then scenes, became established in the early decades of the seventeenth century.[4] It is not known when, or how regularly, act pauses or intervals became customary in the public playhouses. As noted above, Shakespeare appears to have conceived *A Midsummer Night's Dream*, like *The Comedy of Errors*, as a single continuous action, and there is no evidence to show when it became habitual to play it with one or more intervals.

Here the word 'Act' in the direction *They sleepe all the Act* becomes crucial. It has three possible meanings. One is 'interval', but the only known uses of the word in this sense, all three doubtful, occur in texts of the 1630s.[5] A second meaning is 'music played between the acts', which is the usual interpretation of stage directions such as those in Marston's *The Malcontent* Act 2, instructing characters to enter 'whilst the act is playing'. This, and the similar direction in his *What You Will* (1601), relate to staging at the private theatres, and could just as well refer to music played to announce the beginning of a new act. According to John Webster's Induction to *The Malcontent* in 1604, the custom of playing music between the acts was 'not-received' at the Globe,[6] and there is no evidence that act-intervals were observed, or that music was played between the acts in early performances of *A Midsummer Night's Dream*,

---

[1] As by Greg, p. 243, and Brooks, p. xxxii.

[2] 'Were there act-pauses on Shakespeare's stage?', in S. Henning, R. Kimbrough and R. Knowles (eds.), *English Renaissance Drama*, 1976, pp. 18, 27.

[3] Greg, p. 145; *Henslowe's Diary*, pp. 100, 103, etc.; the first mention of payments for an act or acts rather than the 'book' of a play is dated 23 October 1598.

[4] Wilfred T. Jewkes, *Act Division in Elizabethan and Jacobean Plays 1583–1616*, 1958, pp. 100–3, argued that act-division became accepted in the public theatres mainly after about 1607; but he does not seem to have noticed the practice, well-established among Henslowe's authors, of sharing the writing of plays by acts.

[5] Greg, pp. 143–4. All three are in the peculiar phrase 'Act long', and two occur in a manuscript of Philip Massinger's *Believe as You List* marked up for the stage by Edward Knight, book-keeper for the King's Men from 1624 or 1625 (Greg, pp. 78–9). These, and the curious direction in Thomas Middleton's *The Changeling* (1624; first published in 1653), Act 3, instructing De Flores to hide a rapier in the 'act-time', suggests that the word 'interval' was as yet not used in the theatre, and, indeed, that they had no word for the time between the acts, perhaps because such a word had not been needed. Shakespeare once uses the Latin form 'intervallums' (*2H4* 5.1.81), when Falstaff refers to vacations between law-terms, quibbling perhaps on the Latin meaning of a space between ramparts, and it would appear that 'interval' had not yet passed into common use.

[6] The King's Men hired John Webster to provide additions to Marston's play, written for the Children of the Queen's Revels at Blackfriars, 'in order to abridge the not-received custom of music at our theatre', i.e. the Globe (Induction, lines 83–4).

though the King's Men could have adopted this practice after they took over and began to use the Blackfriars Theatre in 1609. Music is used so pointedly within the action of Shakespeare's play (for instance, to wake Titania, who lies asleep between Acts 2 and 3, at 3.1.107, and to rouse the lovers at 4.1.135), that additional music in intervals might be thought superfluous. The third, and in my view most plausible, meaning of 'Act' is its usual sense of a section of a play in performance, and this direction may be a prompter's reminder that the lovers are to remain on stage asleep when Titania enters, and throughout the next part of the action. It would then link with the further direction *Sleepers Lye still* (i.e. the sleepers continue to lie on stage) in the Folio at 4.1.98. In the absence of other evidence, this is the natural way to interpret these two directions. However, all interpretation has to be speculative, since we do not know whether the act-markings in the Folio text relate to playhouse usage, and we do not know when the prompt-copy used by the editor was marked up for use in the theatre, or whether it had been in use over a long period; and most commentators have preferred to believe that 'Act' here refers to a break between acts,[1] even though it seems to have been customary at the Blackfriars Theatre for members of the audience sitting on the stage to 'Rise up between the *Acts*' to display themselves, so that it would hardly have done to leave actors lying on stage pretending to be asleep.[2]

The text of the present edition is based on that of the Q1, supplemented by what appear to be the authoritative additions and changes in the Folio, and the, by now, traditional scene-divisions added by the eighteenth-century editors, Rowe and Capell. It would be interesting to know how far Shakespeare was himself involved in any of the changes and additions in the prompt-copy, but in the absence of information, it seems best to retain, for instance, the quarto's assignment of 5.1.44–60 to Theseus, while recognising that the Folio arrangement may represent the way these lines were played. It is a pity that the editor of the Folio text was so casual, though editors have over-reacted to what Brooks calls his 'demonstrable negligence and clumsiness'.[3] There is in fact no reason to doubt that what changes he made came from the prompt-book, but he may not have altered or added in the right place, and his casual treatment of the text suggests that he may have overlooked a good deal. An editor who allowed text printed as stage directions in Q2 at 1.1.24 and 26 ('Stand forth, Demetrius!...Stand forth, Lysander!') to remain so in the Folio, and who only managed to restore the correct lineation here and there in the first part of Act 5, was doing a half-hearted job, and this makes it the more difficult to interpret the meaning and placing of a puzzling entry like *They sleepe all the Act*.

---

[1] So G. K. Hunter says of the lovers, 'The progressive and parallel awakenings of Act IV requires [*sic*] the presence of the lovers on the stage, but their silence and apparent invisibility for the first sixty lines of the act is a mode of absence sufficient to justify an act-pause' ('Were there act-pauses on Shakespeare's stage?', p. 28).

[2] Ben Jonson, *The Devil is an Ass* (1616), 1.6.33; see also G. E. Bentley, *The Jacobean and Caroline Stage*, VI, 1968, pp. 6–8.

[3] Brooks, p. xxxi.

APPENDIX: A FURTHER NOTE ON SOURCES

The sources of *A Midsummer Night's Dream* have been treated at length by Bullough (1957), Muir (1977) and Brooks (1979). All three, but especially Brooks, detect influences on Shakespeare beyond those discussed at pp. 4–12 above. It is difficult to draw a line between genuine sources, consciously used as such, and the common stock of images, ideas and lore available to writers of the period. Authors at any time are likely to have read widely, and it would be surprising if Shakespeare did not know the major works of the past, as well as the publications of his notable contemporaries, like Marlowe and Spenser. So Brooks suggests, pp. lxi–lxii, that Spenser's *Shepheardes Calender* (1579) was a source for Shakespeare's play, contributing both to the 'sylvan beauty of the setting' and to 'Titania's foul-weather speech' in 2.1. It is, of course, more than probable that Shakespeare had read Spenser's influential poem, and absorbed its pastoral imagery, but it does not therefore follow that he had it in mind in referring to 'fragrant flowers', to 'flowerets' (4.1.49–52), to 'eglantine' (2.1.252), or in thinking of Phoebe, the moon, as 'silver' (1.1.209–10). Brooks lists more parallels, but most are from what by the 1590s was a common stock of imagery, and together they do not, in my view, establish that Spenser's poem can be regarded as a source for *A Midsummer Night's Dream*.

   Among the other works that have been claimed as sources for the play are three which deserve mention. These are as follows:

   1. Jorge de Montemayor, *Diana Enamorada* (1542; translated by Bartholomew Yong, 1598). This sequence of stories includes one which Shakespeare certainly used for *The Two Gentlemen of Verona*, and which includes a discourse by the wise Felicia on love and reason, and the cause why Cupid is painted blind (Bullough, 1, 248–9). The sage, Felicia, who devotes herself on behalf of Diana to curing the passions of love, also uses herbs to reverse a spell cast on a lover (Brooks, p. lxxxi). Shakespeare may have known the original, and Yong's translation, finished about 1582, in manuscript. His use of it for *The Two Gentlemen of Verona* perhaps left him with memories of it which he could exploit in *A Midsummer Night's Dream*, in which the relation of love to reason is an important issue (see, for example, 1.1.232–9).

   2. Seneca, *Oedipus*, *Medea* and *Hippolytus*. Shakespeare's use of the tragedies of Seneca for images and sentences in his own tragedies has long been taken for granted (see J. A. K. Thomson, *Shakespeare and the Classics*, 1951, and Percy Simpson, *Studies in Elizabethan Drama*, 1955, esp. pp. 49–54), so that it would not be surprising to find echoes in the comedies, as in Portia's speech on mercy in *The Merchant of Venice* (Simpson, pp. 54–5). Shakespeare may well have read Seneca in Latin, but he also knew the translation of *Seneca his Tenne Tragedies* by Jasper Heywood, John Studley, T. Nuce and Thomas Newton (1581), for he parodied the opening of John Studley's translation of *Hercules Oetaeus* in Bottom's lines, 1.2.24–31. Brooks, pp.

lxii–lxiii, 139–45, has noticed further links, between Titania's speech on disorder in nature (2.1.88 ff.) and Medea's invocation of Hecate, *Medea*, lines 750–94, as well as *Oedipus*, lines 36–185; between Oberon's speech on Cupid shooting at a 'fair vestal' (2.1.155 ff.) and passages in *Hippolytus*, lines 192–203, 294–5, 331–7 and 351; and between the speeches of Theseus and Hippolyta on hounds and hunting (4.1.100 ff.) and Hippolytus's directions to his huntsmen, lines 1–43. All of these echoes are plausible, and perhaps reflect again Shakespeare's absorption of images and motifs into his capacious memory and transforming imagination, rather than a conscious use of Seneca as a source.

3. Antony Munday, *John a Kent and John a Cumber* (?1590 or 1596). There are analogies, for example, in rustics contriving an entertainment for an aristocratic patron, and Brooks thinks Puck is related to Munday's character Shrimp, and Oberon to John a Kent 'in commanding events by means of magic' (Brooks, p. lxxxiii). Brooks was persuaded by Nevill Coghill's discussion in *Shakespeare's Professional Skills*, 1964, pp. 50–4, but the connection between the two plays seems tenuous to me; in any case, the date of Munday's play remains uncertain, and it may have been written after *A Midsummer Night's Dream* (see Brooks, pp. lxiv–lxvi).

READING LIST

This list provides details of the more important books and articles referred to in the Introduction or Commentary, together with a few additional items, and may serve as a guide to those who wish to undertake further study of the play.

Arthos, John. *Shakespeare's Use of Dream and Vision*, 1977
Barber, C. L. *Shakespeare's Festive Comedy*, 1959
   (Emphasising the play's links with traditional summer festivities, Barber's chapter on it also illustrates its formal design; an important essay)
Berry, Ralph. *Shakespeare's Comedies: Explorations in Form*, 1972
   (A rather sombre view of Shakespeare's comedies as preparations for the tragedies that were to follow)
Briggs, Katharine M. *The Anatomy of Puck*, 1959
   (On the background lore relating to the fairies)
Peter Brook's Production of William Shakespeare's A Midsummer Night's Dream for the Royal Shakespeare Company, 1974
   (Comments of the director and various actors who took part, together with the text of the play, as staged by Brook)
Brown, John Russell. *Shakespeare and his Comedies*, 1957
   (One of the first books to treat the play seriously in terms of its thematic content, specifically in relation to love)
Calderwood, J. L. *Shakespeare's Metadrama*, 1971
   (Incorporates his essay on the play, published as 'The illusion of drama', *MLQ* 26 (1965), 506–22)
Cope, Jackson. *The Theater and the Dream*, 1973
   (A long, wide-ranging work, suggestive in its exploration of ideas and images that bear upon the play)
Dent, R. W. 'Imagination in *A Midsummer Night's Dream*', *SQ* 15 (1964), 115–29
   (An interesting account of the play as 'a delightful exposition of the follies produced by excessive imagination in love, and the pleasures produced by controlled imagination in art', p. 128)
Shakespeare's Proverbial Language, 1981
   (A revision and expansion of the listings in M. P. Tilley's *Dictionary*, referred to in the Commentary; this is an essential reference guide for all interested in Shakespeare's use of proverb lore)
Fender, Stephen. *Shakespeare: A Midsummer Night's Dream*, 1968
   (A good, level-headed, general introduction to the play)
Garber, Marjorie. *Dream in Shakespeare*, 1974

Hunter, G. K. *John Lyly: The Humanist as Courtier*, 1962
    (An excellent study of Lyly's plays, with an analysis of their influence on
    Shakespeare)
Huston, J. Dennis. *Shakespeare's Comedies of Play*, 1981
    (Goes overboard in presenting Shakespeare as a self-conscious dramatist, turning
    A Midsummer Night's Dream into a play of parodies)
Kermode, Frank, 'The mature comedies', in J. R. Brown and B. Harris (eds.), *Early
    Shakespeare*, 1961, pp. 211–27
Kott, Jan. *Shakespeare Our Contemporary*, 1964
    (His stress on the potentially cruel and bestial elements in the play greatly
    influenced some critics, and Peter Brook as director of the play)
Latham, M. W. *The Elizabethan Fairies*, 1930
Leggatt, Alexander. *Shakespeare's Comedy of Love*, 1974
    (Contains a sturdy, well-balanced account of the play)
McFarland, Thomas. *Shakespeare's Pastoral Comedy*, 1972
    (In contrast to Kott, sees the play as the happiest of Shakespeare's comedies)
Olson, Paul H. '*A Midsummer Night's Dream* and the meaning of court marriage',
    ELH 24 (1957), 95–119
Richmond, Hugh. *Shakespeare's Sexual Comedy*, 1971
    (Influenced by Kott, Richmond finds sadomasochistic sexual passions released
    in the play)
Scragg, Leah. 'Shakespeare, Lyly and Ovid: the influence of "Gallathea" on "A
    Midsummer Night's Dream"', *S.Sur.* 30 (1977), 125–34
    The Metamorphosis of Gallathea: A Study in Creative Adaptation, 1982
    (Presses rather too strenuously her claims for the influence of Lyly on
    Shakespeare)
Siegel, Paul N. '*A Midsummer Night's Dream* and the wedding guests', *SQ* 4 (1953),
    139–44
    (Claims that we only recapture the full experience of the play by becoming
    wedding guests in imagination, and reading the play as if it were being performed
    at a wedding celebration)
Styan, J. L. *The Shakespeare Revolution*, 1977
    (Provides the best account of the seminal production of the play by Harley
    Granville-Barker in 1914)
Thompson, Ann. *Shakespeare and Chaucer*, 1978
Turner, Robert K., Jr. 'Printing methods and textual problems in *A Midsummer
    Night's Dream* Q1', *Studies in Bibliography* 15 (1962), 33–55
Wickham, Glynne, '*A Midsummer Night's Dream*: the setting and the text' in
    Shakespeare's Dramatic Heritage, 1969
Williams, Gary Jay. '"The concord of this discord": music in the stage history of
    A Midsummer Night's Dream', *Yale/Theatre* 4 (1973), 40–68
    'Madame Vestris, *A Midsummer Night's Dream* and the web of Victorian tradition',
    Theatre Survey 18 (1977), 1–22

Young, David P. *Something of Great Constancy: The Art of A Midsummer Night's Dream*, 1966
(An important book, extending Barber's account of the play, notably in dealing with the integration of courtly and popular elements, and in exploring attitudes to dreams and the imagination in Shakespeare's age)